# THE ENNEAGRAM OF MIRACLES

## THE ENNEAGRAM OF "A COURSE IN MIRACLES"

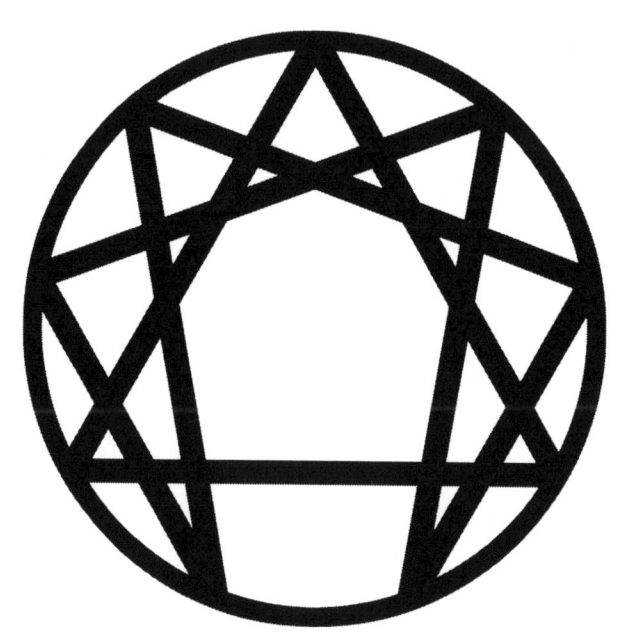

### TIM L. MORGAN Ph.D.

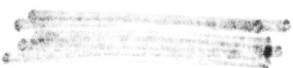

Copyright © 2013 by Tim L. Morgan PHD
All rights reserved.

ISBN: 1492227900
ISBN 13: 9781492227908

*This book is dedicated to my son and daughter.
Love always.*

The purpose of this book is to be a general rule of thumb in cross-referencing Enneagram character types with A Course in Miracles channeled material and the wisdom therein. It is not to be considered an encyclopedia of Course issues and references "set in stone."

It is also the purpose of this book to expand the rationalizations of A Course in Miracles to better see an ancient framework of wisdom used in the Gospels of Jesus and to understand how he enabled individuals to be saved from themselves. A Course in Miracles exhorts us to seek peace and then turn from fear in our lives to love. The Enneagram shows us the characters' paths of dematerialization and what is unhealthy in each specific character.

The paths of growth and dematerialization will be forthcoming in my next book, Miracle Transformations. This volume will explain the enneatypical growth and degeneration lines in terms of A Course in Miracles Workbook for Students.

# THE ENNEAGRAM OF MIRACLES

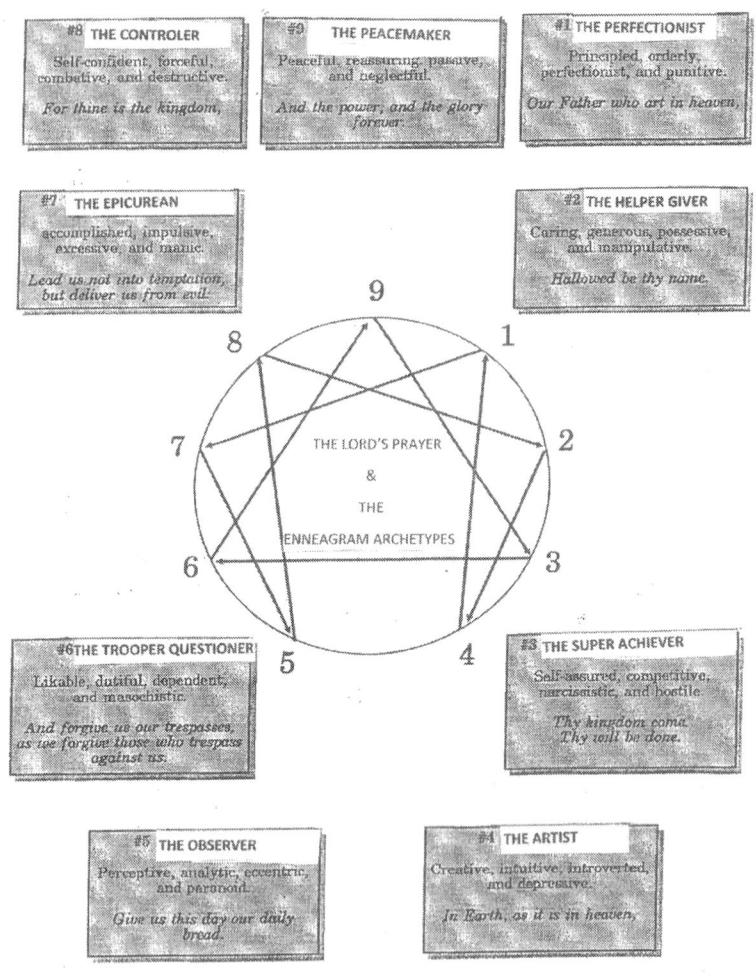

# THE LORD'S PRAYER AND THE ENNEAGRAM

At the earliest the *enneagram* is credited to the Sarmoun Brotherhood in Persia, circa 2500BC and the Desert Fathers in Egypt between 77 and 400 AD. They" fleshed out" the Lord's

Prayer into the distinct psychological archetypes of the *enneagram* as it is known today.

The Jewish Kabbalastic Sefirote and the Lord's Prayer are one in the same syncretized body of knowledge communicating to the initiate the existence of these divine psychological keys in being able to know people and allowing people to know themselves.

In our time, with thanks to George Gurdjieff, IIchazo, and Charles Tart of The Transpersonal School of Psychology to which the "A Course In Miracles" is a part, we have the marriage of these seemingly different bodies of knowledge but they truly are of the same family.

The *enneagram* interpretation of the Lord's Prayer originally is at one. The Enneagram of "A Course In Miracles" is now also...... finally......at ONE.

## A NOTE FROM THE AUTHOR

It has always been my opinion that A Course in Miracles has had a need for an invasive legend to identify "character object relations" as defined by Melany Cline, MD. The Enneagram of Miracles endeavors to be the object relations framework to sort out the character issues related in the Course process.

The *Enneagram* serves as the "cartographic legend," as it were, in sorting out the *Course* descriptions and expanding the enneatype interpretations within the character archetype.

This has been my six-year labor of love. I hope you, my reader, will enjoy the character-matrix cross-referencing. As the

*Enneagram* has gained wide acceptance in behavioral circles as a very reliable test and measure of character, so too has *A Course in Miracles* been accepted as a viable therapy tool for in-depth examination of "soul stuff" for individuals examining their lives.

It was my purpose to marry the two schools of thought. The *Enneagram* serves as a guide to best understand the *Course* issues, and the *Course* issues serve to expand the philosophy of the enneatype in terms of seeking peace and living in God's love.

Yours truly,<br>
Tim

# INTRODUCTION

Our virtues and strengths develop bastions of unconscious kingdoms and principalities over time in our lives. When given free rein, they develop psychotic, "out of control" episodes of either obsessive-compulsive disorder, histrionic personality disorder, narcissistic personality disorder, depressogenic personality disorder, paranoid schizophrenia, schizophrenic nihilistic delusional disorder, manic depression (bipolar disorder), sociopathic personality disorder, and multiple personality disorder.

Our developed discipline and personal choices and perceptions lead us further into illness and dematerialization of health, or into growth, recovery, and optimal health. For perplexed readers of *A Course in Miracles*, this book is a guide through the character traits that belong to the character processes described in the *Course* channeling. This should in no way detract from, add to, or prejudicate the genius of Helen Schucman's work.

*The Enneagram of Miracles* serves only as a character legend similar to that on a maritime map or common road map that identifies sites and locations on one's journey. It is the legend of which character type most likely fits the *Course* process at specific and particular points in the *Course* work, and will take the guesswork out of the mind of the reader as to which issue belongs to which character.

For the in-text parenthetical citations of material from A Course in Miracles (ACIM), Text refers to the text section, Workbook to the workbook for students section, Manual to the manual for teachers section, and Glossary to the glossary.

# TABLE OF CONTENTS

INTRODUCTION ................................................... ix
CHAPTER 1 – THE HEALTHY PERFECTIONIST ..................... 1
CHAPTER 2 – THE HELPER-GIVER ................................ 41
CHAPTER 3 – THE SUPER ACHIEVER ............................. 61
CHAPTER 4 – THE ARTIST ....................................... 99
CHAPTER 5 – THE OBSERVER .................................... 155
CHAPTER 6 – THE QUESTIONER .................................. 197
CHAPTER 7 – THE EPICUREAN ................................... 245
CHAPTER 8 – THE CONTROLLER .................................. 275
CHAPTER 9 – THE PEACEMAKER .................................. 307
CHAPTER 10 – "GOD IS INCOMPLETE WITHOUT ME." ............ 335

## CHAPTER 1
# THE HEALTHY PERFECTIONIST

The ultimate purpose of projection is always to get rid of guilt.
(ACIM Text, 223, 229)

> **Right-mindedness:** the part of our separated minds that contains the Holy Spirit—the Voice of forgiveness and reason; we are repeatedly asked to choose it instead of wrong-mindedness, to follow the Holy Spirit's guidance rather than the ego's, and thus return to the one-mindedness of Christ. (ACIM Glossary, 178)

*As the enneatype literature intimates, the healthy perfectionists are honorable and noble in their intent as they pursue their effortless crusade for justice, as well as exhibiting a can-do sense to "get to the bottom of this." They want to make things right and are natural reformers. Healthy perfectionists will always strive to be fair and will seek out the transcendent high-ground position of perception to maintain the "right." They make excellent teachers, mechanics, bank loan officers, surgeons, and school principals. They are hopeful and humane in their deep concern to be right in love as they aspire to justice.*

*The healthy perfectionist is very charitable and exercises great tolerance for those that are different from him. The healthy perfectionist truly believes that all things will work out for the best over time and ultimately in the end. They will not attempt to manipulate or corral in any insidious way to bring about a better outcome. They give the benefit of the doubt to another individual with the assumption that, of course, he will finally "get it right" over time.*

9. Healing is an ability that developed after the separation before which it was unnecessary. Like all aspects of the belief in space and time, it is temporary. However, as long as time persists, healing is needed as a means of protection. This is because healing rests on charity, and charity is a way of perceiving the perfection of another even if you cannot perceive it in yourself. Most of the loftier concepts of which you are capable now are time-dependent. Charity is really a weaker reflection of a much more powerful love-encompassment that is far beyond any form of charity you can conceive of as yet. Charity is essential to right-mindedness in the limited sense in which it can now be attained.

10. Charity is a way of looking at another as if he had already gone far beyond his actual accomplishments in time. Since his own thinking is faulty he cannot see the Atonement for himself, or he would have no need of charity. The charity that is accorded him is both an acknowledgment that he needs help and recognition that he will accept it. Both of these perceptions clearly imply their dependence on time, making it apparent that charity still lies within the limitations of this world. I said before that only revelation transcends time. The miracle, as an expression of charity, can only shorten it. It must be understood, however, that whenever you offer a miracle to another, you are shortening the suffering of both of you. This corrects retroactively as well as progressively! (Text 2 V. 9, 10)

I myself said, "If I go I will send you another Comforter and he will abide with you." His symbolic function makes the Holy Spirit difficult to understand, because symbolism is open to different interpretations. As a man and also one of God's creations, my right thinking, which came from the Holy Spirit or the Universal Inspiration, taught me first and foremost that this Inspiration is for all. I could not have it myself without knowing this. The word "know" is proper in this context, because the Holy Spirit is so close to knowledge that He calls it forth; or better, allows it to come. I have spoken before of the higher or "true" perception, which is so near to the truth that God Himself can flow across the little gap. "Knowledge is always ready to flow everywhere, but it cannot oppose." Therefore you can obstruct it, although you can never lose it.

5. The Holy Spirit is the Christ Mind which is aware of the knowledge that lies beyond perception. He came into being with the separation as a protection, inspiring the Atonement principle at the same time. Before that there was no need for healing, for no one was comfortless. The voice of the Holy Spirit is the Call to Atonement, or the restoration of the integrity of the mind. When the atonement is complete and the whole Sonship is healed, there will be no call to return, but what God creates is eternal. The Holy Spirit will remain with the sons of God, to bless their creations and keep them in the light of joy.

6. God honored even the miscreation of His children because they had made them. But he also blessed his children with a way of thinking that could raise their perceptions so high they could reach almost back to Him. The Holy Spirit is the Mind of the Atonement. He represents a state of mind close enough to One-mindedness that transfer to it is at last possible. Perception is not knowledge, but it can be transferred to knowledge or cross over into it. It might even be more helpful here to use the literal meaning of transferred or "carried over," since the last step is taken by God.

7. The Holy Spirit, the shared inspiration of all the Sonship, induces a kind of perception in which many elements are like those in the Kingdom of Heaven itself. First, its universality is perfectly clear, and no one who attains it could believe for one instant that sharing it involves anything but gain. Second, it is incapable of attack and is therefore truly open. (Text, 74, 5.1:4.5)

*The healthy perfectionist quintessentially delights in being fair. They are very attracted to high ideals but do not yet feel the compulsion to obsess over them. They are very wise due to the accuracy of their judgment. At this point in their lives they truly are, "a little less than the angels."*

---

*I gave only love to the Kingdom because I believed that was what I was. What you believe you are determines your gifts, and if God created you by extending himself as you, you can only extend yourself as He did. Only joy increases forever, since joy and eternity are inseparable. God extends outward beyond limits and beyond time and you who are co-creator with Him extend His Kingdom forever and beyond limit. Eternity is the indelible stamp of creation, the eternal are in peace and joy forever. (Text, 113)*

---

*The healthy perfectionist automatically exercises a suspension of judgment when regarding others in tolerance. They have a foresight into madness which is uncomfortable for them to initiate and thus they preserve the moment of enjoyment.*

The holy instant is not an instant of creation, but of recognition, for recognition comes of vision and suspended judgment. Then only is it possible to look within and see what must be there plainly in sight, and wholly independent of inference and judgment. Undoing is not your task, but it is up to you to welcome it or not. Faith and desire go hand in hand, for everyone believes in what he wants.

9. We have already said that wishful thinking is how the ego deals with what it wants to make it so. There is no better demonstration of the power of wanting, and therefore of faith, so I make its goals seem real and possible. Faith in the unreal leads to adjustments of reality to make it fit the goal of madness. The goal of sin induces the perception of a fearful world to justify its purpose. What

you desire, you will see, and if its reality is false, you will uphold it by not realizing all the adjustments you have introduced to make.

10. When vision is denied, confusion of cause and effect becomes inevitable. The purpose now becomes to keep obscure the cause of the effect, and make effect appear to be a cause. This seeming independence of effect enables it to be regarded as standing by itself and capable of serving as a cause of the events and feelings its maker thinks it causes. Earlier, we spoke of your desire to create your own creator, and be father and not son to him. This is the same desire. The Son is the Effect, whose Cause he would deny, and so he seems to be the cause, producing real effects. Nothing can have effects without a cause, and to confuse the two is merely to fail to understand them both.

11. It is as needful that you recognize you made the world you see, as that you recognize that you did not create yourself. *They are the same mistake.* Nothing not created by your Creator has any influence over you, and if you think what you have made can tell you what you see and feel, and place your faith in its ability to do so; you are denying your Creator and believing that you made yourself. If you think the world you made has power to make you what it will, you are confusing Son and Father; effect and source.

12. The son's creations are like his father's. "Yet in creating them the Son does not delude himself that he is independent of his source. His union with it is the source of his creating. Apart from this, he has no power to create, and what he makes it mean" (Text, 450).

*This is the practice of the healthy perfectionist. They are able to suspend judgment and give unconditional regard in a vicarious sort of way. They maintain a natural sense of being "right" with equanimity and optimism. They practice a "forth-seeing" into the future with no sense of dread or forbearing guilt.*

## V. BEYOND PERCEPTION

1. I have said that the abilities *you* possess are only shadows of your real strength, and that perception, which is inherently judgmental, was introduced only after the separation. No one has been sure of anything since. I have also made it clear that the resurrection was the means for the return to knowledge, which was accomplished by the union of my will with the father's. We can now establish a distinction that will clarify some of our subsequent statements.

2. Since the separation, the words "create" and "make" have become confused. When you make something, you do so out of a specific sense of lack or need. Anything made for a specific purpose has no true generalizability. When you make something to fill a perceived lack, you are tacitly implying that you believe in separation. The ego has invented many ingenious thought systems for this purpose. None of them is creative; inventiveness is wasted effort even in its most ingenious form. The highly specific nature of invention is not worthy of the abstract creativity of God's creations.

3. Knowing, as we already have observed, does not lead to doing. "The confusion between your real creation and what you have made of yourself is so profound that it has become literally impossible for you to know anything." Knowledge is always stable, and it is quite evident that you are not. Nevertheless, you are perfectly stable as God created you. In this sense, when your behavior is unstable, you are disagreeing with God's idea of your creation. You can do this if you choose, but you would hardly want to do it, if you were in your right mind.

4. The fundamental question you continually ask yourself cannot properly be directed to yourself at all. You keep asking what it is you are. This implies that the answer is not only one you know, but is also one that is up to you to supply. (Text, 44)

*The healthy perfectionists are in perfect balance with themselves. They are extremely realistic and permit their higher awareness to emerge in their greatest expression of their divine humanity. They are not boastful in their unconditional "largesse" of tolerance or natural altruism.*

## LESSON 283
*My true identity abides in You.*

1. Father, I "made an image of myself, and it is this I call the Son of God. Yet it creation as it always was, for Your creation is unchangeable. Let me not worship Idols. I am he my Father loves. My holiness remains the light of Heaven and the Love of God. Is not what is beloved of You secure? Is not the light of Heaven infinite? Is not Your Son my true identity?

2. Now are we one in shared identity, with God our Father as our only source, and everything created part of us, and so we offer blessing to all things, uniting lovingly with all the world, which our forgiveness has made one with us. (Workbook, 439)

*The shadowy stranger, guilt, like unrecognized and unearned iniquity, harbors the possibility of punishment and this causes one to live in shame. Because the healthy perfectionist holds himself to the highest standards of perfection, the natural resultant emotion on the timeline of human events is self-imposed guilt, and resultant anger at the unresolved shame of whatever was not accomplished.*

## IX. THE CLOUD OF GUILT

1. Guilt remains the only thing that hides the Father, for guilt is the attack upon His Son. The guilty always condemn, and having done so they will still condemn, linking the future to the past as

is the ego's law. Fidelity to this law lets no light in, for it demands fidelity to darkness and forbids awakening. The ego's laws are strict, and breaches are severely punished. Therefore give no obedience to its laws, for they are laws of punishment and those who follow them believe that they are guilty, and so they must condemn. Between the future and the past the laws of God must intervene, if you would free yourself. Atonement stands between them, like a lamp shining so brightly that the shame of darkness in which you bound yourself will disappear. (Text, 260, 13.9 1:1)

2. Release from guilt is the ego's whole undoing. *Make no one fearful,* for his guilt is yours, and by obeying the ego's harsh commandments you bring its condemnation on yourself, and you will not escape the punishment it offers those who obey it. The ego rewards fidelity to it with pain, for faith in it is pain. And faith can be rewarded only in terms of the belief in which the faith was placed. Faith makes the power of belief, and where it is invested determines its reward, for faith is always given what is treasured, and what is treasured is returned to you.

3. The world can give you only what you gave it, for being nothing but your own projection, it has no meaning apart from what you found in it and placed your faith in. Be faithful unto darkness and you will not see, because your faith will be rewarded as you gave it. You *will* accept your treasure, and if you place your faith in the past, the future will be like it. Whatever you hold dear you think is yours. The power of your valuing will make it so.

4. Atonement brings a re-evaluation of everything you cherish, for it is the means by which the Holy Spirit can separate the false and the true, which you have accepted into your mind without distinction. Therefore you cannot value one without the other, and guilt has become as true for you as innocence. You do not believe the Son of God is guiltless because you see the past, and see him not. When you condemn a brother you are saying, "I who was guilty choose to remain so." You have denied his freedom, and by so doing

you have denied the witness unto yours. You could as easily have freed him from the past, and lifted from his mind the cloud of guilt that binds him to it, and in his freedom would have been your own.

5. Lay not his guilt upon him, for his guilt lies in his secret thought that he has done this unto you. Would you then teach him he is right in his delusion? The idea that the guiltless Son of God can attack himself and make himself guilty is insane. In any form, in anyone, *believe this not,* for sin and condemnation are the same, and the belief in one is faith in the other, calling for punishment instead of love. Nothing can justify insanity, and to call for punishment upon yourself must be insane.

6. See no one then as guilty, and you will affirm the truth of guiltlessness unto yourself. In every condemnation that you offer the Son of God lies the conviction of your own guilt. If you would have the Holy Spirit make you free of it, accept His offer of Atonement for all your brothers, for so you learn that it is true for you. Remember always that it is impossible to condemn the Son of God in part. Those whom you see as guilty become the witnesses to guilt in you and you will see it there, for it *is* there until it is undone. Guilt is always in your mind, which has condemned itself. Project it not, for while you do it cannot be undone. With everyone you release from guilt, great is the joy in Heaven where the witnesses to your fatherhood rejoice.

7. Guilt makes you blind, for while you see one spot of guilt within you, you will not see the light, and by projecting it, the world seems dark and shrouded in your guilt. You throw a dark veil over it and cannot see it because you cannot look within. You are afraid of what you would see there, but it is not there. *The thing you fear is gone.* If you would look within you would see only the Atonement, shining in quiet and in peace upon the altar to your Father.

8. Do not be afraid to look within. The ego tells you all is black with guilt within you, and bids you not to look. Instead, it bids you look upon your brothers, and see the guilt in them, yet this you cannot do without remaining blind. For those who see their brothers

in the dark, and guilty in the dark in which they shroud them, are too afraid to look upon the light within. Within you is not what you believe is there, and what you put your faith in. Within you is the holy sign of perfect faith your Father has in you. He does not value you as you do. He knows Himself, and knows the truth in you. He knows there is no difference, for He knows not of differences. Can you see guilt where God knows there is perfect innocence? You can deny His knowledge, but you cannot change it. Look, then, upon the light He placed within you, and learn that what you feared was there has been replaced with love. (Text, 262)

*Healthy perfectionists are always expecting the best to transpire from any situation. Their mindfulness is reflected in their idealistic heavenly projection of the best of all outcomes.*

# LESSON 232
*Be in my mind, my Father, through the day.*

1. Be in my mind, my Father, when I wake, and shine on me throughout the day today. Let every minute be a time in which I dwell with You, and let me not forget my hourly thanksgiving that You have remained with me, and always will be there to hear my call to You and answer me. As evening comes, let all my thoughts be still of You and Your love, and let me sleep sure of my safety, certain of Your care, and happily aware I am Your Son.

2. This is as every day should be. Today, practice the end of fear, have faith in Him who is your Father. Trust all things to Him. Let Him reveal all things to you, and be you undismayed because you are His Son. (Text, 408)

*The healthy perfectionists will innocently and naively miss this point of corrected perception. They will assume that they have a "steady* state" of perfect perception and miss the point when their perception is flawed by an obvious lack of information. (Even when they have unconsciously "skewed" their perception to arrive at an outcome that was prejudicated according to what "ought" to be the outcome, given their perfect circumstances.)

## IX. HEALING AS CORRECTED PERCEPTION

1. I said before that the Holy Spirit is the answer. He is the answer to everything, because he knows what the answer to everything is. The ego does not know what a real question is, although it asks an endless number. Yet you can learn this as you learn to question the value of the ego, and thus establish your ability to evaluate its questions. When the ego tempts you to sickness do not ask the Holy Spirit to heal the body, for this would merely be to accept the ego's belief that the body is the proper aim of healing. Ask, rather, that the Holy Spirit teach you the *right perception* of the body, for perception alone can be distorted. Only perception can be sick, because only perception can be wrong.

2. Wrong perception is the wish that things be as they are not. The reality of everything is totally harmless, because total harmlessness is the condition of its reality. It is also the condition of your awareness of its reality. You do not have to seek reality; it will seek you and find you when you meet its conditions. Its conditions are part of what it is, and this part only is up to you. The rest is of itself. You need do so little because your little part is so powerful that it will bring the whole to you. Accept, then, your little part and let the whole be yours. (Text, 157)

*The healthy perfectionist expresses charity and becomes generous only at the "seven" points in the enneagram. Only when they experience abundance can they become charitable.*

6. Only those who have a real and lasting sense of abundance can be truly charitable. This is obvious when you consider what is involved. To the ego, to give anything implies that you will have to do without it. When you associate giving with sacrifice, you give only because you believe that you are somehow getting something better, and can therefore do without the thing you give. "Giving to get" is an inescapable law of the ego, which always evaluates itself in relation to other egos. It is therefore continually preoccupied with the belief in scarcity that gave rise to it. Its whole perception of other egos as real is only an attempt to convince itself that *it* is real. "Self-esteem" in ego terms means nothing more than that the ego has deluded itself into accepting its reality, and is therefore temporarily less predatory. This "self-esteem" is always vulnerable to stress, a term which refers to any perceived threat to the ego's existence.

7. The ego literally lives by comparisons. Equality is beyond its grasp, and charity becomes impossible. The ego never gives out of abundance, because it was made as a substitute for it. That is why the concept of "getting" arose in the ego's thought system. Appetites are "getting" mechanisms, representing the ego's need to confirm itself. This is as true of body appetites as it is of the so-called "higher ego needs." Body appetites are not physical in origin. The ego regards the body as its home, and tries to satisfy itself through the body, but the idea that this is possible is a decision of the mind, which has become completely confused about what is really possible.

8. The ego believes it is completely on its own, which is merely another way of describing how it thinks it originated. This is such a fearful state that it can only turn to other egos and try to unite with them in a feeble attempt at identification, or attack them in an equally feeble show of strength. It is not free, however, to open the premise to question, because the premise is its foundation. The ego is the mind's belief that it is completely on its own. The ego's ceaseless attempts to gain the spirit's acknowledgment and thus establish its own existence are useless. Spirit in its knowledge is

unaware of the ego. It does not attack; it merely cannot conceive of it at all. While the ego is equally unaware of spirit, it does perceive itself as being rejected by something greater than itself. This is why self-esteem in ego terms must be delusional; the creations of God do not create myths.

*The deft thread of existing vitriol, anger, and unexercised iniquity at the subconscious level of the healthy perfectionist inadvertently pours over into the expression of the perfectionist. The expression vacillates from the pure and objective perspective to the dim, pessimistic, and prejudiced perspective. It is perhaps the combination of "scarcity consciousness" that trips off the pessimism and the need to project blame to rid themselves of imperfection that fuels the skewed perception.*

## VI. THE SPECIAL FUNCTION

The grace of God rests gently on forgiving eyes, and everything they look on speaks of Him to the beholder. He can see no evil; nothing in the world to fear, and no one who is different from himself, and as he loves them, so he looks upon himself with love and gentleness. He would no more condemn himself for his mistakes than damn another. He is not an arbiter of vengeance, nor a punisher of sin. The kindness of his sight rests on himself with all the tenderness it offers others. For he would only heal and only bless, and being in accord with what God wills, he has the power to heal and bless all those he looks on with the grace of God upon his sight. Eyes become used to darkness and the light of brilliant day seems painful to the eyes grown long accustomed to the dim effects perceived at twilight, and they turn away from sunlight and the clarity it brings to what they look upon. Dimness seems better, easier to see, and better recognized. Somehow the vague and more obscure seems easier to look upon; less painful to the eyes than what is wholly clear and unambiguous. Yet this is

> *5. The miracle enables you to see your brother without his past, and so perceive him as born again. His errors are all past, and by perceiving him without them you are releasing him. And since his past is yours, you share in this release. Let no dark cloud out of your past obscure him from you, for truth lies only in the present, and you will find it if you seek it there. You have looked for it where it is not, and therefore have not found it. Learn, then, to seek it where it is, and it will dawn on eyes that see. Your past was made in anger, and if you use it to attack the present, you will not see the freedom that the present holds. (Text, 251)*

not what the eyes are for, and who can say that he prefers the darkness and maintain he wants to see?

The wish to see calls down the grace of God upon your eyes, and brings the gift of light that makes sight possible. Would you behold your brother? God is glad to have you look on him. He does not will your savior be unrecognized by you. Nor does He will that he remain without the function that He gave to him. Let him no more be lonely, for the lonely ones are those who see no function in the world for them to fill; no place where they are needed, and no aim which only they can perfectly fulfill. (Text, 529)

## Chapter 4

### THE ILLUSIONS OF THE EGO

3. No one who learns from experience that one choice brings peace and joy while another brings chaos and disaster needs additional convincing. Learning through rewards is more effective than learning through pain,

because pain is an ego illusion and can never induce more than a temporary effect. The rewards of God, however, are immediately recognized as eternal. Since this recognition is made by you and not the ego, the recognition itself establishes that you and your ego cannot be identical. You may believe that you have already accepted this difference, but you are by no means convinced as yet. The fact that you believe you must escape from the ego shows this; but you cannot escape from the ego by humbling it or controlling it or punishing it.

4. The ego and the spirit do not know each other; the separated mind cannot maintain the separation except by dissociating. Having done this, it denies all truly natural impulses, not because the ego is a separate thing, but because you want to believe *that you are*. The ego is a device for maintaining this belief, but it is still only your decision to use the device that enables it to endure. (Text, 68)

*The healthy perfectionists can maintain their healthy perception by forgiving others and double-checking their "big picture" grand scheme of reality, making sure it includes all the correct checks and balances, with no residual baggage of resentment from the past or foreboding pessimistic projections of the future.*

2. Yet consider how strange a solution the ego's arrangement is. You project guilt to get rid of it, but you are actually merely concealing it. You do experience the guilt, but you have no idea why. On the contrary, you associate it with a weird assortment of "ego ideals," which the ego claims you have failed. Yet you have no idea that you are failing the Son of God by seeing him as guilty. Believing you are no longer you, you do not realize that you are failing yourself.

3. The darkest of your hidden cornerstones holds your belief in guilt from your awareness. For in that dark and secret place is the realization that you have betrayed God's Son by condemning him to death. You do not even suspect this murderous but insane idea

lies hidden there, for the ego's destructive urge is so intense that nothing short of the crucifixion of God's Son can ultimately satisfy it. It does not know who the Son of God is because it is blind. Yet let it perceive guiltlessness anywhere, and it will try to destroy it because it is afraid.

4. Much of the ego's strange behavior is directly attributable to its definition of guilt. To the ego, *the guiltless are guilty.* Those who do not attack are its "enemies" because, by not valuing its interpretation of salvation, they are in an excellent position to let it go. They have approached the darkest and deepest cornerstone in the ego's foundation, and while the ego can withstand your raising all else to question, it guards this one secret with its life, for its existence depends on keeping this secret. So it is this secret that we must look upon, for the ego cannot protect you against truth, and in its presence the ego is dispelled.

5. In the calm light of truth, let us recognize that you believe you have crucified God's Son. You have not admitted to this "terrible" secret because you would still wish to crucify him if you could find him. Yet the wish has hidden him from you because it is very fearful, and so you are afraid to find him. You have handled this wish to kill yourself by not knowing who you are, and identifying with someone else. You have projected guilt blindly and indiscriminately, but you have not uncovered its source. For the ego does want to kill you, and if you identify with it, you must believe its goal is yours.

6. I have said that the crucifixion is the symbol of the ego. When it was confronted with the real guiltlessness of God's Son it did attempt to kill him, and the reason it gave was that guiltlessness is blasphemous to God. To the ego, the ego *is* God, and guiltlessness must be interpreted as the final guilt that fully justifies murder. You do not yet understand that any fear you may experience in

connection with this course stems ultimately from this interpretation, but if you will consider your reactions to it you will become increasingly convinced that this is so.

7. This course has explicitly stated that its goal for you is happiness and peace. Yet you are afraid of it. You have been told again and again that it will set you free, yet you sometimes react as if it is trying to imprison you. You often dismiss it more readily than you dismiss the ego's thought system. To some extent, then, you must believe that by not learning the course you are protecting yourself, and you do not realize that it is only your guiltlessness that can protect you.

8. The Atonement has always been interpreted as the release from guilt, and this is correct if it is understood. Yet even when I interpret it for you, you may reject it and do not accept it for yourself. You have perhaps recognized the futility of the ego and its offerings, but though you do not want them, you may not yet look upon the alternative with gladness. In the extreme, you are afraid of redemption and you believe it will kill you. Make no mistake about the depth of this fear, for you believe that, in the presence of truth, you might turn on yourself and destroy yourself.

9. Little child, this is not so. Your "guilty secret" is nothing, and if you will but bring it to the light, the light will dispel it, and then no dark cloud will remain between you and the remembrance of your Father, for you will remember His guiltless Son, who did not die because he is immortal, and you will see that you were redeemed with him and have never been separated from him. In this understanding lies your remembering, for it is the recognition of love without fear. There will be great joy in Heaven on your homecoming, and the joy will be yours; for the redeemed son of man is the guiltless Son of God and to recognize him is your redemption. (Text, 240–241)

> *The very thought of sacrifice is an overused convention in the mind of the perfectionist and gains "a life of its own," past the real-world investment strategies of the business world. This then creates the notion of lack or scarcity to the reality of the perfectionist. Thus, they then are in anxiety or fear for the very notion of sacrifice and investment.*

## THE INNOCENT PERCEPTION

4. Sacrifice is a notion totally unknown to God. It arises solely from fear, and frightened people can be vicious. Sacrificing in any way is a violation of my injunction that you should be merciful even as your Father in Heaven is merciful. It has been hard for many Christians to realize that this applies to themselves. Good teachers never terrorize their students. To terrorize is to attack, and this results in rejection of what the teacher offers. The result is learning failure. (Text, 37)

*Perfectionists were made to grow up too fast and were raised by austere and demanding parents. They were raised by angry sources and always living under the cloud of condemnation and fear of judgment.*

## FINDING THE PRESENT

6. Judgment and condemnation are behind you, and unless you bring them with you, you will see that you are free of them. Look

lovingly upon the present, for it holds the only things that are forever true. (Text, 251)

7. Judgment is but a toy, a whim, the senseless means to play the idle game of death in your imagination, but vision sets all things right, bringing them gently within the kindly sway of Heaven's laws. What if you recognized that this world is a hallucination? What if you really understood you made it up? What if you realized that those who seem to walk about in it, to sin and die, murder and attack, and murder and destroy themselves, are wholly unreal? Could you have faith in what you see if you accepted this? Would you see it?

8. Hallucinations disappear when they are recognized for what they are. This is the healing and the remedy. Believe them not and they are gone, and all you need to do is recognize that *you* did this. Once you accept this simple fact and take unto yourself the power you gave them, you are released from them. One thing is sure; hallucinations serve a purpose, and when that purpose is no longer held, they disappear. Therefore the question never is whether you want them, but always, do you want the Purpose that they serve? This world seems to hold out many Purposes, each different and with different values. Yet they are all the same. Again there is no order; only a seeming hierarchy of values. Only two purposes are possible. One is sin and the other is holiness. Nothing is in between, and which you choose determines what you see, for what you see is merely how you elect to meet your goal; hallucinations serve to meet the goal of madness. They are the means by which the outside world, projected from, adjusts to sin and seems to witness to its reality. It still is. (Text, 443)

*Average perfectionists are, from fear, obsessed with promoting "their" ideal. Because they inadvertently leave out details in their considerations, they find themselves in conflict with those around them. They get mentally entrenched in their "shoulds" and "oughts." At the lower end of average approaching unhealthy, they get totally disconnected from reality in their own sense of superiority, and consequently end up in their inflexible autistic rut.*

## VL. FEAR AND CONFLICT

1. Being afraid seems to be involuntary; something beyond your own control. Yet I have said already that only constructive acts should be involuntary. My control can take over everything that does not matter, while my guidance can direct everything that does, if you so choose. Fear cannot be controlled by me, but it can be self-controlled. Fear prevents me from giving you my control. The presence of fear shows that you have raised body thoughts to the level of the mind. This removes them from my control and makes you feel personally responsible for them. This is an obvious confusion of levels. (Text, 28–29)

2. I do not foster level confusion, but you must choose to correct it. You would not excuse insane behavior on your part by saying you could not help it. Why should you condone insane thinking? There is a confusion here that you would do well to look at clearly. You may believe that you are responsible for what you think, because it is only at this level that you can exercise choice. What you do comes from what you think. You cannot separate yourself from the truth by "giving" autonomy to behavior. This is controlled by me automatically as soon as you place what you think under my guidance. Whenever you are afraid it is a sure sign that you have allowed your mind to miscreate and have not allowed me to guide it.

3. It is pointless to believe that controlling the outcome of mis-thought can result in healing. When you are fearful you have chosen wrongly. That is why you feel responsible for it. You must change your mind, not your behavior, and your willingness. You do not need guidance except at the mind level. Correction belongs

only at the level where change is possible. Change does not mean anything at the symptom level, where it cannot work.

4. The correction of fear is your responsibility. When you ask for release from fear, you are implying that it is not. You should ask, instead, for help in the conditions that have brought the fear about. These conditions always entail a willingness to be separate. At that level, you *can* help it. You are much too tolerant of mind wandering, and are passively condoning your mind's miscreations. The particular result does not matter, but the fundamental error does. The correction is always the same. Before you choose to do anything, ask me if your choice is in accord with mine. If you are sure that it is, there will be no fear.

5. Fear is always a sign of strain, arising whenever what you want conflicts with what you do. This situation arises in two ways. First, you can choose to do conflicting things, either simultaneously or successively. This produces conflicted behavior, which is intolerable to you because the part of the mind that wants to do something else is outraged. Second, you can behave as you think you should, but without entirely wanting to do so. (Text, 29)

## Chapter 2
## THE SEPARATION AND THE ATONEMENT

This produces consistent behavior, but entails great strain. In both cases, the mind and the behavior are out of accord, resulting in a situation in which you are doing what you do not wholly want to do. This arouses a sense of coercion that usually produces rage, and projection is likely to follow. Whenever there is fear, it is because you have not made up your mind. Your mind is therefore split and your behavior inevitably becomes erratic. Correcting at the behavioral level can shift the error from the first to the second type, but will not obliterate the fear.

6. It is possible to reach a state in which you bring your mind under my guidance without conscious effort, but this implies a willingness that you have not developed as yet. The Holy Spirit cannot ask more than you are willing to do. The strength to do comes from your undivided decision. There is no strain in doing God's will as soon as you recognize that it is also your own. The lesson here is quite simple, but particularly apt to be overlooked. The mind will therefore repeat it, urging you to listen. Only your mind can produce fear. It does so whenever it is conflicted in what it wants, producing inevitable strain because wanting and doing are discordant. This can be corrected only by accepting a unified goal.

7. The first corrective step in undoing the error is to know first that the conflict is an expression of fear. Say to yourself that you must somehow have chosen not to love, or the fear could not have arisen. Then the whole process of correction becomes nothing more than a series of pragmatic steps in the larger process of accepting the Atonement as the remedy. These steps may be summarized in this way:

- Know first that this is fear; fear arises from lack of love.
- The only remedy for lack of love is perfect love.
- Perfect love is the Atonement.

8. I have emphasized that the miracle, or the expression of Atonement, is always a sign of respect *from* the worthy *to* the worthy. The recognition of this worth is re-established by the Atonement. It is obvious, then, that when you are afraid, you have placed yourself in a position where you need Atonement. You have done something loveless, having chosen without love. This is precisely the situation for which the Atonement was offered. The need for the remedy inspired its establishment. As long as you recognize only the need for the remedy you will remain fearful. However, as soon as you accept the remedy, you have abolished the fear. This is how true healing occurs. Everyone experiences fear. Yet it would take very little right thinking to realize why fear occurs. Few appreciate the real power of the mind, and no one remains fully aware of it all

the time; however, if you hope to spare yourself from fear there are some things you must realize, and realize fully. The mind is very powerful, and never loses its creative force. It never sleeps. Every instant it is creating. It is hard to recognize that thought and belief combine into a power surge that can literally move mountains. It appears at first glance that to believe such power about yourself is arrogant, but that is not the real reason you do not believe it. You prefer to believe that your thoughts cannot exert real influence because you are actually afraid of them. This may allay awareness of the guilt, but at the cost of perceiving the mind as impotent. If you believe that what you think is ineffectual, you may cease to be afraid of it, but you are hardly likely to respect it. There are no idle thoughts; all thinking produces form at some level. (Text, 30–31)

*When average perfectionists are in the throes of reforming and correcting everything, they are in fear of losing self-control. Their "very rightly structured argumentations" alienate those that are close to them. At this point, they may have a "Javert" moment of depression, as Javert did in Les Misérables. They then need to realize that their remedy is not to treat the body but their perception.*

## IX. HEALING AS CORRECTED PERCEPTION

1. I said before that the Holy Spirit is the answer. He is the answer to everything, because he knows what the answer to everything is. The ego does not know what a real question is, although it asks an endless number. Yet you can learn this as you learn to question the value of the ego, and thus establish your ability to evaluate its questions. When the ego tempts you to sickness, do not ask the Holy Spirit to heal the body, for this would merely be to accept the ego's belief that the body is the proper aim of healing. Ask, rather, that the Holy Spirit teach you the *right perception* of the

> **Wrong-mindedness:** the part of our separated minds that contains the ego—the voice of sin, guilt, fear, and attack; we are repeatedly asked to choose right-mindedness instead of wrong-mindedness, which imprisons us still further in the world of separation. (Glossary, 228)

body, for perception alone can be distorted. Only perception can be sick, because only perception can be wrong. (Text, 157–158)

4. Think of the love of animals for their offspring, and the need they feel to protect them. That is because they regard them as part of themselves. No one dismisses something he considers part of himself. You react to your ego much as God does to His creations—with love, protection, and charity. Your reactions to the self you made are not surprising. In fact, they resemble in many ways how you will react to your real creations, which are as timeless as you are. The question is not how you respond to the ego, but what you believe you are. Belief is an ego function, and as long as your origin is open to belief you are regarding it from an ego viewpoint. When teaching is no longer necessary you will merely know God. Belief that there is another way of perceiving is the loftiest idea of which ego thinking is capable. "That is because it contains a hint of recognition that the ego is not the self." (Text, 57)

> **Illusion:** something that is believed to be real but is not; the ultimate illusion is the separation from God, upon which rest all the manifestations of the separated world which may be understood as distortions in perception; i.e., seeing attack instead of a call for love, sin instead of error; the illusions of the world reinforce the belief that the body has a value in and of itself, a source of either pleasure or pain; forgiveness is the final illusion as it forgives what never was, and leads beyond all illusions to the truth of God. (Glossary, 112)

*The childhood origin of the perfectionist has that individual forever looking in the rearview mirror of his life, with a steady-state parent demanding and expecting everything to be "right" and "in order" before he is allowed to go out to play.*

2. Consciousness, the level of perception, was the first split introduced into the mind after the separation, making the mind a perceiver rather than a creator. Consciousness is correctly identified as the domain of the ego. The ego is a wrong-minded attempt to perceive yourself as you wish to be, rather than as you are. Yet you can know yourself only as you are, because that is all you can be sure of. Everything else is open to question.

3. The ego is the questioning aspect of the post-separation self, which was made rather than created. It is capable of asking questions but not of perceiving meaningful answers, because these would involve knowledge and cannot be perceived. The mind is therefore confused, because only one-mindedness can be without confusion. A separated or divided mind *must* be confused. It

is necessarily uncertain about what it is. It has to be in conflict because it is out of accord with itself. This makes its aspects strangers to each other, and this is the essence of the fear-prone condition, in which attack is always possible. You have every reason to feel afraid as you perceive yourself. This is why you cannot escape from fear until you realize that you did not and could not create yourself. You can never make your misperceptions true, and your creation is beyond your own error. That is why you must eventually choose to heal the separation. (Text, 42)

*Unhealthy perfectionists are dogmatic and inflexible to the point that they refuse to be proved wrong. Even in the light of true and accurate information showing them to be in obvious error, they persevere in their self-righteous and pedantic stupidity.*

The intolerant and obsessive magical thinking of the perfectionists cycles down into inflexibility, and they are angered and "mind blown" when proved wrong. There is a brittle sense of irate fragility and emptiness in their dogmatic, hypocritical judgment based on their preconceived notions of right and wrong. Magical thinking is rumination over a premise of reality that is irrelevant to the true existing circumstances. The obsession with magical thoughts fuels subsequent madness, and there is a continual lowering of serotonin in the brain, which subsequently deepens depression, and later embitters the self-incrimination of self-imposed guilt.

It is the insanity of preoccupation with black and white, right and wrong, and the culpability of everyone else that steers the perfectionist to his or her perceptual demise. There is an accompanying sense of "lack" expressed by the perfectionist. It is expressed very well by a radio talk show host that said, "The nothing you feel, the nothing you love, and the nothing you give...is yourself."

7. You can encounter only part of yourself because you are part of God, who is everything. His power and glory are everywhere, and you cannot be excluded from them. The Holy Spirit teaches that all strength is in God and therefore in you. God wills no one suffer. He does not will anyone to suffer for a wrong decision, including you. That is why He has given you the means for undoing it. Through His power and glory all your wrong decisions are undone completely, releasing you and your brother from every imprisoning thought any part of the Sonship holds. Wrong decisions have no power, because they are not true. The imprisonment they seem to produce is no truer than they are. (Text, 143)

*The unhealthy perfectionist seeks to correct a problem with the use of improper beliefs. Such beliefs can be said to be ideals that do not fit reality. However, the unhealthy perfectionist worships those improper ideals as idols. They are thus identified as "magical thinking."*

## 17. HOW DO GOD'S TEACHERS DEAL WITH MAGIC THOUGHTS?

1. This is a crucial question both for teacher and pupil. If this issue is mishandled, the teacher of God has hurt himself and has also attacked his pupil. This strengthens fear, and makes the magic seem quite real to both of them. How to deal with magic thus becomes a major lesson for the teacher of God to master. His first responsibility in this is not to attack it. If a magic thought arouses anger in any form, God's teacher can be sure that he is strengthening his own belief in sin and has condemned himself. He can be sure as well that he has asked for depression, pain, fear and disaster to come to him. Let him remember, then, it is not this that he would teach, because it is not this that he would learn.

2. There is, however, a temptation to respond to magic in a way that reinforces it. Nor is this always obvious. It can, in fact, be concealed beneath a wish to help. It is this double wish that makes the help of little value, and must lead to undesired outcomes. Nor should it be forgotten that the outcome that results will always come to teacher and to pupil alike. How many times has it been emphasized that you give but to yourself? Where could this be better shown than in the kinds of help the teacher of God gives to those who need his aid? Here is his gift most clearly given him, for he will give only what he has chosen for himself, and in this gift is his judgment upon the holy Son of God.

3. It is easiest to let error be corrected where it is most apparent, and errors can be recognized by their results. A lesson truly taught can lead to nothing but release for teacher and pupil, who have shared in one intent. Attack can enter only if perception of separate goals has entered, and this must indeed have been the case if the result is anything but joy. The single aim of the teacher turns the decided goal of the pupil into one direction, with the call for help becoming his one appeal. This then is easily responded to with just one answer, and this answer will enter the teacher's mind unfailingly. From there it shines into his pupil's mind, making it one with his.

4. Perhaps it will be helpful to remember that no one can be angry at a fact. It is always an interpretation that gives rise to negative emotions, regardless of their seeming justification by what *appears* as facts. (Manual, 44,45)

8. Into this hopeless situation God sends His teachers. They bring the light of hope from God himself. There is a way in which patience and abundant willingness. Given that, the lesson's manifest simplicity stands out like an intense white light against a black horizon, for such it is. If anger comes from an interpretation and not a fact, it is never justified. Once this is even dimly grasped, the

way is open. Now it is possible to take the next step. The interpretation can be changed at last. Magic thoughts need not lead to condemnation, for they really do not have the power to give rise to guilt, and so they can be overlooked, and thus forgotten in the truest sense.

9. Madness but seems terrible. In truth it has no power to make anything. Like the magic which becomes its servant, it neither attacks nor protects. To see it and to recognize its thought system is to look on nothing. Can nothing give rise to anger? Hardly so. Remember, then, teacher of God, that anger recognizes a reality that is not there, yet is the anger certain witness that you do believe in it as fact. Now is escape impossible, until you see you have responded to your own interpretation, which you have projected on an outside world. Let this grim sword be taken from you now. There is no death. This sword does not exist. The fear of God is causeless, but *His* love is cause of everything beyond all fear, and thus forever real and always true. (Manual, 46)

*The unhealthy perfectionists become neurotically preoccupied and furious with the object of their focus. They become "tunnel-visioned" from reality and thus their mind is split off from reality. They become controlled by their impulsive and irrational thoughts having no bearing on reality. They experience a double dichotomy. On the one side is a split between their impulses and the power repressing those impulses. On the other side is the control they exert over themselves and the breakdown of that control.*

## SPLIT

Without enumerating them as such, the Course describes four levels of splits, which are mirrored in the world by our special relationships:

1. The original thought of separation, when we believed we had split ourselves off from God, leading to the belief in two minds: the mind of Christ and the split mind.
2. The further split of the split mind into the wrong and right minds; the homes of the ego and Holy Spirit.
3. The splitting off of the wrong from the right mind through the belief in the ego's thought system of sin, guilt, and fear; the Holy Spirit's love now being buried beneath the ego's specialness, with God feared rather than accepted.
4. The final ontological split wherein the guilt in our minds is denied and projected out, making a separated world of attack and death, a world which appears to be split off from the mind that thought it. (Glossary, 199)

*See dissociation.*

4. You cannot perpetuate an illusion about another without perpetuating it yourself. There is no way out of this, because it is impossible to fragment the mind. To fragment is to break into pieces, and mind cannot attack or be attacked. The belief that it can, an error the ego always makes, underlies its whole use of projection.
5. It does not understand what mind is, and therefore does not understand what *you* are.
6. Yet its existence is dependent on your mind, because the ego is your belief.
7. The ego is confusion in identification.
8. Never having had a consistent model, it never developed consistently.
9. It is the product of the misapplication of the laws of God by distorted minds that are misusing their power. (Text, 130–131)

*The unhealthy perfectionists get hardwired into avoiding guilt with ritual inflexible thinking, and because they already see themselves mixed in a world of guilt, they are in repressed mode to deal with the level of guilt they are already engaged with, and do not wish to deal with anything that would cause them more guilt.*

## Chapter 13
## THE GUILTLESS WORLD

1. If you did not feel guilty, you could not attack, for condemnation is the root of attack. It is the judgment of one mind by another as unworthy of love and deserving of punishment. But herein lies the split. For the mind that judges perceives itself as separate from the mind being judged, believing that by punishing another, it will escape punishment. All this is but the delusional attempt of the mind to deny itself, and escape the penalty of denial. It is not an attempt to relinquish denial, but to hold on to it, for it is guilt that has obscured the Father to you, and it is guilt that has driven you insane.

2. The acceptance of guilt into the mind of God's Son was the beginning of the separation, as the acceptance of the Atonement is its end. The world you see is the delusional system of those made mad by guilt. Look carefully at this world, and you will realize that this is so; for this world is the symbol of punishment, and all the laws that seem to govern it are the laws of death. Children are born into it through pain and in pain. Their growth is attended by suffering, and they learn of sorrow and separation and death. Their minds seem to be trapped in their brain, and its powers to decline if their bodies are hurt. They seem to love, yet they desert and are deserted. They appear to lose what they love, perhaps the most insane belief of all, and their bodies wither and gasp and are laid in the ground, and are no more. Not one of them but has thought that God is cruel. (Text, 236)

3. If this were the real world, God *would* be cruel, for no Father could subject his children to this as the price of salvation and be loving. *Love does not kill to save.* If it did, attack would be salvation, and this is the ego's interpretation, not God's. Only the world of guilt could demand this, for only the guilty could conceive of it. Adam's "sin" could have touched no one, had he not believed it was the Father who drove him out of Paradise. For in that belief the knowledge of the Father was lost, since only those who do not understand Him could believe it.

4. This world is a picture of crucifixion of God's Son, and until you realize that God's Son cannot be crucified, this is the world you will see. Yet you will not realize this until you accept the eternal fact that God's Son is not guilty. He deserves only love because he has given only love. He cannot be condemned because he has never condemned. The Atonement is the final lesson he need learn, for it teaches him that, never having sinned, he has no need of salvation. (Text, 236–237)

*The unhealthy perfectionist does not invite new information to come to bear on his already-made-up mind. If it is offered, it is summarily rejected without even an acknowledgement of its plausibility.*

## VII. CREATION AND COMMUNICATION

1. It is clear that while the content of any particular ego illusion does not matter, its correction is more helpful in a specific context. Ego illusions are quite specific, although the mind is naturally abstract. Part of the mind becomes concrete, however, when it splits. The concrete part believes in the ego, because the ego depends on the concrete. The ego is the part of the mind that believes your existence is defined by separation.

2. Everything the ego perceives is a separate whole, without the relationships that imply being. The ego is thus against communication,

except insofar as it is utilized to establish separateness rather than to abolish it. The communication system of the ego is based on its own thought system, as is everything else it dictates. Its communication is controlled by its need to protect itself, and it will disrupt communication when it experiences threat. This disruption is a reaction to a specific person or persons. The specificity of the ego's thinking, then, results in spurious generalization which is really not abstract at all. It merely responds in certain specific ways to everything it perceives as related. (Text, 69)

*Unhealthy perfectionists rationalize whatever they think and whatever they do, no matter how much their actions or words contradict their stated beliefs. They are so tightly wound in repressed emotions that they explode into fury or guilt as they lean against the negative side of regret. These feelings easily erupt, to the surprise of the perfectionist, who is trying to stay controlled.*

## V. THE EGO'S USE OF GUILT

1. Perhaps some of our concepts will become clearer and more personally meaningful if the ego's use of guilt is clarified. The ego has a purpose, just as the Holy Spirit has. The ego's purpose is fear, because only the fearful can be egotistic. The ego's logic is as impeccable as that of the Holy Spirit, because your mind has the means at its disposal to side with Heaven or Earth, as it elects; but again, remember that both are in you.

2. In Heaven there is no guilt, because the Kingdom is attained through the Atonement, which releases you to create. The word "create" is appropriate here because, once what you have made is undone by the Holy Spirit, the blessed residue is restored and therefore continues in creation. What is truly blessed is incapable of giving rise to guilt, and must give rise to joy. This makes it invulnerable

to the ego because its peace is unassailable. It is invulnerable to disruption because it is whole. Guilt is *always* disruptive. Anything that engenders fear is divisive because it obeys the laws of division. If the ego is the symbol of the separation, it is also the symbol of the guilt. Guilt is more than merely not of God. It is the symbol of attack on God. This is a totally meaningless concept except to the ego, but do not underestimate the power of the ego's belief in it. This is the belief from which all guilt really stems. (Text, 83–84)

3. The ego is the part of the mind that believes in division. How could part of God detach itself without believing it is attacking Him? We spoke before of the authority problem as based on the concept of usurping God's power. The ego believes that this is what you did because it believes that it is you. If you identify with the ego, you must perceive yourself as guilty. Whenever you respond to your ego you will experience guilt, and you will fear punishment. The ego is quite literally a fearful thought. However ridiculous the idea of attacking God may be to the sane mind, never forget that the ego is not sane. It represents a delusional system, and speaks for it. Listening to the ego's voice means that you believe it is possible to attack God, and that a part of Him has been torn away by you. Fear of retaliation from without follows, because the severity of the guilt is so acute that it must be projected.

4. Whatever you accept into your mind has reality for you. It is your acceptance of it that makes it real. If you enthrone the ego in your mind, your allowing it to enter makes it your reality. This is because the mind is capable of creating reality or making illusions. I said before that you must learn to think with God. To think with Him is to think like Him. This engenders joy, not guilt, because it is unnatural. Unnatural thinking will always be attended with guilt, because it is the belief in sin. The ego does not perceive sin as a lack of love, but as a positive act of assault. This is necessary to the ego's survival, because as soon as you regard sin as a lack, you will automatically attempt to remedy the situation, and you will succeed. The ego regards this as doom, but you must learn to regard it as freedom.

> **Scarcity principle:** an aspect of guilt; the belief that we are empty and incomplete, lacking what we need. This leads to our seeking idols or special relationships to fill the scarcity we experience within ourselves; inevitably projected into feelings of deprivation, wherein we believe others are depriving us of the peace which in reality *we* have taken from ourselves; in contrast to God's principle of abundance. (Glossary, 183)

5. The guiltless mind cannot suffer. Being sane, the mind heals the body because it has been healed. The sane mind cannot conceive of illness because it cannot conceive of attacking anyone or anything. I said before that illness is a form of magic. It might be better to say that it is a form of magical solution. The ego believes that by punishing itself, it will mitigate the punishment of God. (Text, 84–85)

*The unhealthy perfectionists operate in an information vacuum and realize that something is missing, but are in denial that it is their mind denying its own capability to allow new information in. They take the scarcity notion to believe that everyone and everything else is lacking.*

## Chapter 2

### THE SEPARATION AND THE ATONEMENT

#### *1. The Origins of Separation*

1. To extend is a fundamental aspect of God which He gave to His Son. In the creation, God extended himself to His creations and

imbued them with the same loving will to create. You have not only been fully created, but have also been created perfect; there is no emptiness in you; because of your likeness to your Creator, you are creative. No child of God can lose this ability because it is inherent in what he is, but he can use it inappropriately by projecting. The inappropriate use of extension, or projection, occurs when you believe that some emptiness or lack exists in you, and that you can fill it with your own ideas instead of truth. This process involves the following steps:

- First, you believe that what God created can be changed by your own mind.
- Second, you believe that what is perfect can be rendered imperfect or lacking.
- Third, you believe that you can distort the creations of God, including yourself.
- Fourth, you believe that you create yourself, and that the direction of your own creation is up to you.

2. These related distortions represent a picture of what actually occurred in the separation, or the "detour into fear." None of this actually existed before the separation, nor does it actually exist now. Everything God created is like Him. Extension, as undertaken by God, is similar to the inner radiance that the children of the Father inherit from Him. Its real source is internal. This is as true of the Son as of the Father. In this sense the creation includes both the creation of the Son by God, and the Son's creations when his mind is healed. This requires God's endowment of the Son with free will, because all loving creation is freely given in one continuous line, in which all aspects are of the same order.

3. The Garden of Eden, or the pre-separation condition, was a state of mind in which nothing was needed. When Adam listened to the "lies of the serpent," all he heard was untruth. (Text, 17)

8. The world but demonstrates an ancient truth; you will believe that others do to you exactly what you think you did to them, but once deluded into blaming them, you will not see the cause of what they do, because you *want* the guilt to rest on them. How childish is the petulant device to keep your innocence by pushing guilt outside yourself, but never letting go. It is not easy to perceive the jest when all around you do your eyes behold its heavy consequences, but without their trifling cause. Without the cause, do its effects seem serious and sad indeed? Yet they but follow, and it is their cause that follows nothing and is but a jest. (Text, 587)

# LESSON 352 (ARCHETYPE STANCE)

*Judgment and love are opposites. From one come all the sorrows of the world, but from the other comes the peace of God Himself.*

1. Forgiveness looks on sinlessness alone, and judges not. Through this I come to you. Judgment will bind my eyes and make me blind. Yet love, reflected in forgiveness here, reminds me; You have given me a way to find Your peace again. I am redeemed when I elect to follow in this way. You have not left me comfortless. I have in me both the memory of You and the one who leads me to it. *Father, I would hear Your voice and find Your peace today; for I would love my own identity and find it in the memory of You.*

# LESSON 301 (DEMATERIALIZATION)

*And God Himself shall wipe away all tears.*

*Father, unless I judge I cannot weep, nor can I suffer pain, or feel I am abandoned or unneeded in the world. This is my home because I judge it not, and therefore is it only what You will. Let me today behold* it uncondemned, through happy eyes forgiveness has released from all distortion. Let me see Your world instead of mine, and all the tears I shed will be forgotten, for their source is gone. Father, I will not judge Your world today.

God's world is happy. Those who look on it can only add their joy to it, and bless it as a cause of further joy in them.

## LESSON 322 (GROWTH LINE)
*I can give up but what was never real.*

1. I sacrifice illusions; nothing more, and as illusions go I find the gifts illusions tried to hide, awaiting me in shining welcome and in readiness to give God's ancient messages to me. His memory abides in every gift that I receive of Him, and every dream serves only to conceal the Self which is God's only Son; the likeness of Himself, the Holy One who still abides in Him forever, as He still abides in me.

2. Father, to You all sacrifice remains forever inconceivable, and so I cannot sacrifice except in dreams. As You created me, I can give up nothing You gave me. What You did not give has no reality. What less can I anticipate except the loss of fear and the return of love into my mind?

# CHAPTER 2
# THE HELPER-GIVER

"Giving to get" [that is, associating giving with sacrifice] is an inescapable law of the ego.

(ACIM Text, 52, 58)

# A HEALTHY HELPER-GIVER ACCORDING TO A COURSE IN MIRACLES

*The healthy two is encouraging, empathetic, and graciously giving. Giving—receiving.*

*The healthy helper-giver is altruistic and truly has the other person's needs and welfare in mind when he offers his help, gifts, and support. He seems to embody the Holy Relationship.*

The Holy Spirit's means to undo the unholy or special relationship by shifting the goal of guilt to the goal of forgiveness or truth; the process of forgiveness by which one who had perceived another as separate joins with him in his mind through Christ's vision. (Glossary, 102)

*The healthy twos truly enjoy doing for others and they nurture the underdog.*

---

**Right-mindedness:** giving and receiving are identical, reflecting Heaven's principle of abundance and the law of extension; spirit can never lose, since when one gives love, one receives it. The Holy Spirit's gifts are qualitative, not quantitative, and thus are increased as they are shared; the same principle works on the ego level, for as one gives guilt away (projection) one receives it. (Glossary, 82)

**Joining:** despite the dreams of separation, the Sons of God remain joined with each other as Christ, and joined with God in perfect oneness; however, since we share the illusion of being separate, we must first share the illusion of joining with each other, which reflects the process of forgiveness occurring in our minds; only then can we awaken and remember that we are already joined; joining with Jesus or the Holy Spirit is the prerequisite for joining with our brothers. (Glossary, 119)

> **Holy Relationship:** the Holy Spirit's means to undo the unholy or special relationship by shifting the goal of guilt to the goal of forgiveness or truth; the process of forgiveness by which one who had perceived another as separate joins with him in his mind through Christ's Vision. (Glossary, 102)

*They are God's perfect mothers and the ideal companion to help, do, provide, and assist in any conceivable way. They join and engage for the good of the people they help.*

*The mind of the two is on the magnanimous focus at this time of health. This magnanimity allows him to love and care freely without any thought of sacrifice on his part or any thought of "giving to get."*

## III. THE DECISION FOR GUILTLESSNESS

1. The happy learner cannot feel guilty about learning. This is so essential to learning that it should never be forgotten. The guiltless learner learns easily because his thoughts are free. Yet this entails the recognition that guilt is interference,

not salvation, and serves no useful function at all. (Text, 274) (#2+3-Transcendence for a 2)

*The healthy twos give the benefit of the doubt to their friend and support them in every way. There seems to be a nonstop aspect to their flow of love, empathy, and support for their friend.*

### Littleness versus Magnitude

11. If you are wholly willing to leave salvation to the plan of God and unwilling to attempt to grasp peace for yourself, salvation will be given you. Yet think not you can substitute your plan for His. Rather, join with me in His that we may release all those who would be bound, proclaiming together that the Son of God is host to him.

12. Call forth in everyone only the remembrance of God, and of Heaven that is in him. For where you would have your brother be, there will you think you are. (Text, 309)

Hear not his appeal to hell and littleness, but only his call for Heaven and greatness. Forget not that his call is yours, and answer him with me. God's power is forever on the side of his host, for it protects only the peace in which he dwells. Lay not littleness before His Holy Altar, which rises above the stars and reaches even to Heaven, because of what is given it. (Text, 309)

*The healthy two truly gives credit and support to his friend. There is no gift held back, no favor not done or forwarded. The helping and giving seem to have no end, and it is for this reason that it is so easy to "just let him do everything," because that is how the helper-giver wants everything to be.*

### *Lifting of the Veil*

17. Give faith to your brother, for faith and hope and mercy are yours to give. Into the hands that give, the gift is given. Look on your brother, and see in him the gift of God you would receive. It is almost Easter, the time of Resurrection. Let us give redemption to each other and share in it, that we may rise as one in resurrection, not separate in death. Behold the gift of freedom that I gave the Holy Spirit for you, and be you and your brother free together, as you offer to the Holy Spirit this same gift. (Text, 423–424)

8. Heaven waits silently, and your creations are holding out their hands to help you cross and welcome them: for it is they you seek. You seek but for your own completion, and it is they who render you complete. The special love relationship is but a shabby substitute for what makes you whole in truth, not in illusion. Your relationship with them is without guilt, and this enables you to look on all your brothers with gratitude, because your creations were created in union with them. Acceptance of your creations is the acceptance of the oneness of creation, without which you could never be complete. No specialness can offer you what God has given, and what you are joined with him in giving. (Text, 339)

## THE AVERAGE TWO ACCORDING TO A COURSE IN MIRACLES

*The average two is gushy, demonstrative, and full of good intentions about everything. There is a dissociation and a disconnect when it comes to people pleasing, and it is that they keep score but cannot truly receive the love and reciprocal feelings of another.*

The body is the ego's home by its own election. It is the only identification with which the ego feels safe, since the body's vulnerability

is its own best argument that you cannot be of God. This is the belief that the ego sponsors eagerly. Yet the ego hates the body because it cannot accept it as good enough to be its home. Here is where the mind becomes actually dazed. Being told by the ego that it is really part of the body and that the body is its protector, the mind is also told that the body cannot protect it. Therefore, the mind asks, "Where can I go for protection?" To which the ego replies, "Turn to me." The mind, and not without cause, reminds the ego that it has itself insisted that it is identified with the body, so there is no point in turning to it for protection. The ego has no real answer to this because there is none, but it does have a typical solution. It obliterates the question from the mind's awareness. Once out of awareness, the question can and does produce uneasiness, but it cannot be answered because it cannot be asked. (Text, 66)
*The two's ego flares and a truth from A Course in Miracles becomes apparent:* "Wherever you act egotistical toward another, you are throwing away the graciousness of your indebtedness and the Holy perception it would produce." (Text, 67, 2.3)

---

*Such is the "and so it goes" of the two. It cannot ask the question of "being" because the mind goes to...the verb state of...doing...for meaning. When the receiver of all this "doing" gets to overwhelm... and the two does not receive the satisfaction of being...loved, appreciated, or recognized, or to the point of being...ignored or attempted gotten rid of because he "doesn't get the point"; thus, the two gets angry and vengeful. Also, at this point twos feel as though they have been "set up" and are anxious about being the object of even small affections.*

---

*The average helper-givers experiences separation from ever being loved because they themselves are in the attitudinal posture of adversarial rejection and don't realize it. Thus, they are in separation and denial at this state of health.*

When and if a two can come to the realization of wrong choices and realize that "your part is merely to return your thinking to the point at which the error was made, and give it over to the Atonement in peace. Say this to yourself as sincerely as you can, remembering that the Holy Spirit will respond fully to your slightest invitation;

> *I must have decided wrongly, because I am not at peace. I made the decision myself, but I can also decide otherwise. I want to decide otherwise because I want to be at peace. I do not feel guilty because the Holy Spirit will undo all the consequences of my wrong decision if I will let Him. I choose to let Him by allowing Him to decide for God for me.*
>
> (Text, 90)

*The average helper-givers feel they are indispensable because they feel they cannot do enough for others. Thus, they are driven by guilt. They experience strange guilt enshrouded in denial, which puts them in separation.*

The belief in sin that affirms an identity separate from our Creator; seemed to happen once, and the thought system which arose from the idea is represented by the ego; results in a world of perception and form, of pain, suffering, and death, real in time, but unknown in eternity.

    4. God's laws will keep your mind at peace because peace is His will, and His laws are established to uphold it. His are the laws of freedom, but yours are the laws of bondage. Since freedom and bondage are irreconcilable, their laws cannot be understood

## THE HELPER-GIVER

together. The laws of God work only for your good, and there are no other laws besides His. Everything else is merely lawless and therefore chaotic. Yet God himself has protected everything He created by His laws. Everything that is not under them does not exist. "Laws of chaos" is a meaningless term. Creation is perfectly lawful, and the chaotic is without meaning because it is without God. You have "given" your peace to the gods you made, but they are not there to take it from you, and you cannot give it to them.

5. You are not free to give up freedom, but only to deny it. You cannot do what God did not intend, because what He did not intend does not happen. Your gods do not bring chaos; you are endowing them with chaos and accepting it of them. All this has never been. Nothing but the laws of God has ever been, and nothing but His will, will ever be. You were created through His laws and by His will, and the manner of your creation established you a creator. What you have made is so unworthy of you that you could hardly want it, if you were willing to see it as it is. You will see nothing at all, and your vision will automatically look beyond it, to what is in you and all around you. Reality cannot break through the obstructions you interpose, but it will envelop you completely when you let them go.

6. When you have experienced the protection of God, the making of idols becomes inconceivable. There are no strange images in the Mind of God, and what is not in His mind belongs to Him. It is yours *because* it belongs to Him, for to Him ownership is sharing, and if it is so for Him, it is so for you. His definitions *are* His laws, for by them He established the universe as what it is. No false gods you attempt to interpose between yourself and your reality affect truth at all. Peace is yours because God created you, and He created nothing else. (Text, 188)

*You cannot be your guide for miracles, for it is you who made them necessary.* (Text, 298)

# Chapter 13
## THE GUILTLESS WORLD

### Introduction

1. If you did not feel guilty, you could not attack, for condemnation is the root of attack. It is the judgment of one mind by another as unworthy of love and deserving of punishment. But herein lies the split. For the mind that judges perceives itself as separate from the mind being judged, believing that by punishing another, it will escape punishment. All this is but the delusional attempt of the mind to deny itself, and escape the penalty of denial. It is not an attempt to relinquish denial, but to hold on to it, for it is guilt that has obscured the Father to you, and it is guilt that has driven you insane.

2. The acceptance of guilt into the mind of God's Son was the beginning of the separation, as the acceptance of the Atonement is its end. The world you see is the delusional system of those made mad by guilt. Look carefully at this world, and you will realize that this is so; for this world is the symbol of punishment, and all the laws that seem to govern it are the laws of death. Children are born into it through pain and in pain. Their growth is attended by suffering, and they learn of sorrow and separation and death. Their minds seem to be trapped in their brain, and its powers to decline if their bodies are hurt. They seem to love, yet they desert and are deserted. They appear to lose what they love, perhaps the most insane belief of all, and their bodies wither and gasp and are laid in the ground, and are no more. Not one of them but has thought that God is cruel.

3. If this were the real world, God *would* be cruel, for no Father could subject his children to this as the price of salvation and be loving. *Love does not kill to save.* If it did, attack would be salvation, and this is the ego's interpretation, not God's. Only the world of guilt could demand this, for only the guilty could conceive of it. Adam's "sin" could have touched no one, had he not believed it was

# THE HELPER-GIVER

the Father who drove him out of Paradise. For in that belief the knowledge of the Father was lost, since only those who do not understand Him could believe it. (Text, 236)

*The average helper-giver descends from altruistically helping and supporting others to power-brokering their praise and support in exchange for attention and reciprocal praise and support. Their helping and supporting is merely a business deal of contractual expectation of reciprocity. Their help really gets expensive.*

    6. Yours is the independence of creation, not of autonomy. Your whole creative function lies in your complete dependence on God, whose function he shares with you. By his willingness to share it, He became as dependent on you as you are on him. Do not ascribe the ego's arrogance on him who wills not to be independent of you. He has included you in his autonomy. Can you believe autonomy is meaningful apart from Him? The belief in ego autonomy is costing you the knowledge of your dependence upon God, in which your freedom lies. The ego sees all dependence as threatening, and has twisted even your longing for God into a means of establishing itself; but do not be deceived by its interpretation of your conflict. (Text, 203–204)

    5. Fear is always a sign of strain, arising whenever what you want conflicts with what you do. This situation arises in two ways. First, you can choose to do conflicting things, either simultaneously or successively. This produces conflicted behavior, which is intolerable to you because the part of the mind that wants to do something else is outraged. Second, you can behave as you think you should, but without entirely wanting to do so. (Text, 641, #3)

*The helper-giver's original altercation with the authority figure results in a resultant unearned guilt that sets up the helper-giver, not fully realizing his motives for doing what he does. The guilt sets a love-hate relationship in motion, where the helper-givers are in denial of their motives and feel more anger and expectation, and at the same time they refuse to accept love and affection from any significant other.*

13. Remember, then, that whenever you look without and react unfavorably to what you see, you have judged yourself unworthy and have condemned yourself to death. The death penalty is the ego's ultimate goal, for it fully believes that you are a criminal, as deserving of death as God knows you are deserving of life. The death penalty never leaves the ego's mind, for that is what it always reserves for you in the end, wanting to kill you as the final expression of its feeling for you. It lets you live but to await death. It will torment you while you live but its hatred is not satisfied till you die; for your destruction is the one end toward which it works, and the only end with which it will be satisfied.

14. The ego is not a traitor to God, to whom treachery is impossible; but it is a traitor to you who believe that you have been treacherous to your Father. That is why the undoing of guilt is an essential part of the Holy Spirit's teaching, for as long as you feel guilty you are listening to the voice of the ego, which tells you that you have been treacherous to God and therefore deserve death. You will think that death comes from God and not from the ego because, by confusing yourself with the ego, you believe you want death, and from what you want, God does not save you. (Text, 232–233)

## THE UNHEALTHY TWO ACCORDING TO A COURSE IN MIRACLES

*Out of the two's desire to conform to be good, the essence of substantial emotional referencing is omitted and there is only the form or appearance established in the mind of the two. The unhealthy two unwillingly becomes a martyr through hypochondriasis and the somatopsychic physical breakdowns of overwork and self-appointed victimization in spite of the (perceived) "others" who disappoint them. It was their self-serving manipulations that created the rejection by others in the first place, trying to instill guilt in others because they did not return the favor.*

## V. THE DENIAL OF GOD

1. The rituals of the god of sickness are strange and very demanding. Joy is never permitted, for depression is the sign of allegiance to him. Depression means that you have forsworn God. Many are afraid of blasphemy, but they do not understand what it means. They do not realize that to deny God is to deny their own identity, and in this sense the wages of sin is death. The sense is very literal; denial of life perceives its opposite, as all forms of denial replace what is with what is not. No one can really do this, but that you think you can and believe you have is beyond dispute.

2. Do not forget, however, that to deny God will inevitably result in projection, and you will believe that others, and not yourself, have done this to yourself. You must receive the message you give because it is the message you want. You may believe that you judge your brothers by the messages they give you, but you have judged them by the message you give to them. Do not attribute your denial of joy to them, or you cannot see the spark in them that would bring joy to you. It is the denial of the spark that brings depression, for whenever you see your brothers without it you are denying God.

3. Allegiance to the denial of God is the ego's religion. The god of sickness obviously demands the denial of health, because health is in direct opposition to its own survival. But consider what this means to you: unless you are sick you cannot keep the gods you made, for only in sickness could you possibly want them. Blasphemy, then, is self-destructive, not God-destructive. It means you are willing not to know yourself in order to be sick. This is the offering

> **Perception:** the world of separation has never left its source in the separated mind, though it appears to be external to it; thus, there is no material world, only a projected illusion of one.
>
> **Wrong-mindedness:** projecting guilt from our minds by attack reinforces its presence in the mind that thought it. (Glossary, 109)

your god demands because, having made him out of your insanity, he is an insane idea; the denial of God. (Text, 190)

4. Sickness and death seemed to enter the mind of God's Son against his will. The "attack on God" made his Son think he was fatherless, and out of his depression he made the god of depression.

5. Your gods are nothing, because your Father did not create them. You cannot make creators who are unlike your Creator, any more than He could have created a Son who was unlike Him. If creation is sharing, it cannot create what is unlike itself. It can share only what it is. Depression is isolation, and so it could not have been created. (Text, 190)

*The unhealthy twos do this "unaware" of their own motivation, like automatic heat-seeking missiles on autopilot. They get resentful and angry in their entitlement-driven vengeance to "get their due." Mentally they have placed their loved ones in their debt. The two's conviction is that God's loving being has no home in the two's life.*

# THE HELPER-GIVER

You have so little faith in yourself because you are unwilling to accept the fact that perfect love is in you; and so you seek without for what you cannot find without. (Text, 314–315)

## SACRIFICE IS THE TWO'S MAJOR "CURRENCY"

4. Sacrifice is a notion totally unknown to God. It arises solely from fear, and frightened people can be vicious. Sacrificing in any way is a violation of my injunction that you should be merciful even as your Father in Heaven is merciful. It has been hard for many Christians to realize that this applies to themselves. God teachers never terrorize their students. To terrorize is to attack, and this results in rejection of what the teacher offers. The result is learning failure. (Text, 37)

*The unhealthy helper-givers, in their original intent to "appear good," separate in their false pride to oftentimes do one thing and give the impression that the motivation was for another thing. Thus, they act and feel in bifurcation and are incongruent in their actions and motivations.*

### *Split*

Without enumerating them as such, the Course describes four levels of splits, which are mirrored in the world by our special relationships:
The original thought of separation, when we believed we had split ourselves off from God, leading to the belief in two minds: the mind of Christ and the split mind.
The further split of the split mind into the wrong and right minds, the laws of the ego and the Holy Spirit.

The splitting off of the wrong from the right mind through the belief in the ego's thought system of sin, guilt, and fear; the Holy Spirit's love now being buried beneath the ego's specialness, with God feared rather than accepted.
The final ontological split wherein the guilt in our minds is denied and projected out, making a separated world of attack and death, a world which appears to be split off from the mind that thought it. (Text, 213)

Yet consider how strange a solution the ego's arrangement is. You project guilt to get rid of it, but you are actually merely concealing it. You do experience the guilt, but you have no idea why. On the contrary, you associate it with a weird assortment of "ego ideals," which the ego claims you have failed. Yet you have no idea that you are failing the Son of God by seeing him as guilty. Believing you are no longer you, you do not realize that you are failing yourself. (Text, 240)

## IV. SEEKING AND FINDING

1. The ego is certain that love is dangerous and this is always its central teaching. It never puts it this way; on the contrary, everyone who believes that the ego is salvation seems to be intensely engaged in the search for love. Yet the ego, though encouraging the search for love very actively, makes one proviso: do not find it. Its dictates, then, can be summed up simply as "seek and do not find." This is the one proviso it will keep, for the ego pursues its goals with fanatic insistence, and its judgment, though severely impaired, is completely consistent. (Text, 240)

*"Ideas leave not their source" is the expression of cause and effect, for cause and effect cannot be separate; an idea cannot leave the mind that thought it.*

Magic is the mindless or miscreative use of mind. Physical medications are forms of "spells," but if you are afraid to use the mind to heal, you should not attempt to do so. The very fact that you are afraid makes your mind vulnerable to miscreation. You are therefore likely to misunderstand any healing that might occur, and because egocentricity and fear usually occur together, you may be unable to accept the real Source of the healing. (Text, 25)

*The unhealthy helper-giver is locked into a denial of arrogance dressed up as humility. Religious systems give the helper-givers a framework of language that enables them to indulge in fantasies where they see themselves as saints and saviors by justifying all their good works and best intentions to sacrifice themselves for the love of others. This then whiplashes into the resultant feelings that they are not appreciated. They allow themselves to become physically broken-down, so as to say, "Look what I have done to myself and what I have become for you."*

The ego, then, raised the first question that was ever asked, but one it can never answer. That question, "What are you?" was the beginning of doubt. The ego has never answered any questions since, although it has raised a great many. The most inventive activities of the ego have never done more than obscure the question, because you have the answer and *the ego is afraid of you.* (Text, 101)

## LESSON 304 (DEMATERIALIZATION)
*Let not my world obscure the sight of Christ.*

1. I can obscure my holy sight, if I intrude my world upon it. Nor can I behold the holy sights Christ looks upon, unless it is His vision that I use. Perception is a mirror, not a fact; and what I look on is my state of mind, reflected outward. I would bless the world

by looking on it through the eyes of Christ, and I will look upon the certain signs that all my sins have been forgiven me.

2. *You lead me from the darkness to the light; from sin to holiness. Let me forgive, and thus receive salvation for the world. It is Your gift, my Father, given me to offer to Your Holy Son, that He may find again the memory of You, and of Your Son as You created Him.*

# LESSON 290 (ARCHETYPE)
*My present happiness is all I see.*

1. Unless I look upon what is not there, my present happiness is all I see. Eyes that begin to open see at last, and I would have Christ's vision come to me this very day. What I perceive without God's Own Correction for the sight I made is frightening and painful to behold. Yet I would not allow my mind to be deceived by the belief the dream I made is real an instant longer. This day I seek my present happiness, and look on nothing else except the thing I seek.

2. With this resolve I come to You, and ask Your strength to hold me up today, while I but seek to do Your will. You cannot fail to hear me, Father. What I ask have You already given me, and I am sure that I will see my happiness today.

# LESSON 308 (GROWTH LINE)
*This instant is the only time there is.*

1. I have conceived of time in such a way that I defeat my aim. If I elect to reach past time to timelessness, I must change my perception of what time is for. Time's purpose cannot be to keep the past and future one. The only interval in which I can be saved from time is now, for in this instant has forgiveness come to set me free. The birth of Christ is now, without a past or future. He has come to

give His present blessing to the world, restoring it to timelessness and love; and love is ever-present, here and now.

2. *Thanks for this instant, Father. It is now I am redeemed. This instant is the time You have appointed for Your Son's release, and for salvation of the world in him.*

## CHAPTER 3
# THE SUPER ACHIEVER

The ego is nothing more than a part of your
    belief about yourself.
                           (*ACIM* Text, 61, 67)

**Wish-Will:** the ego wishes, spirit wills knowledge; willing expresses creation, which is truth, perception; wishing can reflect wrong- or right-mindedness, both inherently illusory, since wishing implies that there exists a reality other than the Unity of Heaven. (Glossary, 82)

# A HEALTHY SUPER ACHIEVER ACCORDING TO A COURSE IN MIRACLES

*The healthy super achiever is often attractive and holds widely admired ideals of position and status. They reflect qualities of authentic inner-directed virtues while preserving for success.*

16. The miracle but calls your ancient Name, which you will recognize because the truth is in your memory, and to this name your brother calls for his release and yours. Heaven is shining on the Son of God. Deny him not that you may be released. Each instant is the Son of God reborn until he chooses not to die again. In every wish to hurt, He chooses death instead of what His Father wills for Him. Yet every instant offers life to him because His Father wills that he should live. (Text, 557)

7. Salvation is a paradox indeed! What could it be except a happy dream? It asks you but you forgive all things that no one ever did; to overlook what is not there, and not to look upon the unreal as

reality. You are but asked to let your will be done, and seek no longer for the things you do not want, and you are asked to let yourself be free of all the dreams of what you never were and seek no more to substitute the strength of idle wishes for the Will of God. (Text, 635)

*Competition is so ingrained for the threes that they only muster up more aggression to overcome the transgressions of others. They see no need for "forgiveness" and thus put no stock in it whatsoever. They need to let go of the vain will to release the tenacity of the past image.*

5. Forgiveness is a symbol, too, but as the symbol of His will alone it cannot be divided, and so the unity that it reflects becomes His will. It is the only thing still in the world in part, and yet the bridge to Heaven.

6. God's will is all there is. We can but go from nothingness to everything; from Hell to Heaven. Is this a journey? No, not in truth, for truth goes anywhere, but illusions shift from place to place; from time to time. The final step is also but a shift. As a perception it is part unreal, and yet this part will vanish; what remains is peace eternal and the Will of God. (Manual, 83)

*The healthy super achiever strives to be in demand, effective, successful, and a "somebody." If they cannot achieve that image they will fake it till they make it. They develop a very tough tenacity to super achieve. In that process they shut down their personal needs and those of everyone else around them to get the work done.*

7. There are no wishes now for wishes change; even the wished-for can become unwelcome. That must be so because the ego cannot be at peace; but will is constant, as the gift of God, and what he gives is always like himself. This is the purpose of the Face

of Christ. It is the gift of God to save His Son; but look on this and you have been forgiven.

8. How lovely does the world become in just that simple instant when you see the truth about yourself reflected there. Now you are sinless and behold your sinlessness. Now you are holy and perceive it so; and now the mind returns to its Creator, the joining of the Father and the Son, the Unity of unities that stands behind all joining but beyond them all. God is not seen but only understood. His Son is not attacked but recognized. (Manual, 83–84)

4. That is why you need to demonstrate the obvious to yourself. It is not obvious to you. You believe that doing the opposite of God's Will can be better for you. You also believe that it is possible to *do* the opposite of God's will; therefore you believe that an impossible choice is open to you, and one which is both fearful and desirable. Yet God wills; he does not wish. Your will is as powerful as His because it is His. The ego's wishes do not mean anything, because the ego wishes for the impossible. You can wish for the impossible, but you can will only with God. This is the ego's weakness and your strength.

5. The Holy Spirit always sides with you and with your strength. As long as you avoid His guidance in any way, you want to be weak; yet weakness is frightening. What else, then, can this decision mean except that you want to be fearful? The Holy Spirit never asks for sacrifice, but the ego always does. Projection is a confusion in motivation, and given this confusion, trust becomes impossible. No one gladly obeys a guide he does not trust, but this does not mean that the guide is untrustworthy. In this case, it always means that the follower is. However, this too is merely a matter of his own belief; believing that he can betray, he believes that everything can betray him. Yet this is only because he has elected to follow false guidance. Unable to follow this guidance without fear, he associates fear with

guidance, and refuses to follow any guidance at all. If the result of this decision is confusion, this is hardly surprising.

6. The Holy Spirit is perfectly trustworthy, as you are. God Himself trusts you, and therefore your trustworthiness is beyond question. It will always remain beyond question, however much you may question it. I said before that you are the Will of God. His Will is not an idle wish, and your identification with His Will is not optional, since it is what you are. Sharing His Will with me is not really open to choice, though it may seem to be. The whole separation lies in this error. The only way out of the error is to decide that you do not have to decide anything. Everything has been given you by God's decision. That is His will, and you cannot undo it.

7. Even the relinquishment of your false decision-making prerogative, which the ego guards so jealously, is not accomplished by your wish. It was accomplished for you by the Will of God, who has not left you comfortless. His voice will teach you how to distinguish between pain and joy, and will lead you out of the confusion you have made. There is no confusion in the mind of a Son of God, whose will must be the will of the Father, because the Father's will is His Son.

8. Miracles are in accord with the Will of God, whose will you do not know because you are confused about what you will. This means that you are confused about what you are. If you are God's will and do not accept his will, you are denying joy. The miracle is therefore a lesson in what joy is. Being a lesson in sharing it is a lesson in love, which *is* joy. Every miracle is thus a lesson in truth, and by offering truth you are learning the difference between pain and joy. (Text, 134–135)

5. Learning is an ability you made and gave yourself. It was not made to do the will of God, but to uphold a wish that it could be opposed, and that a will apart from it was yet more real than it. This is what learning sought to demonstrate, and you have learned what

it was made to teach. Now does your ancient overlearning stand implacable before the Voice of Truth, and teach you that its lessons are not true; too hard to learn, too difficult to see, and too opposed to what is really true. (Text, 646)

4. God is in everything I see. Behind every image I have made, the truth remains unchanged; behind every veil I have drawn across the face of love, its light remains undiminished. Beyond all my insane wishes is my will, united with the will of my Father. God is still everywhere and in everything forever. And we who are a part of Him will yet look past all appearances, and recognize the truth beyond them all. (Workbook, 93)

2. It does not wish to contain God, but wills to extend His being. (Text, 132)

*The super achiever overlearns the image of success to the point that self-evident truths are seen through the jaded eyes of prejudicated realities and have given those truths altered weights of evidence. Thus, they do not share the same deference with other individuals. (Pilate asked Jesus, "What is truth?")*

6. It is impossible that one illusion be less amenable to truth than are the rest, but it is possible that some are given greater value, and less willingly offered to truth for healing and for help. No illusion has any truth in it, yet it appears some are more true than others, although this clearly makes no sense at all. All that a hierarchy of illusions can show is preference, not reality. What relevance has preference to truth? Illusions are illusions and are false. Your preference gives them no reality. Not one is true in any way, and all must yield with equal ease to what God gave as answer to them all. God's will is one; and any wish that seems to go against His will has no foundation in the truth. (Text, 554–555)

9. The world you perceive is a world of separation. Perhaps you are willing to accept even death to deny your Father. Yet he would not have it so, and so it is not so. You still cannot will against Him, and that is why you have no control over the world you have made. It is not a world of will because it is governed by the desire to be unlike God, and this desire is not will. The world you made is therefore totally chaotic, governed by arbitrary and senseless "laws," and without meaning of any kind. For it is made out of what you do not want, projection from your mind because you are afraid of it. Yet this world is only in the mind of its maker, along with his real salvation. Do not believe it is outside of yourself, for only by recognizing where it is will you gain control over it; for you do have control over your mind, since the mind is the mechanism for decision. (Text, 222–223)

2. These related distortions represent a picture of what actually occurred in the separation, or the "detour into fear." None of these existed before the separation, nor does it actually exist now. Everything God created is like Him. Extension as undertaken by God is similar to the inner radiance that the children of the Father inherit from Him. Its real source is internal. This is as true of the Son as of the Father. In this sense the creation includes both the Creation of the Son of God and the Son's creations when his mind is healed. This requires God's endowment of the Son with free will, because all loving creation is freely given in one continuous line in which all aspects are of the same order. (Text, 17)

3. The Garden of Eden, or the pre-separation condition, was a state of mind in which nothing was needed. When Adam listened to the "lies of the serpent," all he heard was untruth. You do not have to continue to believe what is not true unless you choose to do so. All that can literally disappear in the twinkling of an eye because it is merely a misperception; what is seen in dreams to be very real.

# THE SUPER ACHIEVER

> **Free will (1):** existent only in the illusory world of perception where it appears that the Son of God has the power to separate himself from God; since on the perceptual level we chose to be separate, we can also choose to change our minds; this freedom of choice—between wrong- and right-mindedness—is the only one possible in this world; in the non-dualistic state of Heaven's perfect oneness, choosing cannot exist, and therefore free will as it is usually understood is meaningless in reality.
>
> **(NOTE:** not to be confused with "freedom of will," which reflects that the Will of God *cannot* be imprisoned by the ego, and therefore must always remain free.)
>
> *See: free will (2)*

Healthy super achievers take on the image of success as their only course of reality. When others fall short of a super achiever's expectations, he does not forgive them, but merely disregards them. The super achiever's efforts are further intensified to make up for the other person's shortcoming by achieving even more. Thus, the super achiever works even harder, disregarding his health, and similarly disregarding the personal aspects of those around them.

## LESSON 73
*I will there be light.*

1. Today we are considering the will you share with God. This is not the same as the ego's idle wishes, out of which darkness and nothingness arise. The will you share with God has all the power of creation in it. The ego's idle wishes are unshared and therefore have no power at all. Its wishes are not idle in the sense that they can make a world of illusions in which your belief can be very strong, but

**Free will (2):** an aspect of our free will within the illusion; we are free to believe what reality is, but since reality was created by God we are not free to change it in any way; our thoughts do not affect reality, but do affect what we believe and experience to be reality. (Text, 146)

*See: free will (1)*

they are idle indeed in terms of creation. They make nothing that is real.

2. Idle wishes and grievances are partners or co-makers in picturing the world you see. The wishes of the ego gave rise to it, and the ego's need for grievances, which are necessary to maintain it, peoples it with figures that seem to attack you and call for "righteous" judgment. These figures become the middlemen the ego employs to traffic in grievances. They stand between your awareness and your brother's reality. Beholding them, you do not know your brothers or your Self.

3. Your will is lost to you in this strange bartering, in which guilt is traded back and forth, and grievances increase with each exchange. Can such a world have been created by the will the Son of God shares with his Father? Did God create disaster for His Son? Creation is the will of both together. Would God create a world that kills Himself?

4. Today we will try once more to reach the world that is in accordance with your will.

The light is in it because it does not oppose the will of God. It is not Heaven, but the light of Heaven shines on it. Darkness has vanished. The ego's idle wishes have been withdrawn, yet the light that shines upon this world reflects your will, and so it must be in you that we will look for it.

5. Your picture of the world can only mirror what is within. The source of neither light nor darkness can be found without. Grievances darken your mind, and you look out on a darkened world. Forgiveness lifts the darkness, reasserts your will, and lets you look upon a world of light. We have repeatedly emphasized that the barrier of grievances is easily passed, and cannot stand between you and your salvation....Do you really want to be in hell? Do you really want to weep and suffer and die?

6. Forget the ego's arguments which seek to prove all this is really Heaven. You know it is not so. You cannot want this for yourself; there is a point beyond which illusions cannot go. Suffering is not happiness, and it is happiness you really want. Such is your will in truth, and so salvation is your will as well. You want to succeed in what we are trying to do today. We undertake it with your blessing and your glad accord.

7. We will succeed today if you remember that you want salvation for yourself. You want to accept God's plan because you share in it. You have no will that can really oppose it, and you do not want to do so. Salvation is for you. Above all else, you want the freedom to remember who you really are. Today it is the ego that stands powerless before your will. Your will is free, and nothing can prevail against it.

8. Therefore, we undertake the exercises for today in happy confidence, certain that we will find what it is your will to find, and remember what it is your will to remember. No idle wishes can detain us, nor deceive us with an illusion of strength. Today let your will be done, and end forever the insane belief that it is hell in place of Heaven that you choose.

9. We will begin our longer practice periods with the recognition that God's plan for salvation, and only His, is wholly in accord with your will. It is not the purpose of an alien power, thrust upon you unwillingly. It is the one purpose here on which you and your Father are in perfect accord. You will succeed today, the time appointed for the release of the Son of God from hell and from all idle wishes. His will is now restored to his awareness. He is willing this very day to look upon the light in him and be saved.

10. After reminding yourself of this, and determining to keep your will clearly in mind, tell yourself with gentle firmness and quiet certainty:

*I will there be light. Let me behold the light that reflects God's will and mine.*

Then let your will assert itself, joined with the power of God and united with your Self. Put the rest of the practice period under their guidance. Join with them as they lead the way.

11. In the shorter practice periods, again make a declaration of what you really want. Say:

*I will there be light. Darkness is not my will.*

This should be repeated several times an hour. It is most important, however, to apply today's idea in this form immediately [if] you are tempted to hold a grievance of any kind. This will help you let your grievances go, instead of cherishing them and hiding them in darkness. (Workbook, 127–129)

*Many people aspire to achieve the three's ambition, self-direction, and tough-minded stick-to-it-iveness. They reach the highest education levels and wind up being in control of their profession.*

No force except your own free will is strong enough to guide you. In this you are as free as God and must remain so forever. Let us ask the Father in my name to keep you mindful of His love for you and yours for Him. He has never failed to answer this request, because it asks only for what He has already willed. Those who call truly are always answered. Thou shalt have no other gods before Him because there are none. (Text, 61)

5. Do not underestimate the power of the devotion of God's Son, nor the power of the God He worships has over Him; for He places Himself at the altar of His God, whether it be the God he made or the God who created Him. That is why his slavery is as complete as his freedom, for he will obey only the God he accepts. The God of crucifixion demands that he crucify, and his worshippers obey. In His name they crucify themselves, believing that the power of the Son of God is born of sacrifice and pain. The God of resurrection demands nothing, for He does not will to take away. He does not require obedience, for obedience implies submission. He would only have you learn your will and follow it, not in the spirit of sacrifice and submission, but in the gladness of freedom. (Text, 208)

6. Resurrection must compel your allegiance gladly, because it is the symbol of joy. Its whole compelling power lies in the fact that it represents what you want to be. The freedom to leave behind everything that hurts you and humbles you and frightens you cannot be thrust upon you, but it can be offered you through the grace of God, and you can accept it by his grace, for God is gracious to His Son, accepting Him without question as His own. Who, then, is your own? The Father has given you all that He is, and He Himself is yours with them. Guard them in their resurrection, for otherwise you will not awake in God, safely surrounded by what is yours forever. (Text, 208)

The total senselessness of such a curriculum must be fully recognized before a real change in direction becomes possible. You cannot learn simultaneously from two teachers who are in total disagreement about everything. Their joint curriculum presents an impossible learning task. They are teaching you entirely different things in entirely different ways. Which might be possible, but they are teaching you about yourself. Your reality is unaffected by both, but if you listen to both, your mind will be split about what your reality is. (Text, 139)

## SPECIAL HOLY RELATIONSHIPS

Yet Heaven is sure. There is no dream. Its coming means that you have chosen truth, and it has come because you have been willing to let your special relationship meet its conditions. In your relationship the Holy Spirit has gently laid the real world; the world of happy dreams, from which awakening is so easy and natural. For as your sleeping and your waking dreams represent the same wishes in your mind, so do the real world and the truth of Heaven join in the will of God. Dreams of waking are easily transferred to its reality. For this dream reflects your will joined with the will of God; and what this will would have accomplished has never not been done. (Text, 377–378)

# LESSON 239

*The glory of my Father is my own.*

1. Let not the truth about ourselves today be hidden by a false humility. Let us instead be thankful for the gifts our Father gave us. Can we see in those with whom He shares His glory any trace of sin and guilt? Can it be that we are not among them when He loves

> **Idol:** symbol of the substitution of the ego for our true self or God; a false belief that there can be something other than, or more than God, and thus separate from him, a belief which is then projected onto the special relationship; people, ideas, the anti-Christ. (Glossary, 111)

His Son forever and with perfect constancy, knowing he is as He created him?

2. *We thank You, Father, for the light that shines forever in us; and we honor it, because You share it with us. We are one, united in this light and one with You, at peace with all creation and ourselves.*

## LESSON 240

*Fear is not justified in any form.*

1. Fear is deception. It attests that you have seen yourself as you could never be, and therefore look upon a world which is impossible. Not one thing in this world is true. It does not matter what the form in which it may appear. It witnesses but to your own illusions of yourself. Let us not be deceived today. We are the Sons of God. There is no fear in us, for we are each a part of Love itself.

2. How foolish are our fears! Would you allow Your Son to suffer? Give us faith today to recognize Your Son, and set him free. Let us forgive him in Your name, that we may understand

his holiness, and feel the love for him which is Your own as well. (Workbook, 412)

*All super achievers aspire to look their best, wear the best clothes, and drive the best cars. Their houses are the best, and they constantly aspire to be the most affluent, with all the trappings.*

## 3. WHAT IS THE WORLD?

1. The world is false perception. It is born of error, and it has not left its source. It will remain no longer than the thought that gave it birth is cherished. When the thought of separation has been changed to one of true forgiveness, will the world be seen in quite another light; and one which leads to truth, where all the world must disappear and all its errors vanish. Now its source has gone, and its effects are gone as well.

2. The world was made as an attack on God. It symbolizes fear; and what is fear except love's absence? Thus the world was meant to be a place where God could enter not, and where His son could be apart from Him. Here was perception born, for knowledge could not cause such insane thoughts; but eyes deceive, and ears hear falsely. Now mistakes become quite possible, for certainty has gone.

3. The mechanisms of illusions have been born instead, and now they go to find what has been given them to seek. Their aim is to fulfill the purpose which the world was made to witness and make real. They see in its illusions but a solid base where truth exists, upheld apart from lies. Yet everything that they report is but illusion which is kept apart from truth.

4. As sight was made to lead away from truth, it can be redirected. Sounds become the call for God, and all perception can be given a new purpose by the one whom God appointed Savior to the

world. Follow his light, and see the world as he beholds it. Hear His voice alone in all that speaks to you; and let him give you peace and certainty, which you have thrown away, but Heaven has preserved for you in Him.

5. Let us not rest content until the world has joined our changed perception. Let us not be satisfied until forgiveness has been made complete, and let us not attempt to change our function. We must save the world; for we who made it must behold it through the eyes of Christ; that what was made to die can be restored to everlasting life. (Workbook, 413)

2. Never approach the holy instant after you have tried to remove all fear and hatred from your mind. That is its function. Never attempt to overlook your guilt before you ask the Holy Spirit's help. That is *His* function. Your part is only to offer Him a little willingness to let Him remove all fear and hatred, and to be forgiven. On your little faith, joined with His understanding, He will build your part in the Atonement and make sure that you fulfill it easily; and with him you will build a ladder planted in the solid rock of faith, and rising even to Heaven. Nor will you use it to ascend to Heaven alone.

3. Through your holy relationship, reborn and blessed in every holy instant you do not arrange, thousands will rise to Heaven with you. Can you plan for this? Or could you prepare yourself for such a function? Yet it is possible, because God wills it; nor will He change his mind about it. The means and purpose both belong to him. You have accepted one; the other will be provided. A purpose such as this, without the means, is inconceivable. He will provide the means to anyone who shares His purpose.

4. Happy dreams come true, not because they are dreams, but only because they are happy, and so they must be loving. Their message is, "Thy will be done," and not, "I want it otherwise." The alignment of means and purpose is an undertaking impossible for

> **Means-end:** despite the multitude of means in the world, there remain but two ends or goals: truth or illusion; the body can serve either end, as the mind elects.
>
> **Wrong-mindedness:** the body is used as a means to bring about the goal of sin and guilt, reinforcing illusion through the special relationship.
>
> **Right-mindedness:** the body is used as a means to bring about forgiveness, leading us to truth through the holy relationship.
>
> (Glossary, 145)

you to understand. You do not even realize you have accepted the Holy Spirit's purpose as your own, and you would merely bring unholy means to its accomplishment. The little faith it needed to change the purpose is all that is required to receive the means and use them.

5. It is no dream to love your brother as yourself. Nor is your holy relationship a dream. All that remains of dreams within it is that it is still a special relationship. Yet it is very useful to the Holy Spirit, who has a special function here. It will become the happy dream through which He can spread joy to thousands on thousands who believe that love is fear, not happiness. Let Him fulfill the function that He gave to your relationship by accepting it for you and nothing will be wanting that would make of it what he would have it be. (Text, 383–384)

## THE AVERAGE SUPER ACHIEVER ACCORDING TO A COURSE IN MIRACLES

*The career-oriented super achievers are automatically obsessed with*

> **w--m** the dynamics we use to "protect" ourselves from our guilt, fear, and seeming attack of others, the most important of which are denial and projection; by their very nature "defenses do what they would defend" as they reinforce the belief in our own vulnerability which merely increases our fear and belief that we need defense
>
> (Gloss.p.57)

*self-image and how they appear to others. They shut down the needs of others and themselves to "get the work done" and achieve the end they have in mind as fast as possible, even if they cut corners or "cheat."*

Their self-image of a doer is of greater importance than their sense of "being"; thus, their sense of self is the view they accept that others have of them, and that is the only view they ascribe to.

6. It should especially be noted that God has only one Son. If all his creations are his Sons, everyone must be an integral part of the whole Sonship. The Sonship of its Oneness transcends the sum of its parts; however, this is observed as long as any parts are missing. That is why the conflict cannot be ultimately resolved until all the parts of the Sonship have returned. Only then can the meaning of wholeness in the

true sense be understood. Any part of the Sonship can believe in error or incompleteness if he so chooses; however, if he does so, he is believing in the existence of nothingness. The correction of this error is the Atonement.

7. I have already briefly spoken about readiness, but some additional points might be helpful. Readiness is only the prerequisite for accomplishment. The two should not be confused. As soon as a state of readiness occurs, there is usually some degree of desire to accomplish, but it is by no means necessarily undivided. The state does not imply more than a potential for a change of mind. Confidence cannot develop fully until mastery has been accomplished. We have already attempted to correct the fundamental error that fear can be mastered, and have emphasized that the only real mastery is through love. Readiness is only the beginning of confidence. You may think that this implies that an enormous amount of time is necessary between readiness and mastery, but let me remind you that time and space are under my control. (Text, )p.33)

*Threes are competitively calculating and efficiently goal-oriented in their overt pragmatism. They may be bored beyond their better senses; however, they also adopt the attitude of, "don't think about it; just get it over with." They can shut down their feelings to get the job done.*

2. The essence of grandiosity is competitiveness, because it always involves attack. It is a delusional attempt to outdo, but not to undo. We said before that the ego vacillates between suspiciousness and viciousness. It remains suspicious as long as you despair of yourself. It shifts to viciousness when you decide not to tolerate self-abasement and seek relief. Then it offers you the illusion of attack as a "solution."

> **Right-mindedness:** reinterpreted as the means to free us from fear; e.g., denial denies "the denial of truth," and projecting our guilt enables us to be aware of what we have denied, so that we may truly forgive it.
>
> (Glossary, 57)

3. The ego does not understand the difference between grandeur and grandiosity, because it sees no difference between miracle impulses and ego-alien beliefs of its own. I told you that the ego is aware of threat to its existence, but makes no distinctions between these two very different kinds of threat. Its profound sense of vulnerability renders it incapable of judgment except in terms of attack. When the ego experiences threat, its only decision is whether to attack now or to withdraw to attack later. If you accept its offer grandiosity it will attack immediately; if you do not, it will wait.

4. The ego is immobilized in the presence of God's grandeur, because His grandeur establishes your freedom. Even the faintest hint of your reality literally drives the ego from your mind, because you will give up all investment in it. Grandeur is totally without illusions, and because it is real it is compellingly convincing. Yet the conviction of reality will not remain with you unless you do not allow the ego to attack it. The ego will make every effort to recover

and mobilize its energies against your release. It will tell you that you are insane, and argue that grandeur cannot be a real part of you because of the littleness in which it believes. Yet your grandeur is not delusional because you did not make it. You made grandiosity and are afraid of it because it is a form of attack, but your grandeur is of God, who created it of His love.

5. From your grandeur you can only bless, because your grandeur is your abundance. By blessing you hold it in your mind, protecting it from illusions and keeping yourself in the Mind of God. Remember always that you cannot be anywhere except in the Mind of God. When you forget this, you *will* despair and you *will* attack.

6. The ego depends solely on your willingness to tolerate it. If you are willing to look upon your grandeur you cannot despair, and therefore you cannot want the ego. Your grandeur is God's answer to the ego, because it is true. Littleness and grandeur cannot coexist, nor is it possible for them to alternate. Littleness and grandiosity can and must alternate, since both are untrue and are therefore on the same level. Being the level of shift, it is experienced as shifting and extremes are its essential characteristic. (Text, 178)

7. Truth and littleness are denials of each other because grandeur is truth. Truth does not vacillate; it is always true. When grandeur slips away from you, you have replaced it with something you have made. Perhaps it is the belief in littleness; perhaps it is the belief in grandiosity. Yet it must be insane because it is not true. Your grandeur will never deceive you, but your illusions always will; illusions are deceptions. You cannot triumph, but you *are* exalted, and in your exalted state you seek others like you and rejoice with them.

8. It is easy to distinguish grandeur from grandiosity, because love is returned and pride is not. Pride will not produce miracles,

and will therefore deprive you of the true witnesses to your reality. Truth is not obscure nor hidden, but its obviousness to you lies in the joy you bring to its witnesses, who show it to you. They attest to your grandeur, but they cannot attest to pride because pride is not shared. God wants you to behold what He created because it is His joy.

9. Can your grandeur be arrogant when God Himself witnesses to it? What can be real that has no witnesses to it? What good can come of it? If no good can come of it the Holy Spirit cannot use it. What He cannot transform to the Will of God does not exist at all. Grandiosity is delusional, because it is used to replace your grandeur. Yet what God has created cannot be replaced. God is incomplete without you because His grandeur is total, and you cannot be missing from it.

10. You are altogether irreplaceable in the Mind of God. No one else can fill your part in it, and while you leave your part of it empty your eternal place merely waits for your return. God, through His voice, reminds you of it, and God Himself keeps your extensions safe within it. Yet you do not know them until you return to them. You cannot replace the Kingdom, and you cannot replace yourself. God, who knows your value, would not have it so, and so it is not so. Your value is in God's Mind, and therefore not in yours alone. To accept yourself as God created you cannot be arrogance, because it is the denial of arrogance. To accept your littleness *is* arrogant, because it means that you believe your evaluation of yourself is truer than God's. (Text, 179)

*Prestige and status are the goals and motives beneath the thin veneer of the super achiever's "for others' well-being" façade. Their career and success are the currency of their entire being.*

2. True denial is a painful protective device. You can and should deny any belief that error can hurt you. This kind of denial is not concealment but a correction. Your right mind depends on it. Denial of error is a strong defense of truth, but denial of truth results in miscreation, the projections of the ego. In the service of the right mind the denial of error frees the mind, and reestablishes the freedom of will. When the will is really free it cannot miscreate because it recognizes only truth. (Text, 19)

*The average super achiever is affectless and icily calculating, with no (or muted) sympathy. The senses of empathy, mirth, or altruism are simply nonexistent in any of their machinations.*

## DENIAL
### The Totality of the Kingdom

1. Whenever you deny a blessing to a brother you will feel deprived, because denial is as total as love. It is as impossible to deny part of a Sonship as it is to love it in part. Nor is it possible to love it totally at times. You cannot be totally committed sometimes. Denial has no power in itself, but you can give it the power of your mind, when power is without limit. If you use it to deny reality, reality is gone for you. Reality cannot be partly appreciated. That is why denying any part of it means you have lost the awareness of all of it. Yet denial is a defense, and so it is capable of being used positively as well as negatively. Used negatively it will be destructive, because it will be used for attack; "but in the service of the Holy Spirit, it can help you recognize part of reality, and thus appreciate all of it." Mind is too powerful to be subject to exclusion. You will never be able to exclude yourself from your thoughts. (Text, 127)

# THE SUPER ACHIEVER

**Illusion:** something that is believed to be real but is not; the ultimate illusion is the Separation from God, upon which rest all the manifestations of the separated world which may be understood as distortions in perception; i.e., seeing attack instead of a call for love, sin instead of error; the illusions of the world reinforce the belief that the body has a value in and of itself, a source of pleasure and of pain; forgiveness is the final illusion, as it forgives what never was and leads beyond all illusions to the Truth of God. (Glossary, 112)

## OVERLEARNING

5. Learning is an ability you made and gave yourself. It was not made to do the will of God, but to uphold a wish that it could be opposed, and that a will apart from it was yet more real than it. This is what learning sought to demonstrate, and you have learned what it was made to teach. Now does your ancient overlearning stand implacable before the Voice of Truth, and teach you that its lessons are not true; too hard to learn, too difficult to see, and too opposed to what is really true; yet you will learn them, for their learning is the only purpose for your learning skill the Holy Spirit sees in all the world. His simple lessons in forgiveness have a power mightier than yours, because they call from God and from yourself to you. (Text, 646)

*They make themselves sound better than they truly are, trying to maintain the image of success at all costs. Even in the face of defeat, bad luck, or ill health, still...the show goes on. Average super achievers always have that "packaged-friendly" façade,*

> **Attack:** the attempt to justify the projection of guilt onto others, demonstrating their sinfulness and guilt so that we may feel free of it, because attack is always a projection of responsibility for the separation, it is never justified; also used to denote the thought of separation from God, for which we believe God will attack and punish us in return. (Glossary, 34)

and give others the sense that they are there but their hearts are not. (There are no hearts to find.)

### Body

4. Yet space between you and your brother is apparent only in the present now and cannot be perceived in future time; no more can it be overlooked except for the present. Future loss is not your fear, but present joining is your dread. Who can feel desolation except now? A future cause (as of yet) has no effects, and therefore it must be that if you have fear, there is a present cause, and it is this that needs correction, not a future state. (Text, 559)

*With their arrogant façade of pretentiousness they delve into the disease of narcissism. At this point, hostility and a surprising contempt for others surface as a source from total surprise.*

## THE UNHEALTHY SUPER ACHIEVER ACCORDING TO A COURSE IN MIRACLES

*When a super achiever reaches the point of unhealthy, a pathological liar emerges from this "out for himself" opportunistic and exploitative spoiler of others' successes—because he could not attain success himself.*

4. The ego speaks in judgment, and the Holy Spirit reverses its decision, much as a higher court has the power to reverse a lower court's decisions in this world. The ego's decisions are always wrong, because they were based on the error they were to uphold. Nothing the ego perceives is interpreted correctly. Not only does the ego cite Scripture for its purpose, but it even interprets Scripture, as a witness for itself. The Bible is a fearful thing in the ego's judgment. Perceiving it as frightening, it interprets it fearfully. Being afraid, you do not appeal to the Higher Court because you believe its judgment would also be against you.

5. There are many examples of how the ego's interpretations are misleading, but a few will suffice to show how the Holy Spirit can reinterpret them in his own light.

6. *"As ye sow, so shall ye reap"* He interprets to mean what you consider worth cultivating you will cultivate in yourself. Your judgment of what is worthy makes it worthy for you.

7. *"Vengeance is mine, sayeth the Lord"* is easily reinterpreted if you remember that ideas increase only by being shared. The statement emphasizes that vengeance cannot be shared. Give it therefore to the Holy Spirit, who will undo it in you because it does not belong in your mind, which is part of God.

8. *"I will visit the sins of the fathers unto the third and fourth generation,"* as interpreted by the ego, is particularly vicious. It becomes merely an attempt to guarantee the ego's own survival. To the Holy Spirit, the statement means that in later generations he can still reinterpret what former generations had misunderstood, and thus release the thoughts from the ability to produce fear. (Text, 87)

*Super achievers become devious and deceptive only to maintain their image.*

### *Depersonalized*

When you meet anyone, remember it is a Holy encounter. As you see him, you will see yourself. As you think of him, you will think of yourself. Never forget this, for in him you will find yourself or lose yourself. (Text, 141, 8)

*Super achievers often become sadistic, psychopathic, and murderous; saboteurs and assassins are frequently super achievers.*

## VI. THE TEST OF TRUTH

1. There is nothing outside you. That is what you must ultimately learn, for the realization that the Kingdom of Heaven is restored to you. For God created only this and he did not depart from it nor leave it separate from Himself. The Kingdom of Heaven is the dwelling place of the Son of God, who left not His Father and dwells not apart from Him. Heaven is not a place or condition. It is merely awareness of perfect Oneness, and the knowledge that there is nothing else; nothing outside this Oneness and nothing else within.

2. What could God give but the knowledge of Himself? What else is there to give? The belief that you could give and get something else, something outside of yourself, has cost you the awareness of Heaven, and of your identity; and you have done a stranger thing than you have yet to realize. You have displaced your guilt from your body to your mind. Yet a body cannot be guilty, for it can do nothing of itself. You who think you hate your body deceive yourself. You hate your mind, for guilt has entered into it, and it would remain separate from your brother's, which it cannot do. (Text, 384)

3. Minds are joined, bodies are not. Only by assigning to the mind the properties of the body does separation seem to be possible;

and it is mind that seems to be fragmented and private and alone. Its guilt, which keeps it separate, is projected to the body, which suffers and dies because it is attacked to hold the separation in the mind, and let it not know its Identity. Mind cannot attack, but it can make fantasies and direct the body to act them out; yet it is never what the body does that seems to satisfy. Unless the mind believes the body is acting out its fantasies, it will attack the body by increasing the projection of its guilt upon it.

4. In this, the mind is clearly delusional. It cannot attack, but maintains that it can, and uses what it does to hurt the body to prove it can. The mind cannot attack, but it can deceive itself, and this is all it does when it believes it has attacked the body. It can project its guilt, but cannot lose it through projection; and though it clearly can misperceive the function of the body, it cannot change its function from what the Holy Spirit establishes it to be. The body was not made up by love; yet love does not condemn it and can use it lovingly, respecting what the Son of God has made and using it to save him from illusions.

5. Would you not have the instruments of separation reinterpreted as means for salvation, and used for purposes of love? Would you not welcome and support the shift of fantasies of vengeance to release from them? "Your perception of the body can clearly be sick, but project not this upon the body. For your wish to make destructive what cannot destroy can have no real effect at all." What God created is only what He would have it be, being His will. You cannot make His will destructive; you can make fantasies in which your will conflicts with His, but that is all.

6. It is insane to use the body as the scapegoat for guilt, directing its attack and blaming it for what you wished it to do. It is impossible to act out fantasies, for it is still the fantasies you want, and they have nothing to do with what the body does. It does not dream of them, and they but make it a liability, where it could be an asset; for fantasies have made your body your enemy: weak, vulnerable,

and treacherous, worthy of the hate that you invest in it. How has this served you? You have identified with this thing you hate, the instrument of vengeance and the perceived source of your guilt. You have done this to a thing that has no meaning, proclaiming it to be the dwelling place of God's Son, and turning it against him. (Text, 385)

7. This is the host of God that *you* have made, and neither God nor His most Holy Son can enter an abode that harbors hate, and where you have sown the seeds of vengeance, violence and death. This thing you made to serve your guilt stands between you and other minds. The minds are joined, but you do not identify with them. You see yourself locked in a separate prison, removed and unreachable, as incapable of reaching out as being reached. You hate this prison you have made and would destroy it, but you would not escape from it, leaving it unharmed, without your guilt upon it.

8. Yet only thus can you escape. The home of vengeance is not yours; the place you set aside to house your hate is not a prison, but an illusion of yourself. The body is a limit imposed on the universal communication that is an eternal property of mind, but the communication is eternal. Mind reaches to itself. It is *not* made up of different parts, which reach each other. It does not go out. Within itself it has no limits and there is nothing outside it. It encompasses everything. It encompasses you entirely; you within it and it within you. There is nothing else, anywhere or ever.

9. The body is outside you, and but seems to surround you, shutting you off from others and keeping you apart from them, and them from you. It is not there. There is no barrier between God and His Son, nor can His Son be separated from Himself except in illusions. This is not his reality, though he believes it is. Yet this could only be if God were wrong. God would have had to create differently, and to have separated Himself from His Son to make this possible. He would have had to create different things, and to establish different orders of reality, only some of which were love.

# THE SUPER ACHIEVER

Yet love must be forever like itself, changeless forever, and forever without alternative: and so it is. (Text ,386)

9. The ego values only what it takes. This leads to the *fourth* law of chaos, which, if the others are accepted, must be true. This seeming law is the belief you have in what you have taken. By this, another's loss becomes your gain, and thus it fails to recognize that you can never take away, save from yourself. Yet all the other laws must lead to this, for enemies do not give willingly to one another, nor would they seek to share the things they value. What your enemies would keep from you must be worth having, because they keep it hidden, from your sight.

10. All of the mechanisms of madness are seen emerging here: the "enemy" made strong by keeping hidden the valuable inheritance that should be yours; your justified position and attack for what has been withheld; and the inevitable loss the enemy must suffer to save yourself. Thus do the guilty ones protest their "innocence." Were they not forced into this foul attack by the unscrupulous behavior of the enemy, they would respond with only kindness, but in a savage world the kind cannot survive, so they must take or else be taken from.

11. And now there is a vague unanswered question, not yet "explained." What is this precious thing, this priceless pearl, this hidden secret treasure, to be wrested in righteous wrath from this most treacherous and cunning enemy? It must be what you want but never found. Now you "understand" the reason why you found it not; for it was taken from you by this enemy and hidden where you would not think to look. He hid it in his body, making the cover from his guilt, the hiding place for what belongs to you. Now must his body be destroyed and sacrificed, that you may have that which belongs to you. His treachery demands his death, which you may live, and you attack only in self-defense. (Text, 491–492)

4. It is hard to perceive sickness as a false witness, because *you* do not realize that it is entirely out of keeping with what you want. This witness, then, appears to be innocent and trustworthy because you have not seriously cross-examined him. If you had, you would not consider sickness such a strong witness on behalf of the ego's views. A more honest statement would be that those who want the ego are predisposed to defend it. Therefore, their choice of witnesses should be suspect from the beginning. The ego does not call upon witnesses who would disagree with its case, nor does the Holy Spirit. I have said that judgment is the function of the Holy Spirit, and one He is perfectly equipped to fulfill. The ego as a judge gives anything but an impartial judgment. When the ego calls on a witness, it has already made the witness an ally.

5. It is still true that the body has no function of itself, because it is not an end. The ego, however, establishes it as an end because, as such, its true function is obscured. This is the purpose of everything the ego does. Its sole aim is to lose sight of the function of everything. A sick body does not make any sense. It could not make sense because sickness is not what the body is for. Sickness is meaningful only if the two basic premises on which the ego's interpretation of the body rests are true; that the body is for attack and that you are a body. Without these premises sickness is inconceivable.

6. Sickness is a way of demonstrating that you can be hurt. It is a witness to your frailty, your vulnerability, and your extreme need to depend on external guidance. The ego uses this as its best argument for your need for its guidance. It dictates endless prescriptions for avoiding catastrophic outcomes. The Holy Spirit, perfectly aware of the same situation, does not bother to analyze it at all. If data are meaningless there is no point in analyzing them. The function of truth is to collect information that is true. Any way you handle error results in nothing. The more complicated the results become, the harder it may be to recognize their nothingness, but it

is not necessary to examine all possible outcomes to which premises give rise in order to judge them truly.

7. A learning device is not a teacher. It cannot tell you how you feel. You do not know how you feel because you have accepted the ego's confusion, and you therefore believe that a learning device *can* tell you how you feel. Sickness is merely another example of your insistence on asking guidance of a teacher who does not know the answer. The ego is incapable of knowing how you feel. When I said the ego does not know anything, I said the one thing about the ego that is wholly true; but there is a corollary: if only knowledge has being and the ego has no knowledge, then the ego has no being.

## X. THE END OF INJUSTICE

1. What, then, remains to be undone for you to realize their presence? Only this; you have a differential view of when attack is justified, and when you think it is unfair and not to be allowed. When you perceive it as unfair, you think that a response of anger now is just, and thus you see what is the same as different. Confusion is not limited. If it occurs at all it will be total, and its presence, in whatever form, will hide their presence. They are known with clarity or not at all. Confused perception will block knowledge. It is not a question of the size of the confusion, or how much it interferes. "Its simple presence shuts the door to theirs, and keeps them there unknown." (Text, 562)

2. What does it mean if you perceive attack in certain forms to be unfair to you? It means that there must be some forms in which you think it fair. For otherwise, how could some be evaluated as unfair? Some, then, are given meaning and perceived as sensible; and only some are seen as meaningless. This denies the fact that all are senseless, equally without a cause or consequence, and cannot have effects of any kind. Their presence is obscured by any veil that

stands between their shining innocence, and your awareness that it is your own and equally belongs to every living thing along with you. God limits not, and what is limited cannot be Heaven...so it must be Hell.

3. Unfairness and attack are one mistake, so firmly joined that where one is perceived the other must be seen. You cannot be unfairly treated. The belief you are is but another form of the idea you are deprived by someone not yourself. Projection of the cause of sacrifice is at the root of everything perceived to be unfair and not your just desserts. Yet it is you who ask this of yourself, in deep injustice to the Son of God. You have no enemy except yourself, and you are enemy indeed to him because you do not know him as yourself. What could be more unjust than that he be deprived of what he is, denied the right to be himself, and asked to sacrifice His Father's love and yours as not his due?

4. Beware of the temptation to perceive yourself unfairly treated. In this view, you seek to find an innocence that is not Theirs but yours alone, and at the cost of someone else's guilt. Can innocence be purchased by the giving of your guilt to someone else? Is it innocence that your attack on him attempts to get? Is it not retribution for your own attack upon the Son of God you seek? Is it not safer to believe that you are innocent of this, and victimized despite your innocence? Whatever way the game of guilt is played, there must be loss. Someone must lose his innocence that someone else can take it from him, making it his own.

5. You think your brother is unfair to you because you think that one must be unfair to make the other innocent. In this game, do you perceive one purpose for your whole relationship? This you seek to add unto the purpose given it. The Holy Spirit's purpose is to let the Presence of your Holy guests be known to you. To this purpose nothing can be added, for the world is purposeless except for this. To add or take away from this one goal is but to take away all purpose from the world and from yourself. (Text, 563–564)

# THE SUPER ACHIEVER

1. You will attack what does not satisfy you, and then you will not see you made it up. You always fight illusions, for the truth behind them is so lovely and so still in loving gentleness, were you aware of it, you could forget defensiveness entirely and rush to its embrace. The Truth could never be attacked, and this you knew when you made idols. They were made that this might be forgotten. You attack but false ideas and never truthful ones. All idols are the false ideas you made to fill the gap you think arose between yourself and what is true, and you attack them for the things you think they represent what lies beyond them cannot be attacked. (Text, p.633, IV #1)

6. sub 7. You have identified with this thing you hate, the instrument of vengeance and the perennial source of your guilt. You have done this to a thing that has no meaning, proclaiming it to be the dwelling place of God's Son, and turning it against him. (Text, p.386 VI 6 sub 7)

*Many times super achievers appear in court after their dirty deed, and they look as innocent as children, which blows the jurors' minds. Threes can make a chameleonlike change into this totally innocent persona.*

### The Function of Reason

2. Reality needs no cooperation from you to be itself, but your awareness of it needs your help, because it is your choice. Listen to what the ego says, and see what it directs you see, and it is sure that you will see yourself as tiny, vulnerable, and afraid. You will experience depression, a sense of unworthiness, and feelings of impermanence and unreality. You will believe that you are helpless prey to forces far beyond your own control and far more powerful than you. You will think the world you made directs your destiny;

for this will be your faith…but never believe, because it is your faith that it makes reality.

## LESSON 288
*Let me forget my brother's past today.  (Dematerialization)*

1. *This is the thought that leads the way to You, and brings me to my goal. I cannot come to you without my brother, and to know my source, I first must recognize what You created one with me. My brother's is the hand that leads me on the way to You. His sins are in the past along with mine, and I am saved because the past is gone. Let me not cherish it within my heart, or I will lose the way to walk to you. My brother is my savior. Let me not attack the savior You have given me, but let me honor him who bears Your name, and so remember that it is my own.*
2. *Forgive me, then, today, and you will know you have forgiven me if you behold your brother in the light of holiness. He cannot be less holy than can I, and you cannot be holier than he.*

## LESSON 227    (GROWTH LINE)
*This is my holy instant of release.*

1. *Father, it is today that I am free, because my will is Yours. I thought to make another will; yet nothing that I thought apart from You exists. And I am free because I was mistaken, and did not affect my own reality at all by my illusions. Now I give them up and lay them down before the feet of truth, to be removed forever from my mind. This is my holy instant of release. Father, I know my will is one with Yours.*
2. *And so today we find our glad return to Heaven, which we never really left. The Son of God this day lays down his dreams. The*

Son of God this day comes home again, released from sin and clad in holiness, with his right mind restored to him at last.

## LESSON 239     (ARCHETYPE)
*The glory of my Father is my own.*

1. Let not the truth about ourselves today be hidden by a false humility. Let us instead be thankful for the gifts our Father gave us. Can we see in those with whom He shares His glory any trace of sin and guilt? Can it be that we are not among them when He loves His Son forever and with perfect constancy, knowing he is as He created him?

2. *We thank You, Father, for the light that shines forever in us; and we honor it, because You share it with us. We are one, united in this light and one with You, at peace with all creation and ourselves.*

## CHAPTER 4
# THE ARTIST

The ego is idolatry, the sign of limited and separated self, born in a body, doomed to suffer and to end its life in death.
(ACIM Workbook, 457, 467)

# A HEALTHY ARTIST ACCORDING TO A COURSE IN MIRACLES

**Awakening:** the Course speaks of the separation as being a dream from which we need to awaken; salvation therefore consists of hearing the Holy Spirit—the call to awaken—in ourselves and in our brothers; thus accepting the oneness with each other that undoes the separation which gave rise to the dream in the beginning. (Glossary, 36)

*The healthy artist is always seeking the original and authentic. Artists never want a succession of boring days. They are intuitive, emotionally strong, rebellious, as well as creative.*

The shadowy figures from the past are precisely what you must escape. They are not real, and have no hold over you unless you bring them with you. They carry the spots of pain in your mind, directing you to attack in the present in retaliation for a past that is no more; and this decision is one of future pain. Unless you learn that past pain is an illusion, you are choosing a future of illusions and losing the many opportunities you could find for release in the present. The ego would preserve your nightmares and prevent you from awakening and understanding they are past. Would you recognize a holy encounter, if you are merely perceiving it as a meeting with your own past? For you would be meeting no one, and the sharing of salvation, which makes the encounter Holy, would be excluded from your sight. The Holy Spirit teaches that you always meet yourself, and the encounter is Holy because you are. The ego teaches that you always encounter your past, and because your dreams were not holy, the future cannot be and the present is without meaning. (Text, 13, FV-6)

*The romantic artists are constantly in search of the self to validate the soul, which leads them on their merry search for the rest of their lives.*

14.We pause but for a moment more, to play our final happy game upon this earth, and then we go to take our rightful place where truth abides and games are meaningless. So is the story ended? Let this day bring the last chapter closer to the world, that everyone may learn the tale he reads of terrifying destiny, defeat of all his hopes, his pitiful defense against a vengeance he cannot escape, is but his own deluded fantasy. God's ministers have come to waken him from the dark dreams this story has evoked in his confused, bewildered memory of this distorted tale. God's Son can smile at last, on learning that it is not true. (Workbook, 286)

*The artist sees through the socially mechanistic behaviors of mixed motives and seeks the "pure." Because they see these mixed motives, they often become mavericks by rejecting society's norms and mores.*

## MY HOLY VISION SEES ALL THINGS AS PURE.

*1. Father, Your mind created all that is, Your spirit entered into it. Your love gave life to it, and would I look upon what you created as if it would be sinful? I would not perceive such dark and fearful images. A madman's dream is hardly fit to be my choice, instead of all*

# THE ARTIST

> **A little willingness:** this, joined with the Holy Spirit, is all the atonement requires; our ego seems to make the undoing of guilt impossible, and on our own it would be, but the willingness to forgive allows the Holy Spirit to undo it for us; looking with the Holy Spirit at our guilt without judgment. (Glossary, 25)

*the loveliness with which you blessed creation; all its purity, its joy, and its eternal quiet home in you.*

2. And while we remain outside of the gate of Heaven, let us look on all we see through holy vision and the eyes of Christ. Let all appearances seem pure to us, that we may pass them by in innocence and walk together to our Father's house as brothers and the Holy Sons of God. (Workbook, 427, #263)

"The real world can actually be perceived. All that is necessary is a willingness to perceive nothing else; for if you perceive both good and evil, you are accepting both the false and the true and making no distinction between them." (Text, 11, p. 210 VII. 2 sub 6)

*Artists are aware of and evocative of the universal state of the human condition and focus on their feelings when making any decisions.*

All you need do to dwell in quiet here with Christ is share his vision. Quickly and gladly is his vision given anyone who is but willing to see his brother sinless; and no one can remain beyond this willingness, if you would be released entirely from all effects of sin. Would you have partial forgiveness for yourself? Can you reach heaven while a single sin still tempts you to remain in misery? Heaven is the house of perfect purity, and God created it for you. Look on your holy brother, sinless as yourself, and let him lead you there. (Text, p.47422vs.13 )

He who has freed you from the past would teach you are free of it. He would but have you accept his accomplishments as yours, because he did them for you; and because he did they are yours. He has made you free of what you made. You can deny Him, but you cannot call on him in vain. He would establish his bright teachings so firmly in your mind that no dark lessons of guilt can abide in what he has established as holy by his presence. Thank God that he is there and works through you, and all his works are yours. He offers you a miracle with every one you let him do through you. (Text, 299)

7. A little while and you will see me, for I am not hidden because you are hiding, I will awaken you as surely as I was awakened myself, for I am awake for you. In my resurrection is your release. Our mission is to escape from crucifixion, not from redemption. Trust in my help, for I didn't walk alone, and I will walk with you as our Father walked with me. Do you not know that I walked with him in peace, and does that not mean that peace goes with us on the journey?

*Artists are sensitive and self-revealing, as well as serious and funny.*

8. There is no fear in perfect love. We will not be making perfect to you what is already perfect in you. You do not fear the unknown but the known. You will not fail in your mission because I did not fail in mine. Give me but a little trust in the name of the

complete trust I have in you, and we will easily accomplish the goal of perfection together. For perfection is, and cannot be denied. To deny the denial of perfection is not so difficult as to deny truth, and what we accomplish together will be behind when you see it as accomplished. (Text, 219–220)

# Chapter 29
# THE AWAKENING

## IX. THE FORGIVING DREAM

1. The slave of idols is a willing slave. For willing he must be to let himself bow down in worship to what has no life, and seek for power in the powerless. What happened to the Holy Son of God that this could be his wish; to let himself fall lower than the stones upon the ground, and look to idols that they raise him up? Hear, then, your story in the dream you made, and ask yourself if it be not the truth that you believe that it is not a dream.

2. A dream of judgment came into the mind that God created perfect as Himself, and in that dream was Heaven changed to Hell and God made enemy unto His Son, how can God's son awaken from the dream? It is a dream of judgment so must he judge not, and he will waken, for the dream will seem to last while he is part of it. Judge not, for he who judges will have need of idols, which will hold the judgment off from resting on himself, or can he know the Self he has condemned. Judge not, because you make yourself a part of evil dreams, where idols are your "true" identity and your salvation from the judgment laid in terror and in guilt upon yourself.

3. All figures in the dream are idols, made to save you from the dream. Yet they are part of what they have been made to save you from. Thus does an idol keep the dream alive and terrible, for who could wish for one unless he were in terror and despair? This is

what the idol represents, and so its worship is the worship of despair and terror, and the dream from which they come. Judgment is an injustice to God's son, and it is justice that who judges him will not escape the penalty he laid upon himself within the dream he made. God knows of justice not penalty; but in the dream of judgment you attack and are condemned; and wish to be the slave of idols, which are interposed between your judgment and the penalty it brings.

4. There can be no salvation in the dream as you are dreaming it. For idols must be part of it to save you from what you believe you have accomplished, and have done to make you sinful and put out the light within you. Little child, the light is there. You do but dream, and idols are the toys you dream you play with. Who has need of toys but children? They pretend they rule the world, and give their toys the power to move about, and talk and think and feel and speak for them. Yet everything their toys appear to do is in the minds of those who play with them, but they are eager to forget that they made up the dream in which their toys are real, nor recognize their wishes are their own.

5. Nightmares are childish dreams. The toys have turned against the child who thought he made them real. Yet can a dream attack? Or can a toy grow large and dangerous and fierce and wild? This does the child believe, because he fears his thoughts and gives them to the toys instead, and their reality becomes his own because they seem to save him from his thoughts. Yet do they keep his thoughts alive and real, but seen outside himself, where they can turn against him for his treachery to them. He thinks he needs them that he may escape his thoughts, because he thinks the thoughts are real. So he makes of anything a toy, to make his world remain outside himself, and play that he is but a part of it.

6. There is a time when childhood should be passed and gone forever. Seek not to retain the toys of children. Put them all away, for you have need of them no more. The dream of judgment is a children's game, in which the child becomes the father, powerful,

but with the little wisdom of a child. What hurts him is destroyed; what helps him, blessed. Except he judges this as does a child, who does not know what hurts and what will heal. Bad things seem to happen, and he is afraid of all the chaos in a world he thinks is governed by the laws he made. Yet is the real world unaffected by the world he thinks is real, for have its laws been changed because he does not understand?

7. The real world still is but a dream; except the figures have been changed. They are not seen as idols which betray. It is a dream in which no one is used to substitute for something else, nor interposed between the thoughts the mind conceives and what it sees. No one is used for something he is not, for childish things have all been put away, and what was once a dream of judgment now has changed into a dream where all is joy, because that is the purpose that it has. Only forgiving dreams can enter here, for time is almost over, and the forms that enter in the dream are now perceived as brothers, not in judgment, but in love.

8. Forgiving dreams have little need to last. They are not made to separate the mind from what it thinks. They do not seek to prove the dream is being dreamed by someone else, and in these dreams a melody is heard that everyone remembers, though he has not heard it since before all time began. Forgiveness, once complete, brings timelessness so close the song of Heaven can be heard, not with the ears, but with the holiness that never left the altar that abides forever deep within the Son of God, and when he hears this song again, he knows he never heard it not. Where is time, when dreams of judgment have been put away?

9. Whenever you feel fear in any form (and you are fearful if you do not feel a deep content, a certainty of help, a calm assurance Heaven goes with you) be sure you made an idol, and believe it will betray you. For beneath your hope that it will save you, lay the guilt and pain of self-betrayal and uncertainty, so deep and bitter that the dream cannot conceal completely all your sense of doom. Your

self-betrayal must result in fear, for fear is judgment, leading surely to the frantic search for idols and for death.

10. Forgiving dreams remind you that you live in safety and have not attacked yourself. So do your childish terrors melt away, and dreams become a sign that you have made a new beginning, not another try to worship idols and to keep attack. Forgiving dreams are kind to everyone who figures in the dream, and so they bring the dreamer full release from dreams of fear. He does not fear his judgment for he has judged no one, nor has sought to be released through judgment from what judgment must impose, and all the while he is remembering what he forgot, when judgment seemed to be the way to save him from its penalty. (Text, 624)

*The healthy artist is obsessed with a dark and beautiful death. He imagines the beatific drama of the most intricate and theatrical scenario of an unusual ending to his life.*

## XI. THE PEACE OF HEAVEN

1. Forgetfulness and sleep and even death become the ego's best advice for dealing with the perceived and harsh intrusion of guilt on peace. Yet no one sees himself in conflict and ravaged by a cruel war unless he believes that both opponents in the war are real. Relieving this he must escape, for such a war would surely end his peace of mind, and so destroy him. Yet if he could but realize the war is between real and unreal powers, he could look upon himself and see his freedom. No one finds himself ravaged and torn in endless battles if he himself perceives them as wholly without meaning.

2. God would not have His son embattled, and so His Son's imagined "enemy" is totally unreal. You are but trying to escape a bitter war from which you have escaped. The war is gone; for you have heard the hymn of freedom rising unto Heaven. Gladness and

## THE ARTIST

joy belong to God for your release, because you made it not. Yet as you made not freedom, so you made not a war that could endanger freedom. Nothing destructive was or ever will be. The war, the guilt, and the past are gone as one into the unreality from which they came.

3. When we are all united in Heaven, you will value nothing that you value here, for nothing that you value here do you value wholly, and so you do not value it at all. Value is where God placed it, and the value of what God esteems cannot be judged, for it has been established. It is wholly of value; it can merely be appreciated or not. To value it partially is not to know its value. In Heaven is everything God values, and nothing else. Heaven is perfectly unambiguous. Everything is clear and bright, and calls forth one response. There is no darkness and there is no contrast. There is no variation. There is no interruption. There is a sense of peace so deep that no dream in this world has ever brought even a dim imagining of what it is.

4. Nothing in this world can give this peace, for nothing in this world is wholly shared. Perfect perception can merely show you what is capable of being wholly shared. It can also show you the results of sharing, while you still remember the results of not sharing. The Holy Spirit points quietly to the contrast, knowing that you will finally let Him judge the difference for you; allowing him to demonstrate which must be true. He has perfect faith in your final judgment, because He knows that He will make it for you. To doubt this would be to doubt that His mission will be fulfilled. How is this possible, when His mission is of God?

5. You whose mind is darkened by doubt and guilt remember this: God gave the Holy Spirit to you, and gave Him the mission to remove all doubt and every trace of guilt that His dear Son has laid upon himself. It is impossible that this mission fail. Nothing can prevent what God would have accomplished from accomplishment. Whatever your reactions to the Holy Spirit's voice may be, whatever voice you choose to listen to, whatever strange thoughts may

occur to you. God's will is done. You will find the peace in which He has established you, because He does not change His mind. He is invariable as the peace in which you dwell, and of which the Holy Spirit reminds you.

8You will not remember change and shift in Heaven. You have need of contrast only here. Contrast and difference are necessary teaching aids, for by them you learn what to avoid and what to seek. When you have learned this, you will find the answer that makes the need for any differences disappear. Truth comes of its own will unto its own. When you have learned that you belong to truth, it will flow lightly over you without a difference of any kind. For you will need no contrast to help you realize this is what you want, and only this. Fear not the Holy Spirit fail in what your Father has given him to do. (Text, 267)

# Chapter 13
## THE GUILTLESS WORLD

### XI. THE PEACE OF HEAVEN - GOD CAN FAIL IN NOTHING

7. Have faith in only this thing and it will be sufficient; God wills you be in Heaven, and nothing can keep you from it or it from you. Your wildest misperceptions, your weird imaginings, your blackest nightmares all mean nothing. They will not prevail against the peace God wills for you. The Holy Spirit will restore your sanity because insanity is not the Will of God. If that suffices Him, it is enough for you. You will not keep what God would have removed, because it breaks communication with you with whom He would communicate. His voice *will* be heard.

8. The Communication Link that God himself placed within you, joining your mind with His, cannot be broken. You may believe

you want it broken, and this belief does interfere with the deep peace in which the sweet and constant communication God would share with you is known. Yet His channels of reaching out cannot be wholly closed and separated from Him. Peace will be yours because His peace still flows to you from Him whose will is peace. You have it now; the Holy Spirit will teach you how to use it and by extending it, to learn that it is in you. God willed you Heaven, and will always will you nothing else. The Holy Spirit knows only of His will. There is no chance that Heaven will not be yours, for God is sure, and what He wills is as sure as He is.

9. You will learn salvation because you will learn how to save. It will not be possible to exempt yourself from what the Holy Spirit wants to teach you. Salvation is as sure as God. His certainty suffices; learn that even the darkest nightmare that disturbs the mind of God's sleeping Son holds no power over him. He will learn the lesson of awaking. God watches over him and light surrounds him.

10. Can God's Son lose himself in dreams, when God has placed within him the glad call to waken and be glad? He cannot separate himself from what is in him. His sleep will not withstand the call to wake. The mission of redemption will be fulfilled as surely as the creation will remain unchanged throughout eternity. You do not have to know that Heaven is yours to make it so; it is so. Yet to know it, the will of God must be accepted as your will.

11. The Holy Spirit will undo for you everything you have learned that teaches that what is not true must be reconciled with truth. This is the reconciliation the ego would substitute for your reconciliation to sanity and to peace. The Holy Spirit has a very different kind of reconciliation in His mind for you, and one He will affect as surely as the ego will not affect what it attempts. "Failure is one of the ego, not of God." From him you cannot wander, and there is no possibility that the plan the Holy Spirit offers to everyone, for the salvation of everyone, will not be perfectly accomplished. You will be released, and you will not remember anything you made

that was not created for you and by you in return. For how can you remember what was never true, or not remember what has always been? It is this reconciliation with truth, and only truth, in which the peace of Heaven lies. (Text, 269)

# Chapter 30
## THE NEW BEGINNING

### III. BEYOND ALL IDOLS

1. Idols are quite specific, but your will is universal, being limitless, and so it has no form, nor is it content for its expression in the terms of form. Idols are limits. They are the belief that there are forms that will bring happiness, and that, by limiting, is all attained. It is as if you said, "I have no need of everything. This little thing I want, and it will be as everything to me," and this must fail to satisfy, because it is your will that everything be yours. Decide for idols and you ask for loss. Decide for truth and everything is yours.

2. It is not form you seek. What form can be a substitute for God the Father's love? What form can take the place of all the love in the Divinity of God the Son? What idol can make two of what is one, and can the limitless be limited? You do not want an idol. It is not your will to have one. It will not bestow on you the gifts you seek. When you decide upon the form of what you want, you lose the understanding of its purpose. So you see your will within the idol, thus reducing it to a specific form. Yet this could never be your will, because what shares in all creation cannot be content with small ideas and little things.

3. Behind the search for every idol lies the yearning for completion. Wholeness has no form because it is unlimited. To seek a special person or a thing to add to you to make yourself complete,

# THE ARTIST

can only mean that you believe some form is missing, and by finding this, you will achieve completion in a form you like. This is the purpose of an idol; that you will not look beyond it, to the source of the belief that you are incomplete. Only if you had sinned could this be so. For sin is the idea you are alone and separated off from what is whole, and thus it would be necessary for the search for wholeness to be made beyond the boundaries of limits on yourself.

4. It never is the idol that you want, but what you think it offers you, you want indeed and have the right to ask for. Nor could it be possible it be denied. Your will to be complete is but God's will, and this is given you by being His. God knows not form. He cannot answer you in terms that have no meaning, and your will could not be satisfied with empty forms, made but to fill a gap that is not there. It is not this you want. Creation gives no separate person and no separate thing the power to complete the Son of God. What idol can be called upon to give the Son of God what he already has?

5. Completion is the function of God's Son. He has no need to seek for it at all. Beyond all idols stand His Holy Will to be but what he is, for more than whole is meaningless. If there were change in him, if he could be reduced to any form and limited to what is not in him, he would not be as God created him. What idol can he need to be himself? For can he give a part of him away? What is not whole cannot make whole, but what is really asked for cannot be denied. Your will is granted. Not in any form that would content you not, but in the whole completely lovely thought God holds of you.

6. Nothing that God knows not exists, and what He knows exists forever, changelessly. For thoughts endure as long as does the mind that thought of them, and in the mind of God there is no ending, nor a time in which His thoughts were absent or could suffer change. Thoughts are not born and cannot die. They do not share the attributes of their creator, nor have they a separate life apart from his. The thoughts you think are in your mind, as you are in the mind which thought of you, and so there are no separate parts

in what exists within God's mind. It is forever One, eternally united and at peace. (Text, 631)

7. Thoughts seem to come and go. Yet all this means is that you are sometimes aware of them, and sometimes not. An unremembered thought is born again to you when it returns to your awareness. Yet it did not die when you forgot it. It was always there, but you were unaware of it. The thought God holds of you is perfectly unchanged by your forgetting. It will always be exactly as it was before the time when you forgot, and will be just the same when you remember. It is the same within the interval when you forgot.

8. The thoughts of God are far beyond all change and shine forever. They await not birth. They wait for welcome and remembering. The thought God holds of you is like a star, unchangeable in an eternal sky. So high in Heaven is it set that those outside of Heaven know not it is there. Yet still and white and lovely will it shine though all eternity. There was no time it was not there; no instant when its light grew dimmer or less perfect ever was.

9. Who knows the Father knows this light, for He is the eternal sky that holds it safe, forever lifted up and anchored sure. Its perfect purity does not does not depend on whether it is seen on Earth or not. The sky embraces it and softly holds it in its perfect place, which is as far from Earth as Earth from Heaven. It is neither the distance nor the time that keeps this star invisible to Earth, but those who seek for idols cannot know the star is there.

10. Beyond all idols is the thought God holds of you. Completely unaffected by the turmoil and the terror of the world, the dreams of birth and death that here are dreamed, the myriad of forms that fear can take; quite undisturbed, the thought God holds of you remains exactly as it always was. Surrounded by a stillness so complete no sound of battle comes remotely near, it rests in certainty and perfect peace. Here is your one reality kept sage, completely unaware of all the world that worships idols, and that knows not God. In perfect sureness of its changelessness and of its rest in its

eternal home, the thought God holds of you has never left the mind of its creator whom it knows, as its creator knows that it is there.

11. Where could the thought God holds of you exist but where you are? Is your reality a thing apart from you, and in a world which your reality knows nothing of? Outside you there is no eternal sky, no changeless star and no reality. The mind of Heaven's son in Heaven is, for there the mind of Father and of Son joined in creation which can have no end. You have not two realities, but one. Nor can you be aware of more than one. An idol or the thought God holds of you is your reality. Forget not, then, that idols must keep hidden what you are, not from the mind of God, but from your own. The star shines still; the sky has never changed, but you, the Holy Son of God himself, are unaware of your reality. (Text, 632)

## III. REALITY OF THE KINGDOM

1. The Holy Spirit teaches one lesson and applies it to all individuals in all situations. Being conflict-free, He maximizes all efforts and all results. By teaching the power of the Kingdom of God himself, He teaches you that all power is yours. Its application does not matter. It is always maximal. Your vigilance does not establish it as yours, but it does enable you to use it always and in all ways. When I said, "I am with you always," I meant it literally. I am not absent to anyone in any situation. Because I am always with you, you are the way, the truth and the life. You did not make this power, any more than I did. It was created to be shared, and therefore cannot be meaningfully perceived as belonging to anyone at the expense of another. Such a perception makes it meaningless by eliminating or overlooking its real and only meaning.

2. God's meaning waits in the kingdom, because that is where he placed it. It does not wait in time. It merely rests in the Kingdom, because it belongs there, as you do. How can you who are God's

meaning perceive yourself as absent from it? You can see yourself as separated from your meaning only by experiencing yourself as unreal. This is why the ego is insane; it teaches that you are not what you are. That is so contradictory it is clearly impossible. It is therefore a lesson you cannot really learn, and therefore cannot really teach. Yet you are always teaching. You must, therefore, be teaching something else, even though the ego does not know what it is. The ego, then, is always being undone, and does suspect your motives. Your mind cannot be unified in allegiance to the ego, because the mind does not belong to it. Yet what is "treacherous" to the ego is faithful to peace. The ego's "enemy" is therefore your friend.

3. I said before that the ego's friend is not part of you, because the ego perceives itself at war and therefore in need of allies. You who are not at war must look for brothers and recognize all whom you see as brothers, because only equals are at peace. Because God's equal sons have everything, they cannot compete. Yet if they perceive any of their brothers as anything other than their perfect equals, the idea of competition has entered their minds. Do not underestimate your need to be vigilant against this idea, because all your conflicts come from it. It is the belief that conflicting interests are possible, and therefore you have accepted the impossible as true. Is that different from saying you perceive yourself as unreal? (Text, 116)

4. To be in the Kingdom is merely to focus your full attention on it. As long as you believe you can attend to what is not true, you are accepting conflict as your choice. Is it really a choice? It seems to be, but seeming and reality are hardly the same. You who are the Kingdom are not concerned with seeming. Reality is yours because you are reality. This is how having and being are ultimately reconciled, not in the Kingdom, but in your mind. The altar there is the only reality. The altar is perfectly clear in thought, because it is a reflection of perfect thought. Your right mind sees only brothers, because it sees only in own light.

**Perception:** forgiveness, healing, salvation, and the acceptance of the Atonement for ourselves; our "special function" is to forgive our special relationships; the function of the Holy Spirit is to carry out the plan of the Atonement, reminding each son of God of his special function. (Glossary, 78)

**Magic:** the attempt to solve a problem where it is not; trying to solve a problem in the mind through physical or "mindless" measures: the ego's strategy to keep the real problem—the belief in separation—from God's answer; guilt is projected outside our minds onto others (attack) or our bodies (sickness) and sought to be corrected there, rather than being undone in our minds by bringing it to the Holy Spirit; referred to as "false healing" in "The Song of Prayer." (Glossary, 143)

5. God has lit your mind Himself, and keeps your mind lit by his light because his light is what your mind is. This is totally beyond question, and when you question it you are answered. The answer merely undoes the question by establishing the fact that to question reality is to question meaninglessly. That is why the Holy Spirit never questions. His sole function is to undo the questionable and thus lead to certainty. The certain are perfectly calm, because they are not in doubt. They do not raise questions, because nothing questionable enters their minds. This holds them in perfect serenity, because this is what they share, knowing what they are. (Text, 117)

## THE AVERAGE ARTIST ACCORDING TO A COURSE IN MIRACLES

*The average four, a tragic romantic, exhibits his idea of specialness by dressing distinctively, communicating cryptically, and,*

> **Scarcity Principle:** an aspect of guilt; the belief that we are empty and incomplete, lacking what we need; this leads to our seeking idols or special relationships to fill the scarcity we experience within ourselves; inevitably projected into feelings of deprivation, wherein we believe others are depriving us of the peace which in reality we have taken from ourselves; in contrast to God's principle of abundance. (Glossary, 133)

at the lower end, communicating through dogmatic opinion.

A Course in Miracles relates the behaviors and exhibitions with remarkable insight and with a host of freeing resultant considerations.

*The average fours dwell in the past or the future, in a cloud of impossible dreams about themselves and others; in some cases they out-dream Cecil B. DeMille in their fantasies.*

## The Two Pictures

1. God established his relationship with you to make you happy, and nothing you do that does not share his purpose can be real. The purpose God ascribed to anything is its only function. Because of his reason for creating His relationship with you, the function of relationships becomes forever "to make happy," and nothing else... (Text, F3)

*Average fours have a romantic orientation to life, as they are impractical and unproductive.*

*When they are in the presence of the object of their desire, their feelings and affect usually go flat because that individual does not conjure up the specialness he has been imagined to be. The average four has created an idol of his dream, and the unsuspecting "friend" has no clue of the expectations surrounding him.*

*Average fours feel exempt and immune from living as others do. So, they wish to be rescued from the humdrum and ordinary.*

*Average fours create the cloud of fantasy because it is easier to feel the elation of their dreams than to deal with what appears to be a scarcity of substantial realization of their expectations.*

## I. BRINGING FANTASY TO TRUTH

1. The betrayal of the Son of God lies only in illusions, and all his "sins" are but his own imagining. His reality is forever sinless. He need not be forgiven but awakened. In his dreams, he has betrayed himself, his brothers, and his God. Yet what is done in dreams has not been really done. It is impossible to convince the dreamer that this is so, for dreams are what they are because of their illusion of reality. Only in waking is the full release from them, for only then does it become perfectly apparent that they had no effect upon reality at all, and did not change it. Fantasies change reality. That is their purpose. They cannot do so in reality, but they can do so in the mind that would have reality be different.

2. It is, then, only your wish to change reality that is fearful, because by your wish you think you have accomplished what you wish. This strange position, in a sense, acknowledges your power. Yet by distorting it and devoting it to "evil," it also makes it unreal. You cannot be faithful to two masters who ask conflicting things of

you. What you use in fantasy you deny to truth. Yet what you give to truth to use for you is safe from fantasy.

3. When you maintain that there must be an order of difficulty in miracles, all you mean is that there are some things you would withhold from truth. You believe truth cannot deal with them only because you would keep them from truth. Very simply; our lack of faith in the power that heals all pain arises from you to retain some aspects of reality for fantasy. If you but realize what this must do to your appreciation of the whole! What you reserve for yourself, you take away from Him who would release you. Unless you give it back, it is inevitable that your perspective on reality be warped and unconnected.

4. As long as you would have it so, so long will the illusion of an order of difficulty in miracles remain with you. For you have established this order in reality by giving some of it to one teacher, and some to another, and so you learn to deal with part of the truth in one way, and in another way the other part. To fragment truth is to destroy it by rendering it meaningless. Orders of reality is a perspective without understanding; a frame of reference for reality to which it cannot really be compared at all.

5. Think you that you can bring truth to fantasy, and learn what truth means from the perspective of illusions? Truth has no meaning in illusion. The frame of reference for its meaning must be itself. When you try to bring truth to illusions, you are trying to make illusions real, and keep them by justifying your belief in them; but to give illusions to truth is to enable truth to teach that the illusions are unreal, and thus enable you to escape from them. Reserve not one idea aside from truth, or you establish orders of reality that must imprison you. There is no order in reality, because everything there is true.

6. Be willing, then, to give all you have held outside the truth to Him who knows the truth, and in whom all is brought to truth. Salvation from separation would be complete, or will not be at all. Be

not concerned with anything at all except your willingness to have this be accomplished. He will accomplish it; not you. But forget not this: when you become disturbed and lose your peace of mind because another is attempting to solve his problems through fantasy, you are refusing to forgive yourself for just this same attempt, and you are holding both of you away from truth and salvation. As you forgive him, you restore to truth what was denied by both of you, and you will see forgiveness where you have given it. (Text, 352)

*The average tragic romantic artist cannot stay in the "now" in any of his concentrations. When he is in the presence of any individual, the romantic artist projects into the past or future and totally disregards the import, value, and significance of the present experience.*

4. Yet space between you and your brother is apparent only in the present, now, and cannot be perceived in the future time. No more can it be overlooked except within the present future loss is not your fear; but present joining is your dread. Who can feel desolation except now? A future cause as yet has no effects, and therefore must it be that if you fear, there is a present cause, and it is this that needs correction, not a future state. (Text, 559)

# Chapter 17
## *FORGIVENESS AND THE HOLY RELATIONSHIP*

1. To fulfill this function you relate to your creations as God to His. For nothing God created is apart from happiness, and nothing God created but would extend happiness as its creator did. Whatever does not fulfill this function cannot be real.

2. In this world it is impossible to create. Yet it is possible to make happy. I have said repeatedly that the Holy Spirit would not

deprive you of your special relationships, but would transform them; and all that is meant by that is that he will restore to them the function given them by God. The function you have given them is clearly not to make happy, but the holy relationship shares God's purpose, rather than aiming to make a substitute for it. Every special relationship you have made is a substitute for God's Will, and glorifies yours instead of His because of the illusion that they are different.

3. You have made very special relationships even in this world. Yet you do not recognize them because you have raised their substitutes to such predominance that, when truth calls to you, as it does constantly, you answer with a substitute. Every special relationship you have made has, as its fundamental purpose, the aim of occupying your mind so completely that you will not hear the call of truth.

4. In a sense, the special relationship was the ego's answer to the creation of the Holy Spirit, who was God's answer to the separation; for although the ego did not understand what had been created, it was aware of threat. The whole defense system the ego evolved to protect the separation from the Holy Spirit was in response to the gift with which God blessed it, and by His blessing enabled it to be healed. This blessing holds within itself the truth about everything; and the truth is that the Holy Spirit is in close relationship with you, because in him is your relationship with God restored to you. The relationship with Him has never been broken, because the Holy Spirit has not been separate from anyone since the separation, and through Him have all your holy relationships been carefully preserved, to serve God's purpose for you.

5. The ego is always alert to threat, and the part of your mind into which the ego was accepted is very anxious to preserve its reason, as it sees it. It does not realize that it is totally insane, and you must realize just what this means if you would be restored to sanity. The insane protect their thought systems, but they do so insanely,

## THE ARTIST

and all their defenses are as insane as what they are supposed to protect. The separation has nothing in it, no part, no "reason," and no attribute that is not insane. It's "protection" is part of it, as insane as the whole. The special relationship, which is its chief defense, must therefore be insane. (Text, 358)

6. You have but little difficulty now in realizing that the thought system the special relationship protects is but a system of delusions. You recognize, at least in general terms, that the ego is insane. Yet the special relationship still seems to you somehow to be "different"; yet we have looked at it far closer than we have at many other aspects of the ego's thought system that you have been more willing to let go. While this one remains, you will not let the others go, for this one is not different. Retain this one, and you have retained the whole. (Text, 359)

7. It is essential to realize that all defenses do what they would defend. The underlying basis for their effectiveness is that they offer what they would defend. What they defend is placed in them for safe keeping, and as they operate they will bring it to you. Every defense operates by giving gifts, and the gift is always a miniature of the thought system the defense protects, set in a golden frame. The frame is very elaborate, all set with jewels, and deeply carved and polished. Its purpose is to be of value in itself...and to divert your attention from what it encloses. But the frame without the picture you cannot have, defenses operate to make you think you can.

8. The special relationship has the most imposing and deceptive frame of all the defenses the ego uses. It's thought system is offered her, surrounded by a frame so heavy and so elaborate that the picture is almost obliterated by its imposing structure. Into the frame are woven all sorts of fanciful and fragmented illusions of love, set with dreams of sacrifice and self-aggrandizement, and interlaced with gilded threads of self-destruction. The glitter of blood shines like rubies, and the tears are faceted like diamonds and gleam in the dim light in which the offering is made.

9. Look at the picture. Do not let the frame distract you. This gift is given you for your damnation, and if you take it you will believe that you are damned. You cannot have the frame without the picture. What you value is the frame, for there you see no conflict. Yet the frame is only the wrapping for the gift of conflict. The frame is not the gift: be not deceived by the most superficial aspects of this thought system, for these aspects enclose the whole, complete in every aspect. Death lies in this glittering gift. Let not your gaze dwell on the hypnotic gleaming of the frame. Look at the picture, and realize that death is offered you.

10. That is why the holy instant is so important in the defense of truth. The truth itself needs no defense, but you do need defense against your acceptance of the gift of death. When you who are truth accept an idea so dangerous to truth, you threaten truth with destruction, and your defense must now be undertaken, to keep the truth whole. The power of Heaven, the love of God, the tears of Christ, and the joy of His Eternal Spirit are marshaled to defend you from your own attack; for you attack them, being part of them, and they must save you for they love themselves.

11. The Holy Instant is a miniature of Heaven, sent you from Heaven. It is a picture, too, set in a frame. Yet if you accept this gift, you will not see the frame at all, because the gift can only be accepted through your willingness to focus all you attention on the picture. The Holy Instant is a miniature of Eternity. It is a picture of timelessness, set in a frame of time. You focus on the picture; you will realize that it was only the frame that made you think it was a picture. Without the frame, the picture is seen as what it represents, for as the whole thought system of the ego lies in its gifts, so the whole of Heaven lies in this instant, borrowed from eternity and set in time for you.

12. Two gifts are offered you. Each is complete, and cannot be impartially accepted. Each is a picture of all that you can have, seen very differently. You cannot compare their value by comparing a

## THE ARTIST

picture to a frame. It must be the pictures only that you compare, or the comparison is wholly without meaning. Remember that it is the picture that is the gift, and only on this basis are you really free to choose. Look at the pictures: both of them. One is a tiny picture, hard to see at all beneath the heavy shadows of its enormous and disproportionate enclosure. The other is lightly framed and hung in light, lovely to look up for what it is. (Text, 360)

13. You have tried so hard, and are still trying to fit the better picture into the wrong frame and so combine what cannot be combined, accept this and be glad. These pictures are each framed perfectly for what they represent: one is framed to be out of focus and not seen. The other is framed for perfect clarity. The picture of darkness and of death grows less convincing as you search it out amid its wrappings. As each senseless stone that seems to shine from the frame in darkness is exposed to light, it becomes dull and lifeless, and ceases to distract you from the picture. Finally you look upon the picture itself, seeing at last that, unprotected by the form, it has no meaning.

14. The other picture is lightly framed, for time cannot contain eternity, there is no distraction here. The picture of Heaven and eternity grows more convincing as you look at it, and now, by real comparison, a transformation of both pictures can at last occur. Each is given its rightful place when both are seen in relation to each other. The dark picture, brought to light, is not perceived as fearful, but the fact that it is just a picture, is brought home at last. What you see there you will recognize as what it is; a picture of what you thought was real, and nothing more; for beyond this picture you will see noting.

15. The picture of light, in clear-cut and unmistakable contrast, is transformed into what lies beyond the picture. As you look on this, you realize that it is not a picture, but a reality. This is no figured representation of a thought system, but the thought itself. What it represents is there, the frame fades gently and God rises to

your remembrance, offering you the whole of creation in exchange for your little picture, wholly without value and entirely deprived of meaning.

16. As God ascends into His rightful place and you to yours, you will experience again the meaning of relationship and know it to be true. Let us ascend in peace together to the Father, by giving Him ascendance in our minds. We will gain everything by giving Him the power and the glory, and keeping no illusions of where they are. They are in us, through His ascendance. What He has given is His. It shines in every part of Him as in the whole. The whole reality of your relationship with Him lies in our relationship to one another. The Holy Instant shines alike on all relationships, for in it they are one. For here is only healing, already complete and perfect. For here is God, and where He is only the perfect and complete can be. (Text, 361)

3. An idol is a false impression, or a false belief; some form of anti-Christ that constitutes a gap between the Christ and what you see. An idol is a wish, made tangible and given form, and thus perceived as real and seen outside the mind. Yet it is still thought, and cannot leave the mind that is its source; nor is its form apart from the idea it represents. All forms of anti-Christ oppose the Christ, and fall before His face like a dark veil that seems to shut you off from Him, alone in darkness. Yet the light is there. A cloud does not put out the sun; no more a veil can banish what it seems to separate, nor darken by one without the light itself.

4. This world of idols is a veil across the face of Christ, because its purpose is to separate your brother from yourself. A dark and fearful purpose, yet a thought without the power to change one blade of grass from something living to a sign of death. Its form is nowhere, for its source abides within your mind where God abideth not. Where is this place where what is everywhere has been excluded and been kept apart? What hand could not be held up to

block God's way? Whose voice could make demand He enter not? The "more-than-everything" is not a thing to make you tremble and to quail in fear. Christ's enemy is nowhere. He can take no form in which he ever will be real.

5. What is an idol? Nothing! It must be believed before it seems to come to life, and given power that it may be feared. Its life and power are its believer's gift, and this is what the miracle restores to what has life and power worthy of the gift of Heaven and eternal peace. The miracle does not restore the truth, the light the veil between has not put out. It merely lifts the veil, and lets the truth shine unencumbered, being what it is. It does not need belief to be itself, for it has been created; so it is.

6. An idol is established by belief, and when it is withdrawn, the idol "dies." This is the anti-Christ; the strange idea that there is a power past omnipotence, a place beyond the infinite, a time transcending the eternal. Here the world of idols has been set by the idea this power and place and time are given form, and shape the world where the impossible has happened. Here the deathless come to die, the all-encompassing to suffer loss, the timeless to be made the slaves of time. Here does the changeless change; the peace of God, forever given to all living things, give way to chaos; and the Son of God, as perfect, sinless, and as loving as His Father, come to hate a little while; to suffer and finally to die.

7. Where is an idol: Nowhere! Can there be a gap in what is infinite; a place where time can interrupt eternity? A place of darkness set where all is light, a dismal alcove separated off from what is endless, has no place to be. An idol is beyond where God has set all things forever, and has left no room for anything to be except His will. Nothing and nowhere must an idol be, while God is everything and everywhere.

8. What purpose has an idol, then? What is it for? This is the only question that has many answers, each depending on the one of whom the question has been asked. The world believes in idols. No

one comes unless he worshipped them, and still attempts to seek for one that yet might offer him a gift reality does not contain. Each worshipper of idols harbors hopes his special deities will give him more than other men possess. It must be more. It does not really matter more of what: more beauty, more intelligence, more wealth, or even more affliction and more pain; but more of something is an idol for. When one fails, another takes its place with hope of finding more of something else. Be not deceived by forms the "something" takes. An idol is a means for getting more, and it is this that is against God's will.

9. God has not many Sons, but only one. Who can have more, and who be given less? In Heaven would the Son of God but laugh, if idols could intrude upon his peace. It is for him the Holy Spirit speaks, and tells you idols have no purpose here; for more than Heaven can you never have. If Heaven is within, why would you seek for idols that would make Heaven less to give you more than God bestowed on your brother and on you, as one with Him? God gave you all there is, and to be sure you could not lose it, did He also give the same to every living thing as well. Thus is every living thing a part of you, as of Himself. No idol can establish you as more than God, but you will never be content with being less. (Text, 620–621)

*The average artist dwells on the past and/or future, and thus makes idols of "what used to be" or "what could have been." They then foster impossible dreams about themselves and others in fantastic cinematic fantasies. Because they have a romantic notion and orientation toward life, they will become impractical and unproductive. Average artists totemize their creations and place in them the import to life and their reason to produce and exist. Thus, they create idols, and make idols of people, events, and notions they have developed a feeling about. Because they feel exempt from the rules of life, they also feel immune from social expectations and living as other people do.*

*The average artists totemize not only the creations they have made; they also totemize relationships as "special," and in effect put them in the same category as their "Special (exempt from all normal expectations) Relationship." Their mind magnifies the import of their relationship; however, in reality they limit and truly make less of its magnificent and dynamic reality.*

## VII. THE NEEDLESS SACRIFICE

1. Beyond the poor attraction of the special love relationship, and always obscured by it, is the powerful attraction of the father for His son. There is no other love that can satisfy you, because there is no other love. This is the only love that is fully given and fully returned. Being complete, it asks nothing. Being wholly pure, everyone joined in it has everything. This is not the basis for any relationship in which the ego embarks is special.

2. The ego establishes relationships only to get something, and it would keep the giver bound to itself through guilt. It is impossible for the ego to enter into any relationship without anger, for the ego believes that anger makes friends. This is not its statement, but it is its purpose. For the ego really believes that it can get and keep by making guilty. This is its one attraction; an attraction so weak that it would have no hold at all, except that recognizes it. For the ego always seems to attract through love, and has no attraction at all to anyone who perceives that it attracts through guilt. (Text, 317)

3. The sick attraction of guilt must be recognized for what it is. For having been made real to you, it is essential to look at it clearly, and by withdrawing your investment in it, to learn to let it go. No one would choose to let go what he believes has value. Yet the attraction of guilt has value to you only because you have not looked at what it is, and have judged it completely in the dark. As we bring it to light, your only question will be why it was you ever wanted it.

You have nothing to lose by looking open-eyed, for ugliness such as this belongs not in your holy mind. This host of God can have no real investment here.

4. We said it before that the ego attempts to maintain and increase guilt, but in such a way that you do not recognize what it would do to you. For it is the ego's fundamental doctrine that what you do to others you have escaped. The ego wishes no one well. Yet its survival depends on your belief that you are except from its evil intentions. It counsels, therefore, that if you are host to it, it will enable you to direct its anger outward, thus protecting you; and thus it embarks on an endless, unrewarding chain of special relationships, forged out of anger and dedicated to but one insane belief; that the more anger you invest outside yourself, the safer you become.

5. It is this chain that binds the Son of God to guilt, and it is this chain the Holy Spirit would remove from his Holy mind. For the chain of savagery belongs not around the chosen host of God, who cannot make himself host to the ego. In the name of his release, and in the name of him who would release him, let us look more closely at the relationships the ego contrives, and let Holy Spirit judge them truly. For it is certain that if you will look at them, you will offer them gladly to Him. What he can make of them you do not know, but you will become willing to find out, if you are willing first to perceive what you have made of them.

6. In one way or another, every relationship the ego makes is based on the idea that by sacrificing itself, it becomes bigger. The "sacrifice," which it regards as purification, is actually the root of its bitter resentment; for it would prefer to attack directly, and avoid delaying what it really wants. Yet the ego acknowledges "reality" as it sees it, and recognizes that no one could interpret direct attack as love. Yet to make guilty is direct attack, although it does not seem to be. For the guilty expect attack, and having asked for it they are attracted to it.

7. In such insane relationships, the attraction of what you do not want seems to be much stronger that the attraction of what you do want. For each one thinks that he has sacrificed something to the other, and hates him for it. Yet this is what he thinks he wants. He is not in love with the other at all. He merely believes he is in love with sacrifice; and for this sacrifice, which he demands of himself, he demands that the other accept the guilt and sacrifice himself as well. Forgiveness becomes impossible, for the ego believe that to forgive another is to lose him. It is only by attack without forgiveness that the ego can ensure the guilt that holds all its relationships together.

8. Yet they only seem to be together. For relationships, to the ego, mean only that bodies are together. It is always this that the ego demands, and it does not object where the mind goes or what it thinks, for this seems unimportant. As long as the body is there to receive its sacrifice, it is content. To the ego, the mind is private and only the body can be shared. Ideas are basically of no concern, except as they bring the body of another closer or farther; and it is in these terms that it evaluates ideas as good or bad. What makes another guilty and holds him through guilt is "good." What releases him from guilt is "bad," because he would no longer believe that bodies communicate, and so he would be "gone."

9. Suffering and sacrifice are the gifts with which the ego would "bless" all unions, and those who are united at its altar accept suffering and sacrifice as the price of union. In their angry alliances, born of the fear of loneliness and yet dedicated to the continuance of loneliness, each seeks relief from guilt by increasing it in the other. For each believes that this decreases guilt in him. The other seems always to be attacking and wounding him, perhaps in little ways, perhaps "unconsciously," yet never without demand of sacrifice. The fury of those joined at the ego's altar far exceeds your awareness of it; for what the ego really wants, you do not realize.

10. Whenever you are angry, you can be sure that you have formed a special relationship, which the ego has "blessed," for anger is it blessing. Anger takes many forms, but it cannot long deceive those who will learn that love brings no guilt at all, and what brings quilt cannot be love and must be anger. All anger is nothing more than an attempt to make someone feel guilty, and this attempt is the only basis the ego accepts for special relationships. Guilt is the only need the ego has, and as long as you identify with it, guilt will remain attractive to you but remember this; to be with a body is not communication; and if you think it is, you will feel guilty about communication and will be afraid to hear the Holy Spirit, recognizing in His voice you own need to communicate.

11. The Holy Spirit cannot teach though fear, and how can He communicate with you, while you believe that by communicating you will be abandoned; and yet many do believe it. For they think their minds must be kept private or they will lose them, but if their bodies are together their minds remain their own. The union of bodies thus becomes the way in which they would keep minds apart. For bodies cannot forgive; they can only do as the mind directs.

12. The illusion of the autonomy of the body and its ability to overcome loneliness is but the working of the ego's plan to establish its own autonomy. As long as you believe that to be with a body is companionship, you will be compelled to attempt to keep your brother in his body, held there by guilt; and you will see, in guilt and danger in communication. For the ego will always teach that loneliness is solved by guilt, and that communication is the cause of loneliness and despite the evident insanity of this lesson, many have learned it.T.p.320

*The average artist has a need to be reclusive, to be alone. The artist also needs to communicate, but can't do both at the same time. The average artist is given to cryptic communication laced with subjective emotionalism and symbolic self-referencing emotional referents. This by definition keeps the artists in their solitude and maintaining their reclusive posture.*

## Chapter 15
## THE HOLY INSTANT

13. Forgiveness lies in communication as surely as damnation lies in guilt. It is the Holy Spirit's teaching function to instruct those who believe communication to be damnation that communication is salvation, and He will do so, for the power of God in Him and you is joined in a real relationship so holy and so strong, that it can overcome even this without fear.

14. It is through the holy instant that what seems impossible is accomplished, making it evident that it is not impossible. In the holy instant guilt holds no attraction, since communication has been restored. Guilt, whose only purpose is to disrupt communication, has no function here. Here there is no concealment, and no private thoughts. The willingness to communicate

---

**"Ideas leave not their source"**

**Perception:** the world of separation has never left its source in the separate mind, though it appears to be external to it; thus, there is no material world, only a projected illusion of one.

**Wrong-mindedness:** projecting guilt from our minds by attack reinforces its presence in the mind that thought it.

(Glossary, 109)

attracts communication to it, and overcomes loneliness completely. There is complete forgiveness here, for there is no desire to exclude anyone from your completion, in sudden recognition of the value of his part in it. In the protection of your wholeness, all are invited and made welcome, and you understand that your completion is God's, whose only need is to have you be complete. For your completion makes you His in your awareness, and here it is that you experience yourself as you were created, and as you are. (Text, 320)

## THE UNHEALTHY ARTIST ACCORDING TO *A COURSE IN MIRACLES*

*The unhealthy artists are emotionally paralyzed and confused, and in their need to be alone they have alienated everyone around them.*

*In their desire to be alone, they have also alienated themselves through their self-reproaches and self-hatred. They inhibit themselves and get lost in their poor thinking, thus leaving themselves depressed and in a lifestyle of regret.*

3.An idol is a false impression, or false belief; some form of anti-Christ that constitutes a gap between the Christ and what you see. An idol is a wish, made tangible and given form, and thus perceived as being real and seen outside the mind. Yet it is still a thought and cannot leave the mind that is its source. Nor is its form apart from the idea that it represents. All forms of anti-Christ opposes the Christ, and all fall before His face like a dark veil that seems to shut you off from Him, alone in darkness. Yet the light is there. A cloud does not put out the sun. No more a veil can banish what it seems to separate, nor darken by one with the light itself.T.p 620

> **Perception:** the world of separation has never left its source in the separate mind, though it appears to be external to it; thus, there is no material world, only a projected illusion of one. (Glossary, 109)

### *Love-fear*

1. Although you can love the Sonship only as one, you can perceive it as fragmented. It is impossible, however, to see something in part of it that you will not attribute to all of it. That is why attack is never discreet, and why it must be relinquished entirely. If it is not relinquished entirely it is not relinquished at all. Fear and love make or create, depending on whether the ego or the Holy Spirit begets or inspires them, but they will return to the mind of the thinker and they will affect his total perception. That includes his concept of God, of his creations and of his own. He will not regard any of them if he regards them fearfully. He will appreciate all of them with love. (Text,p. 123)

### *Projection*

4. Perception laws are opposite to truth, and what is true of knowledge is not true of anything that is apart from it. Yet has God given answers to the world of sickness, which applies to all its forms. God's answer is eternal, though it

works in time, where it is needed. Yet because it is of God, the laws of time do not affect its workings. It is in this world, but not a part of it. For it is real, and dwells where all reality must be. Ideas leave not their source and their effects but seem to be apart from them. Ideas are of the mind. What is projected out, and seems to be external to the mind, is not outside at all, but an effect of what is in, and has not left its source.

12. Let us consider what the error is, so it can be corrected, not protected. Sin is belief attack can be projected outside the mind where the belief arose. Here is the firm connection that ideas can leave their source made real and meaningful, and from this error does the world of sin and sacrifice arise. This world is an attempt to prove your innocence while cherishing attack. Its failure lies in that you still feel guilty though without understanding why. Effects are seen as separate from their source, and seen to be beyond your control or to prevent. What is thus kept apart can never join.

13. Cause and effect are one, not separate. God wills you learn what always has been true: that he created you as part of Him, and this must still be true because ideas leave not their source. Such is creative law; that each idea the mind conceives but adds to its abundance, never takes away. This is as true of what is idly wicked as what is truly willed, because the mind can wish to be deceived, but cannot make it be what it is not; and to believe ideas can leave their source is to invite illusions to be true without success. For never will success be possible in trying to deceive the Son of God. (Text, p.556)

*The fours totemize objects, people, and circumstances. They imbue objects of their creation with their personal essence—their four-hood specialness, so to speak. They cast their prejudicated form of aspersions on people and circumstances as well.*

## THE ARTIST

3. An idol is a false impression, or a false belief; some form of anti-Christ that constitutes a gap between the Christ and what you see. An idol is a wish, made tangible and given form, and thus perceived as real and seen outside the mind. Yet it is still a thought, and cannot leave the mind that is its source. Nor is its form apart from the idea it represents. All forms of anti-Christ oppose the Christ, and fall before His face like a dark veil that seems to shut you off from Him, alone in darkness. Yet the light is there. A cloud does not put out the sun. No more a veil can banish what it seems to separate, nor darken by one with the light itself. (Text, 620)

*A true saying for the four is that you are only the feeling you act upon. Since the artists cannot pick their feelings, they can have some measure of control deciding which actions to anchor their feelings to, thus compounding and magnifying the feelings they are already experiencing.*

14. We said you can begin a happy day with the determination not to make decisions by yourself. The only question really is with what you choose to make them. That is really all. The first rule, then, is not coercion, but a simple statement of a simple fact. You will not make decisions by yourself whatever you decide. For they are made with idols or with God. And you ask help of anti-Christ or Christ,and which you choose will join with you and tell you what to do.T.p.628.

### IV. The Quiet Answer

The world asks but one question. It is but this: of these illusions which of them are true? Which one establishes peace and offer joy? Which can offer escape from all the pain of which the world is made? Whatever the form the question takes, its purpose is the

> **Anti-Christ:** symbol for the ego and the belief that there is a power that can oppose the omnipotence of God and deny the reality of Christ. (Glossary, 31)

same. It asks but to establish sin is real and answers in the form of preference. Which sin do you prefer? That is the one you should choose. The others are not true. (Text, 575, 4:4)

## VII. THE TOTALITY OF THE KINGDOM

1. Whenever you deny a blessing to a brother you will feel deprived, because denial is as total as love. It is as impossible to deny part of the Sonship as it is to love it in part. Nor is it possible to love it totally at times. You cannot be totally committed sometimes. Denial has no power in itself, but you can give it the power of your mind, whose power is without limit. If you use it to deny reality, reality is gone for you. Reality cannot be partly appreciated. That is why denying any part of it means you have lost the awareness of all of it. Yet denial is a defense, and so it is as capable of being used positively as well as negatively. Used negatively it will be destructive, because it will be used for attack; but in the service of the Holy

# THE ARTIST

Spirit, it can help you recognize part of reality, and thus appreciate all the Holy Spirit, it can help you recognize part of reality, and thus appreciate all of it. Mind is too powerful to be subject to exclusion. You will never be able to exclude yourself from your thoughts.

2. When a brother acts insanely he is offering you an opportunity to bless him. His need is yours. You need the blessing you can offer him. There is no way for you to have it except by giving it. This is the law of God, and it has no exceptions. What you deny you lack, not because it is lacking, but because you have denied it in another and are therefore not aware of it in yourself. Every response you make is determined by what you think you are, and what you want to be is what you think you are. What you want to be, then, must determine every response you make.

3. You do not need God's blessing because that you have forever, but you do need yours. The ego's picture of you is deprived, unloving and vulnerable. You cannot love this. Yet you can very easily escape from this image by leaving it behind. You are not there, and that is not you. Do not see this picture in anyone, or you have accepted it as you. All illusions about the Sonship are dispelled together as they were made together. Teach no one that he is what you would not want to be. Your brother is the mirror in which you see the image of yourself as long as perception lasts; and perception will last until the Sonship knows itself as whole. You made perception and it must last as long as you want it.

4. Illusions are investments. They will last as long as you value them. Values are relative, but they are powerful because they are judgments. (Text, 127)

*The unhealthy fours exercise their sense of scarcity as projection. They adopt the feeling of scarcity as a sense of hopelessness and fatalism. Feeling they have no control over anything, they cannot choose any other possible outcome, nor do they try to imagine a possible outcome.*

*The unhealthy four must learn that living in the belief of irrational specific blindness, unspecific senses of scarcities, and favorite denials is an unhealthy posture for dealing with reality and with rational (as well as irrational) people.*

# THE GIFTS OF THE KINGDOM

## VIII. THE UNBELIEVABLE BELIEF

1. We have said that without projection there can be no anger, but it is also true that without extension there can be no love. These reflect a fundamental law of the mind, and therefore one that always operates. It is the law by which you create and were created. It is the law that unifies the Kingdom, and keeps it in the mind of God. To the ego, the law is perceived as a means of getting rid of something it does not want. To the Holy Spirit, it is the fundamental law of sharing, by which you give what you value in order to keep it in your mind. To the Holy Spirit it is the law of extension. To the ego it is the law of deprivation. It therefore produces abundance or scarcity, depending on how you choose to apply it. This choice is up to you, but it is not up to you to decide whether or not you will utilize the law. Every mind must project or extend, because this is how it lives, and every mind is life.

2. The ego's use of projection must be fully understood before the inevitable association between projection and anger can be finally undone. The ego always tries to preserve conflict. It is very ingenious in devising ways that seem to diminish conflict because it does not want you to find conflict so intolerable that you will insist on giving it up. The ego therefore tries to persuade you that it can free you of conflict lest you give the ego up and free yourself. Using its own warped version of the law of God, the ego utilizes the power of the mind only to defeat the mind's real purpose. It projects

# THE ARTIST

conflict from your mind to other minds, in an attempt to persuade you that you have gotten rid of the problem.

3. There are two major errors involved in this attempt. First, strictly speaking, conflict cannot be projected because it cannot be shared. Any attempt to keep part of it and get rid of another part does not really mean anything. Remember that a conflicted teacher is a poor teacher and a poor learner. His lessons are confused, and their transfer value is limited by his confusion. The second error is the idea that you can get rid of something you do not want by giving it away. Giving it is how you keep it. The belief that by seeing it outside you have excluded it from within is a complete distortion of the power of extension. That is why those who project are vigilant for their own safety. They are afraid that their projections will return and hurt them. Believing they have blotted their projections from their own minds, they also believe their projections are trying to creep back in. Since the projections have not left their minds, they are forced to engage in constant activity in order not to recognize this.

4. The only way to dispel illusions is to withdraw all investment from them, and they will have no life for you because you will have put them out of your mind. While you include them in it, you are giving life to them; except there is nothing there to receive your gift.

5. The gift of life is yours to give, because it was given you. You are unaware of your gift because you do not give it. You cannot make nothing live, since nothing cannot be enlivened, therefore you are not extending the gift you both have and are, and so you do not know your being. All confusion comes from not extending life, because that is not the will of your Creator, you can do nothing apart from Him, and you *do* do nothing apart from Him. Keep His way to remember yourself, and teach His way lest you forget yourself. Give only honor to the Sons of the living God, and count yourself among them gladly.

6. Only honor is a fitting gift for those whom God himself created worth of honor and whom He honors. Give them the appreciation God accords them always, because they are His beloved Sons in whom he is well pleased. You cannot be apart from them because you are not apart from Him. Rest in His love and protect your rest by loving. But love everything He created, of which you are a part, or you cannot learn of His peace and accept His gift for yourself and as yourself. You cannot know your own perfection until you have honored all those who were created like you.

7. One child of God is the only teacher sufficiently worthy to teach another. One teacher is in all minds and He teaches the same lesson to all. He always teaches you the inestimable worth of every Son of God, teaching it with infinite patience born of the infinite love for which He speaks. Every attack is a call for His patience, since His patience can translate attack into blessing. Those who attack do not know they are blessed, and only attack because they believe they are deprived. Give, therefore, of your abundance, and teach your brothers theirs. Do not share their illusions of scarcity, or you will perceive yourself as lacking.

8. Attack could never promote attack unless you perceived it as a means of depriving you of something you want. Yet you cannot lose anything unless you do not value it and therefore do not want it. This makes you feel deprived of it, and by projecting your own rejection you them believe that others are taking it from you. You must be fearful if you believe that others are taking it from you. You must be fearful if you believe that your brother is attacking you to tear the Kingdom of Heaven from you. This is the ultimate basis for all the ego's projection.

9. Being the part of your mind that does not believe it is responsible for itself, and being without allegiance to God, the ego is incapable of trust projecting its insane belief that you have been treacherous to your Creator, it believes that your brothers, who are as incapable of this as you are, are out to take God from

# THE ARTIST

you. Whenever a brother attacks another that is what he believes. Projection always sees your wishes in others. You choose to separate yourself from God. That is what you will think others are doing to you.

10. You are the Will of God. Do not accept anything else as your will, or you are denying what you are. Deny this and you will attack, believing you have been attacked; but see the Love of God is in you, and you will see it everywhere because it is everywhere. See His abundance in everyone, and you will know that you are in Him with them. They are part of you, as you are part of God. You are as lonely without understanding this as God Himself is lonely when His sons do not know Him. The peace of God is understanding this; there is only one way out of the world's thinking, just as there was only one way out into it. Understand totally by understanding totality.

11. Perceive any part of the ego's thought system as wholly insane, wholly delusional and wholly undesirable, and you have correctly evaluated all of it. This correction enables you to perceive any part of creation as wholly real, wholly perfect and wholly desirable. Wanting this only you will have this only, and giving this only you will be only this. The gifts you offer to the ego are always experienced as sacrifices, but the gifts you offer to the Kingdom are gifts to you. They will always be treasured by God because they belong to His beloved Sons, who belong to Him. All power and glory are yours because the Kingdom is His. (Text, 129)

4. You cannot perpetuate an illusion about another without perpetuating it about yourself. To fragment is to break into pieces, and mind cannot attack or be attacked. The belief that it can, an error the ego always makes, underlies its whole use of projection. It does not understand what mind is, and therefore does not understand what you are. Yet its existence is dependent on your mind, because the ego is your belief. The ego is a confusion in identification. Never

having had a consistent model, it never developed consistently. It is the product of the misapplication of the laws of God by distorted minds that are misusing their power.

5. Do not be afraid of the ego. It depends on your mind, and as you made it by believing in it, so you can dispel it by withdrawing belief from it. Do not project the responsibility for your belief in it onto anyone else, or you will preserve the belief. When you are willing to accept sole responsibility for the ego's existence you will have laid aside all anger and all attack, because they come from an attempt to project responsibility for your own errors; but having accepted the errors as yours, do not keep them. Give them over quickly to the Holy Spirit to be undone completely, so that all their effects will vanish from your mind and from the Sonship as a whole.

6. The Holy Spirit will teach you to perceive beyond your belief, because truth is beyond belief and His perception is true, the ego can be completely forgotten at any time, because it is a totally incredible belief, and no one can keep a belief. The whole purpose of this course is to teach you that the ego is unbelievable and will forever be unbelievable. You who made the ego by believing the unbelievable cannot make this judgment alone. By accepting the atonement for yourself, you are deciding against the belief that you can be alone, thus dispelling the idea of separation and affirming your true identification with the whole Kingdom as literally part of you. This identification is as beyond doubt as it is beyond belief. Your wholeness has no limits because being is infinity. (Text, P.129-131)

*The unhealthy artists are given to believe in their "specialness," and anyone who can feed and embellish on their sense of specialness is adopted as their "sycophant in residence."*

5. You can defend your specialness, but never will you hear the Voice for God beside it. They speak a different language and they fall on different ears. To every special one a different message, and

## THE ARTIST

one with different meaning, is the truth. Yet how can truth be different to each one? The special messages the special hear convince them they are different and apart; each in his special sins and "safe" from love, which does not see his specialness at all. Christ's vision is their "enemy," for it sees not what they would look upon, and it would show them that the specialness they think they see is an illusion. (Text, 503, #5)

*The unhealthy artists have the need to withdraw and be reclusive, and at the same time have the need to communicate, but cannot do both simultaneously. It is their sense of fear and dread of helplessness that causes them not to decide anything, and their neglect of details leads them to be victims of their own negligence.*

4. Yet space between you and your brother is apparent only in the present, now, and cannot be perceived in future time. No more can it be overlooked except within the present. Future loss is not your fear, but present joining is your dread. Who can feel desolation except now? A future cause as yet has no effects, and therefore must it be that if you fear there is a present cause. It is this that needs correction, not a future state. (Text, P.559,

## LESSON 135
*If I defend myself I am attacked.*

1. Who would defend himself unless he thought he were attacked, that the attack were real, and that his own defense could save himself? Herein lies the folly of defense; it gives illusions full of reality, and then attempts to handle them as real. It adds illusions to illusions, thus making correction doubly difficult; and it is this you do when you attempt to pan the future, activate the past, or organize the present as you wish.

2. You operate from the belief you must protect yourself from what is happening, because it must contain what threatens it. A sense of threat is an acknowledgment of an inherent weakness; a belief that there is danger which has power to call on you to make appropriate defense. The world is based on this insane belief, and all its structures, all its thoughts and doubts, its penalties and heavy armaments, its legal definitions and its codes, its ethics and its leaders and its gods, all serve but to preserve its sense of threat. For no one walks the world in armature, but must have terror striking at his heart.

3. Defense is frightening. It stems from fear, increasing fear as each defense is made. You think it offers safety. Yet it speaks of fear mad real and terror justified. Is it not strange you do not pause to ask, as you elaborate your plans and make your armor thicker and you locks more tight, what you defend, and how, and against what?

4. Let us consider first what you defend. It must be something that is very weak, and easily assaulted. It must be something made easy prey, unable to protect itself and needing your defense. What but the body has such frailty that constant care and watchful, deep concern are needful to protect its little life? What but the body falters and must fail to serve the Son of God as worthy host?

5. Yet it is not the body that can fear, nor be a thing of fear. It has no needs but those which you assign to it. It needs no complicated structures of defense, no health-inducing medicine, no care and no concern at all. Defend its life, or give it gifts to make it beautiful or walls to make it safe, and you but say your home is open to the thief of time, corruptible and crumbling, so unsafe it be guarded with your very life.

6. Is not this picture fearful? Can you be at peace with such a concept of your home? Yet what endowed the body with the right to serve you thus except your own belief? It is your mind which gave the body all the functions that you see in it, and set its value

far beyond a little pile of dust and water. Who would make defense of something that he recognized as this?

7. The body is in need of no defense. This cannot be too often emphasized, a will be strong and healthy if the mind does not abuse it by assigning it to roles it cannot dill, to purposes beyond its scope, and to exalted aims which it cannot accomplish. Such attempts, ridiculous yet deeply cherished, are the sources for the many mad attacks you make upon it. For it seems to fail your hopes, your needs, your values, and your dreams.

8. The self that needs protection is not real. The body, valueless and hardly worth the least defense, need merely be perceived as quite apart from you, and it becomes a healthy, serviceable instrument through which the mind can operate until its usefulness is over. Who would want to keep it when its usefulness is done?

9. Defend the body and you have attacked your mind. For you have seen in it the faults, the weaknesses, the limits and the lacks from which you think the body must be saved. You will not see the mind as separate from bodily conditions; and you will impose upon the body all the pain that comes from the conception of the mind as limited and fragile, and apart from other minds and separate from its Source.

10. These are the thoughts in need of healing, and the body will respond with health when they have been corrected and replaced with truth. This is the body's only real defense. Yet is this where you look for its defense? You offer it protection of a kind from which it gains no benefit at all, but merely adds to your distress of mind. You do not heal, but merely take away the hope of healing, for you fail to see where hope must lie if it be meaningful.

11. A healed mind does not plan. It carries out the plans that receives through listening to wisdom that is not its own. It waits until it has been taught what should be done, and then proceeds to do it. It does not depend upon itself for anything except its adequacy to fulfill the plans assigned to it. It is secure in certainty that

obstacles cannot impede its progress to accomplishment of any goal that serves the greater plan established for the good of everyone.

12. A healed mind is relieved of the belief that it must plan although it cannot know the outcome which is best, the means by which it is achieved, not how to recognize the problem that the plan is made to solve. It must misuse the body in its plans until it recognizes this is so; but when it has accepted this as true, then it is healed, and lets the body go.

13. Enslavement of the body to the plans the unhealed mind sets up to save itself must make the body sick. It is not free to be the means of helping in a plan which far exceeds its own protection and which needs its service for a little while. In this capacity it is health assured. For everything the mind employs for this will function flawlessly, and with the strength that has been give it and cannot fail.

14. It is, perhaps, not easy to perceive that self-initiated plans are but defenses, with the purpose all of them were made to realize. They are the means by which a frightened mind would undertake its own protection, at the cost of truth. This is not difficult to realize in some forms which these self-deceptions take, where denial of reality is very obvious. Yet planning is not often recognized as a defense.

15. The mind engaged in planning for itself is occupied in setting up control of future happenings. It does not think that it will be provided for, unless it makes its own provisions. Time becomes a future emphasis, to be controlled by learning and experience obtained from past events and previous beliefs. It overlooks the present; for it rests on the idea the past has taught enough to let the mind direct its future course.

16. The mind that plans is thus refusing to allow for change. What it has learned before becomes the basis for its future goals. Its past experience directs its choice of what will happen, and it does not see that here and now is everything it needs to guarantee

a future quite unlike the past, without a continuity of any old ideas and sick beliefs. Anticipation plays no part at all, for present confidence directs the way.

17. Defenses are the plans you undertake to make against the truth. Their aim is to select what you approve, and disregard what you consider incompatible with your beliefs of your reality. Yet what remains is meaningless indeed; for it is your reality that is the "threat" which your defenses would attack, obscure, and take apart and crucify.

18. What could you not accept, if you but knew that everything that happens, all events, past, present and to come, are gently planned by One whose only purpose is your good? Perhaps you have misunderstood His plan, for He would never offer pain to you; but your defenses did not let you see His loving blessing shine in every step you ever took. While you made plans for death, He led you gently to Eternal Life.

19. Your present trust in Him is the defense that promises a future undisturbed, without a trace of sorrow, and with joy that constantly increases, as this life becomes a holy instant, set in time, but heeding only immortality. Let no defenses but your present trust direct the future, and this life becomes a meaningful encounter with the truth that only your defenses would conceal.

20. Without defenses, you become a light which Heaven gratefully acknowledges to be its own; and it will lead you on in ways appointed for your happiness according to the ancient plan, begun when time was born. Your followers will join their light with yours, and it will be increased until the world is lighted up with joy; and gladly will our brothers lay aside their cumbersome defenses, which avail them nothing and could only terrify.

21. We will anticipate that time today with present confidence, for this is part of what was planned for us. We will be sure that everything we need is given us for our accomplishment of this today. We make no plans for who it will be done, but realize that our

defenselessness is all that is required for the truth to dawn upon our minds with certainty.

22. For fifteen minutes twice today we rest from senseless planning, and from every thought that blocks the truth from entering our minds. Today we will receive instead of plan, that we may give instead of organize. We are given truly, as we say:

*If I defend myself I am attacked, but in defenselessness I will be strong and learn what my defenses hide.*

23. Nothing but that. If there are plans to make, you will be told of them. They may not be the plans you thought were needed, or indeed the answers to the problems which you thought confronted you; but they are the answers to another kind of question, which remains unanswered yet in need of answering, until the answer comes to you at last.

24. All your defenses have been aimed at not receiving what will receive today, and in the light and joy of simple trust, will but wonder why you ever thought that you must be defeated from release. Heaven asks nothing. It is Hell that makes extravagant demands for your sacrifice. You give up nothing in these times today when, undefended, you present yourself to the Creator as you really are.

25. He has remembered you. Today we will remember Him. For this is Eastertime in your salvation and you rise again in what was seeming death and hopelessness. Now is the light of hope reborn in you, for now you come without defense, to the part for you within the plan of God. What little plans; magical beliefs can still have value, when you have received your function from the Voice for God himself?

26. Try not to shape this day as you believe would benefit you most; for you cannot conceive of all the happiness that comes to you without your planning. Learn today: all the world will take this

giant stride, and celebrate your Eastertime with you. Throughout the day, as foolish little things appear to raise defensiveness in you and tempt you to engage in weaving plans, remind yourself this is a special day for learning, and acknowledge it with this:

*This is my Eastertime, and I would keep it Holy. I will not defend myself, because the Son of God needs no defense against the truth of his reality.* (Workbook, 256)

*The unhealthy artists get stuck in their feelings of hopelessness and despair. They become self-effacing and suicidal. Their emotional breakdowns lead to chronic illness, depression, unearned shame, and escapism (possibly through drugs and alcohol), and especially obsession with the past. Their confusion with time being the past and the future leads them to be emotionally blocked.*

### 4. What is sin?

1. Sin is insanity. It is the means by which the mind is driven, and seeks to let illusions take the place of truth; and being mad, it sees illusions where the truth should be, and where it really is. Sin gave the body eyes, for what is there the sinless would behold? What need have they of sights or sounds or touch? What would they hear or reach to grasp? What would they sense at all? To sense is not to know, and truth can be but filled with knowledge and with nothing else.

2. The body is the instrument the mind mad in its efforts to deceive itself. Its purpose is to strive. Yet can the goal of striving change, and now the body serves a different aim for striving. What it seeks for now is chosen by the aim the mind has taken as replacement for the goal of self-deception, truth can be its aim as well as lies. The senses then will seek instead for witnesses to what is true.

3. Sin is the home of all illusions, which but stand for things imagined, issuing from thoughts that are untrue. They are the proof that what has no reality is real. Sin "proves" God's Son is evil; timelessness must have an end; eternal life must die. God himself has lost the Son He loves, with but corruption to complete Himself, His will forever overcome by death, love, slain by hate, and peace to be no more.

4. A madman's dreams are frightening, and sin appears indeed to terrify. Yet what sin perceives is but a childish game. The Son of God may play he has become a body; prey to evil and to guilt, with but a little life that ends in death. All the while His Father shines on Him, and loves Him with an everlasting love which His pretenses cannot change at all.

5. How long, O Son of God, will you maintain the game of sin? Shall we not put away these sharp-edged children's toys? How soon will you be ready to come home: perhaps today? There is no sin. Creation is unchanged. Would you still hold return to Heaven back? How long, O Holy Son of God, how long? (Workbook, 419)

# LESSON 242 (GROWTH LINE)
*This is God's day. It is my gift to Him.*

1. I will not lead my life alone today. I do not understand the world, and so to try to lead my life alone must be but foolishness. There is one who knows all that is best for me, and He is glad to make no choices for me but the ones that lead to God. I give this day to Him, for I would not delay my coming home and it is He who knows the way to God.

2. *So we give today to you. We come with wholly open minds. We do not ask for anything that we may think we want. Give us what You would have received by us. You know all our desires and our wants, and You will give us everything we need in helping us to find the way to You.*

## LESSON 290  (DEMATERIALIZATION LINE)
*My present happiness is all I see.*

1. Unless I look upon what is not there, my present happiness is all I see. Eyes that begin to open see at last, and I would have Christ's vision come to me this very day. What I perceive without God's Own Correction for the sight I made is frightening and painful to behold. Yet I would not allow my mind to be deceived by the belief the dream I made is real an instant longer. This day I seek my present happiness, and look on nothing else except the thing I seek.

2. *With this resolve I come to You, and ask Your strength to hold me up today, while I but seek to do Your will. You cannot fail to hear me, Father. What I ask have You already given me, and I am sure that I will see my happiness today.*

## LESSON 308  (ARCHETYPE)
*This instant is the only time there is.*

1. I have conceived of time in such a way that I defeat my aim. If I elect to reach past time to timelessness, I must change my perception of what time is for. Time's purpose cannot be to keep the past and future one. The only interval in which I can be saved from time is now, for in this instant has forgiveness come to set me free. The birth of Christ is now, without a past or future. He has come to give His present blessing to the world, restoring it to timelessness and love; and love is ever-present, here and now.

2. *Thanks for this instant, Father. It is now I am redeemed. This instant is the time You have appointed for Your Son's release, and for salvation of the world in him.*

## CHAPTER 5
# THE OBSERVER

"The ego is unbelievable and will forever be unbelievable."
T.122/131 ACIM

Enneatype presenting: Dissociated, Paranoid, Seperated.

## THE HEALTHY OBSERVER "5" ACCORDING TO A COURSE IN MIRACLES

Grace:

Our natural state as spirit, awareness of which returns to us when we complete our lessons of forgiveness: an aspect of God's love in this world; past learning for it can not be taught, but the goal of learning, for all lessons point to it's love.

*The Healthy Observer is a professional student reading voraciously, always taking another workshop, class, reading another book, theorizing probable reality matrixes upon some section of the world and creating innovative patents and inventions.*

Lesson 313 (WP.457)

Now let a new perception come to me

1. Father there is a vision which beholds all things as sinless, so that fear is gone, and where it was is love invited in. And love will come wherever it is asked. This mission is your gift The eyes of Christ look on a world forgiven. In his sight are all it's sins forgiven for he sees no sin in anything he looks upon. Now let his true perception come to me, that I may awaken from the dream of sin and look within upon my sinlessness, which you have

kept completely undefiled upon the alter of your Holy Son, the self with which I would identify.

2. Let us today behold each other in the sight of Christ How beautiful we are! How Holy and how loving! Brother come and join with me today. We save the world when we have joined for in our vision it becomes as holy as the light in us.

*Healthy observers are visionary, resourcefull, and ahead of their time. They are easily bored and short of patience with the uninformed or the "not as" informed , (subtly scorning the stupid ones.)*

I Seek A Future Different From The Past

1. From new perception of the world there comes a future very different from the past. The future is now recognized as but extension of the present. Past mistakes can cast no shadows on it, so that fear has lost it's idols and images, and being formless it has no effects. Death will not claim the future now for life is now it's goal, and all the means are happily provided. We can grieve or suffer when the present has been freed, extending it's security and peace into a quiet future filled with joy? (Lesson 314 W.P.457)

*Observers have the ability to learn anything they put their concentration on. Observers revolutionize and mainstream processes and products as well as introduce brand new perceptions key to innovation.*

Awakening

The Course speaks of the separation being a dream from which we need to awaken: salvation therefore consists of hearing the Holy Spirit-call to awaken- in ourselves and in our brothers: thus accepting the oneness with each other that undoes the separation which gave rise to the dream in the beginning. (Glossary p. 36)


## V. The Dynamics Of The Ego

1. No one can escape from illusions unless he looks at them, for not looking is the way they are protected. There is no reason to shrink from illusions for they can not be dangerous. We are ready to look more closely at the ego's thought system because together we have the lamp to dispel it, since you realize you do not want it, you must be ready. Let us be very calm in doing this, for we are merely looking honestly for truth. The dynamics of the ego will be our lesson for a while, for we must look first at this to see beyond it, since you have made it real. We will undo this error quietly together, and then look beyond it to truth. (T.p. 202)


Seeing through the eyes of Christ, the mission of forgiveness which corrects the ego's misperceptions of separation by reflecting the true unity of the Son of God: not to be equated with physical sight, it is the attitude that undoes the projections of guilt, allowing us to look upon the real world in place of the world of sin, fear, suffering, and death. (T.p. 215)

*Observers devote their whole life to the pursuit of truth and "getting to the bottom" of things. They hold the attitude of doubt and stay reserved so as to not waste energy by making mistakes while justifying not taking action on anything. They are smart, resourceful, and pride themselves in achieving the true perception.*

Perception Versus Knowledge

11. It can not be emphasized too often that correcting perception is merely a temporary expedient. It is necessary only because misperception is a block to knowledge, while accurate perception is a stepping stone towards it. The whole value of right perception lies in the ineveitable realization that all perception is unnecessary. This removes the block entirely. You may ask how this is possible as long as you appear to be living in this world. That is a reasonable question. You must be careful however that you really understand it. Who is the "you" you are living in this world? Spirit is immortal and immortality is a constant state It is as tru now as it ever was or ever will be, because it implies no change at all. It is not a continuum, nor is it understood by being compared to an opposite. Knowledge never involves comparisons. That is it's main difference from everything else the mind can grasp (T.p. 59)

From Perception To Knowledge

2. The very real difference between perception and knowledge becomes quite apparent if you consider this: There is nothing partial about knowledge. Every aspect is whole, and therefore no aspect is separate. You are an aspect of knowledge, being in the mind of God, who knows you. All knowledge must be yours, for in you is all knowledge. Perception at it's loftiest is never complete. Even

## THE OBSERVER

the perception of the Holy Spirit, as perfect as perception can be, is without meaning in Heaven. Perception can reach everywhere under his guidance, for the vision of Christ beholds everything in light. Yet no perception, however holy, will last forever. (T.p. 258)

You act according to The particular order of needs you establish This in turn depends on your perception of what you are.
A sense of separation from God is the only lack you really need correct. This sense of separation would never have arisen if you had not distorted your perception of the truth, and had thus perceived yourself asa lacking. The idea of order of needs arose bedcause, having made this fundamental error, you had already fragmented yourself into levels with different needs. As you integrate you become one, and your needs become one accordingly. Unified needs lead to unified action, because this produces a lack of conflict.
The idea of orders of need, which follows from the original error that one can be separated from God, requires correction at it's own level before the the error of perceiving levels at all can be corrected. You can not behave effectively while you function on different levels. However, while you do, correction must be introduced vertically from the bottom up. This is because you think yo live in space, where concepts such as "up" and "down" are meaningful. Ultimately, space is as meaningless as time. Both are merely beliefs.
The real purpose of this world is to use it to correct your unbelief you can never control the effects of fear yourself, because you made fear, and you believe in what you have made In attitude, then though not in content, you

resemble your Creator,Who has perfect faith in his creations *because*
He created them. Belief produces the acceptance of existence. That is why you can believe what no one else thinks is true. It is true for you because it was made by you.

All aspects of fear are untrue because they do not exist at the creative level, and therefore do not exist at all. To whatever extent you are willing to submit your beliefs to this test, to that extent are your perceptions corrected. In sorting out the false from the true, the miracle proceeds along these lines:

> *Perfect love casts out fear.*
> *If fear exists,*
> *Then there is not perfect love.*
> *But:*
> *Only perfect love exists.*
> *If there is fear,*
> *It produces a state that does not exist.*

Believe this and you will be free. Only God can establish this solution, and this faith *is* his gift. (T.p 13,15)

Extension
   Knowledge: the ongoing process of creation, wherein spirit extends itself: God creating Christ; since Heaven is beyond time and space,"extension" cannot be understood as a temporal or spatial process.

   True perception; extending the Holy Spirit or Christ's vision in the form of forgiveness or peace; the Holy Spirit's use of the law of mind, contrasted with the ego's projection; since ideas leave not their source, what is extended remains in the mind, where it is reflected in the world of illusion. (Glossary p.67)

Lesson #304

Let not my world obscure the sight of Christ.
    1.I can obscure my holy sight, if I intrude my world upon it. Nor can I behold the holy sights Christ looks upon, unless it is this vision that I use. Perception is a mirror not a fact. And what I look on is my state of mind, reflecting outward. I would bless the world by looking on it through the eyes of Christ. And I will look upon the certain signs that all my sins have been forgiven me

3. You lead me from darkness into light. Let me forgive and receive salvation for the world. It is your gift, my father, given me to offer to your holy Son, that he again may find the memory of you, and of your son as you created him (W.p.451)

## VI. THE ILLUSION OF NEEDS

    1. You who want peace can find it only by complete forgiveness. No learning is acquired by anyone unless he wants to learn it and believes in some way that he needs it. While lack does not exist in the creation of God, it is very apparent in what you have made, it is, in fact the essential difference between them. Lack implies that you would be better off in a state somehow different from the one you are in. Untill the" separation", which is the meaning of the "fall"

Nothing was lacking. There were no needs at all. Needs arise only when you deprive yourself. (T.p.13)

II. Revelation, Time, and Miracles

1. Revelation induces complete but temporary suspension of doubt and fear. It reflects the original form of communication between God and His creations, involving the extremely personal sense of creation sometimes sought in physical relationships. Physical closeness cannot achieve it. "Miracles", however, are genuinely impersonal, and result in true closeness to others. Revelation unites you directly with God. "Miracles" unite you directly with your brother.
Neither emanates from consciousness, but both are experienced there. Consciousness is the state that induces action, though it does not inspire it. You are free to believe what you choose, and what you do attests to what you believe.

2. Revelation is intensely personal and cannot be meaningfully translated. That is why any attempt to describe it in words is impossible. Revelation only induces experience, miracles on the other hand, induce action. They are more useful now because of their interpersonal nature. This phase of learning, working miracles is important because freedom from fear cannot be thrust upon you Revelation is literally unspeakable because it is an experience of unspeakable love.

3. Awe should be reserved for revelation, to which it is perfectly and correctly applicable. It is not appropriate for miracles because a state of awe is worshipful, implying that one of a lesser order stands before his Creator. You are a perfect creation, and should experience awe only in the Presence of the Creator of perfection. The

miracle therefore is a sign of love among equals. Equals should not be in awe of one another because awe implies inequality. It is therefore an inappropriate reaction to me. An elder brother is entitled to respect for his greater experience, and obedience for his greater wisdom. He is also entitled to love because he is a brother, and to devotion if he is devoted. It is only my devotion that entitles me to yours. There is nothing about rate that you cannot attain. I have nothing that does not come from God. The difference between us now is that I have nothing else. This leaves me in a state which is only potential in you.

4. "No man cometh unto the Father but by me" does not mean that I am in any way separate or different from you except in time, and time does not really exist. The statement is more meaningfull in terms of a vertical rather than a horizontal axis. You stand below me and I stand below God.In the process of "rising up" I am higher because without me the distance between God and man would be too great for you to encompass. I bridge the difference as an elder brother to you on the one hand, and as a Son of God on the other. My devotion to my brothers has placed me in charge of the Sonship, which I render complete because I share it. This may appear to contradict the statement,"I and my Father are one," but there are two parts to the statement in recognition that the Father is greater.

5. Revelations are indirectly inspired by me because I am close to the Holy Spirit, and alert to the revelation=readiness of my brothers. I can thus bring down to them more than they can draw down to themselves The Holy Spirit mediates higher to lower communication, keeping the direct channel from God to you open for revelation. Revelation is

not reciprocal. It proceeds from God to you, but not from you to God.

6. The miracle minimizes the need for time. In the longitudinal or horizontal plane the recognition of the equality of the members of the Sonship appears to involve almost endless time. However, the miracle entails a sudden shift from horizontal to vertical perception. This introduces an interval from which the giver and receiver both emerge farther along in time than they would otherwise have been. The miracle thus has the unique property of abolishing time to the extent that it renders the interval of time it spans unnecessary. There is no relation between the time a miracle takes and the time it covers. The miracle substitutes for learning that might have taken thousands of years It does so by the underlying recognition of perfect equality of giver and receiver on which the miracle rests. The miracle shortens time by collapsing it, thus eliminating certain intervals within it. It does this, however, within the larger temporal sequence. (T.p.8)

*The healthy observer is concerned with getting to the heart of reality. Dealing with facts and figures to understand the general world. The observer is consumed with reading, studying, and theorizing on different planes of reality*

## III. PERCEPTION VERSUS KNOWLEDGE

1. We have been emphasizing perception, and have said very little about knowledge as yet. This is because perception must be straightened out before you can know anything. To know is to be certain. Uncertainty means that you do not know. Knowledge is

power because it is certain, and certainty is strength. Perception is temporary. As an attribute of the belief of space and time, it is subject to either fear or love. Misperceptions produce fear and true perceptions foster love, but neither brings certainty because all perception varies. That is why it is not knowledge. True perception is the basis for knowledge, but knowing is the affirmation of truth and beyond all perceptions.

2. All your difficulties stem from the fact that you do not recognize yourself, your brother or God. To recognize means ,"to know again," implying that you knew before. You can see in many ways because your perception involves interpretation, and this means that it is not whole or consistent. The miracle, being a way of perceiving, is not knowledge. It is the right answer to a question, but you do not question when you know. Questionng illusions is the first step in undoing them. The miracle or , the right answer, corrects them. Since perceptions change, their dependence on time is obvious. How you perceive at any given time determines what you do, and actions must occur in time. Knowledge is timeless, because certainty is not questionable. You know when you have ceased to ask questions.

3. The questioning mind perceives itself in time, and therefore looks for future answers. The closed mind believes the future and the present will be the same. This establishes a seemingly stable state that is usually an attempt to countewract an underlying fear that the future will be worse than the present. This fear inhibits the tendency to question at all.

4. True vision is the natural perception of spiritual sight, but it is still a correction rather than a fact. Spiritual sight is symbolic, and therefore not a device for knowing. It is however a means of right perception, which brings it into the proper domain of the miracle. A "vision of God" would be a miracle rather than a revelation. The fact that perception is involved at all removes the experience from the realm of knowledge. This is why visions, however holy, do not last. (T.p.40)

*The Healthy Observer recognizes that knowledge is power and that it is an invisible attribute of the mind to "know." The observer becomes a horder of knowledge and is able to be quite prophetic and can be wise to the true essence of the issue regardless of other people's tangents in their approaches.*

VII. Looking within

1. Miracles demonstrate that learning has occurred under the right guidance, for learning is invisible and what has been learned can be recognized only by it's results. It's generalization is demonstrated as you use it in more and more situations You will recognize that you have learned there is no order of difficulty in miracles when you apply them to all situations. There is no situation to which miracles do not apply, and by applying them to all situations you will gain the real world. For in this holy perception you will be made whole, and the Atonement will radiate from your acceptance of it for yourself to everyone the Holy Spirit sends you for your blessing. In every child of God His blessing lies, and in your blessing of the children of God is his blessing to you.
2. Everyone in the world must play his part in its redemption in order to recognize that the world has been redeemed. You cannot see the invisible. Yet if you see its effects you know it must be there. By perceiving what it does, you recognize its being. And by what it does, you learn what it is. You cannot see your strengths, but you gain confidence in their existence as they enable you to act. And the results of your actions you *can* see.
3. The Holy Spirit is invisible but you can see the results of His presence, and through them you will learn that He is there. What he enables you to do is clearly not of this world, for miracles violate every law of reality as this world judges it. Every law of time and space, of magnitude and mass is transcended, for what the Holy Spirit enables you to do is clearly beyond all of them. Percieving

## THE OBSERVER

His results, you will understand where he must be, and finally know what He is.

4. You cannot see the Holy Spirit but you can see his manifestations. And unless you do, you will not realize He is there. Miracles are His witnesses, and speak for His Presence. What you cannot see becomes real to you only through the witnesses that speak for it. For you can be aware of what you cannot see, and it can become compellingly real to you as its presence becomes manifest through you. Do the Holy Spirits work, for you share in His function. As your function in Heaven is creation, so your function on earth is healing. God shares his function with you in Heaven, and the Holy Spirit shares his function with you on earth. As long as you believe you have other functions, so long will you need correction. For this belief is the destruction of peace, a goal in direct opposition to the Holy Spirit's purpose.

5. You see what you expect, and you expect what you invite. Your perception is the result of your invitation, coming to you as you sent for it. Whose manifestations would you see? Of whose presence would you be convinced? For you will believe in what you manifest, and as you look out so you will see in. Two ways of looking at the world are in your mind, and your perception will reflect the guidance you have chosen.

6. I am the manifestation of the Holy Spirit, and when you see me it will be because you have invited Him. For He will send you his witnesses if you will but look upon them. Remember always that you see what you seek, for what you seek you will find. The ego finds what it seeks, and only that. It does not find love, for that is not what it is seeking. Yet seeking and finding are the same, and if you seek for two goals you will find them, but you will recognize neither. You will think they are the same because you want both of them. The mind always strives for integration, and if it is split and wants to keep the split, it will still believe it has one goal by making it seem to be one. (T.p.231)

## V. WHOLENESS AND SPIRIT

1. The miracle is much like the body in that both are learning aids for facilitating a state in which they become unnecessary. When spirit's original state of direct communication is reached, neither the body nor the miracle serves any purpose. While you believe you are in a body, however, you can choose between loveless and miraculous channels of expression. You can make an empty shell but you cannot express nothing at all. You can wait, delay, paralyze yourself, or reduce your creativity to almost nothing. But you cannot abolish it. You can destroy your medium of communication, but not your potential. You did not create yourself.
2. The basic decision of the miracle-minded is not to wait on time any longer than necessary. Time can waste as well as be wasted. The miracle worker, therefore accepts the time- control factor gladly. He recognizes that every collapse of time brings everyone closer to the ultimate release from time, in which the Father and the Son are one. Equality does not imply equality *now*. When everyone recognizes that he has everything, individual contributions to the Sonship will no longer be necessary.
3. When the Atonement has been completed, all talents will be shared by all the Sons of God. God is not partial. All his children have his total Love, and all his gifts are freely given to everyone alike. "Except ye become as little children" means that unless you fully recognize your complete dependence on God, you cannot know the real power of the Son in his true relationship with the Father. The specialness of God's Sons dos not stem from exclusion but from inclusion. All my brothers are special. If they believe they are deprived of anything, their reception gets distorted. When this occurs

## THE OBSERVER

the whole family of God, or the Sonship is impaired in its relationships.

4. Ultimately every member of the family of God must return. The miracle calls him to return because it blesses and honors him, even though he may be absent in spirit. "God is not mocked" is not a warning but a reassurance. God *would* be mocked if any of his creation lacked holiness. Creation is whole and the mark of wholeness is holiness. Miracles are affirmations of Sonship, which is a state of completion and abundance.

5. Whatever is true is eternal, and cannot change or be changed. Spirit is therefore unalterable because it is already perfect, but the mind can elect what it chooses to serve. The only limit put on its choice is that it cannot serve two masters. If it elects to do so, the mind can become the medium by which spirit creates along the line of its own creation. If it does not freely elect to do so, it retains its creative potential but places itself under tyrannous rather than Authoritative control. As a result it imprisons, because such are the dictates of tyrants. To change your mind means to place it at the disposal of *true* authority.

6. The miracle is a sign that the mind has chosen to be led by me in Christ's service. The abundance of Christ is the natural result of choosing to follow Him. All shallow roots must be uprooted, because they are not deep enough to sustain you. The illusion that shallow roots can be deepened, and thus made to hold, is one of the distortions on which the reverse of the Golden Rule rests. As these false underpinnings are given up, the equilibrium is temporarily experienced as unstable, However, nothing is less stable than an upside down orientation. Nor can anything that holds it up side down be conducive to increased stability. (T.p.13)

# THE AVERAGE OBSERVER ACCORDING TO A COURSE IN MIRACLES

*The Average Observer compartmentalizes their mind and it becomes distant and "taken up" in their work because of the maximal degree of concentration devoted to their work. They shun emotional involvements because it "blows their mind" and cannot stand the distraction or pain or needless bothers.*

Creations

His extension of our spirit; the effects of our creating, analogous to the creation when God created His Son by extending Himself;as extension of Christ, our creations are part of the Second Person of the Trinity, creation is ongoing in Heaven, beyond time and space, and independent of the Son's lack of awareness of it in this world. (Gloss.P.51)

Creation

The extension of God's being or spirit, the Cause, that resulted in his Son, the effect, described as the first coming of Christ; it is the Son's function in Heaven to create, as it was God's in creating Him. (Gloss.P.50)

*The Average observer is involved in intellectual pursuits, researching scholastic findings and fleshing out complicated theories and interpretations. These are the normal endeavors of the genius observer.*

I offer only miracles today for I would have them returned to me. Father, a miracle reflects your gifts to me, your Son. And everyone I give returns to me, reminding me the law of love is universal (W 345)

*As a result of imposing ideas or fads and corroborating the historicity of the truth of the matter, the logic of the Observer leads to iconoclastic and radically extreme positions in attitude and interpretation of reality.*

*The intellectual leaves other people" in the dust" with their analytic scientific style of thinking, leading them to deeper truths and levels of understanding. With that deeper level of understanding they have to defend themselves from the less informed to not be considered as irrelevant to the germaine issue. Yet they do not always wish to show their opponent as "disinherited."*

Defenses
    w-m the dynamics we use to" protect "ourselves from our guilt, fear and seeming attack on others, the most important of which are denial and projection; by their very nature "defenses do what they would defend", as they reinforce the belief in our own vulnerability which merely increases our fear and belief that we need defense. (Gloss.P.57)

## I. RIGHT TEACHING AND RIGHT LEARNING

1. A good teacher clarifies his own ideas and strengthens them by teaching them. Teacher and pupil are alike in the learning process. They are in the same order of learning, and unless they share their lessons conviction will be lacking. A good teacher must believe in the ideas he teaches, but he must meet another condition; he must believe in the students to whom he offers the ideas.

2. Many stand guard over their ideas because they want to protect their thought systems as they are, and learning means change. Change is always fearful to the separated because they cannot conceive of it as a move towards healing the separation. They always perceive it as a move toward further separation, because separation was their first experience of change. You believe that if you allow no change to enter your ego you will find peace. This profound confusion is possible only if you maintain that same thought system can stand on two foundations. Nothing can reach the spirit from the ego and nothing can reach the ego from spirit. Spirit can neither strengthen the ego nor reduce the conflict within it. The ego is a contradiction. Your self and God's self are in opposition. They are opposed in source, in direction, and outcome. They are profoundly irreconcilable, because spirit cannot perceive and the ego cannot know. They are therefore not in communication and can never be in communication. Nevertheless the ego can learn, even though its maker can be misguided. He cannot, however, make the totally lifeless out of the life-given.
3. Spirit need not be taught, but the ego must be. Learning is ultimately perceived as frightening because it leads to the relinquishment, not the destruction, of the ego to the light of spirit. This is the change the ego must fear, because it does not share my charity. My lesson was like yours, and because I learned it I can teach it. I will never attack your ego, but I am trying to teach you how its thought system arose. When I remind you of your true creation, your ego cannot but respond with fear.
4. Teaching and learning are your greatest strengthsnow, because they enable you to change your mind and help others to change theirs. Refusing to change your mind

## THE OBSERVER

will not prove that the separation has not occurred. The dreamer who doubts the reality of his dream while he is still dreaming is not really healing his split mind. You dream of a separated ego and believe in a world that rests upon it. This is very real to you. You cannot undo it by not changing your mind about it. If you are willing to renounce the role of guardian of your thought system and open it to me, I will correct it very gently and lead you back to God.

5. Every good teacher hopes to give his students so much of his own learning that they will one day no longer need him. This is the one true goal of the teacher. It is impossible to convince the ego of this, because it goes against all of its own laws. But remember laws are set up to protect the continuity the system of which the lawmaker believes. It is natural for the ego to try and protect itself once you have made it, but it is not natural for you to want to obey its laws unless *you* believe them. The ego cannot make this choice because of the nature of its origin. You can because of the nature of yours.

6. Egos can clash in any situation but the spirit can not clash at all. If you perceive a teacher as merely" a larger ego"you will be afraid, because to enlarge an ego would be to increase anxiety about separation. I will teach with you and live with you if you will think with me, but my goal will always be to absolve you finally from the need for a teacher. This is the opposite of the ego-oriented teacher's goal. He is concerned with his effect of his ego on other egos, and therefore interprets their interaction as a means of ego preservation. I would not be able to devote myself to teaching if I believed this, and you will not be a devoted teacher as long as you believe it. I am constantly being perceived as a teacher either to be

exalted or rejected, but I do not accept either perception for myself.
7. Your worth is not established by teaching or learning. Your worth is established by God. As long as you dispute this everything you do will be fearful, particularly any situation that lends itself to the belief in superiority and inferiority. Teachers must be patient and repeat their lessons until they are learned. I am willing to do this, because I have no right to set your learning limits for you. Again,-
Nothing you do or think or wish or make is necessary to establish your worth. This point is not debatable except in delusions. Your ego is never at stake because He did. Any confusion on this point is delusional, and no form of devotion is possible as long as this delusion lasts.
8. The ego trys to exploit all situations into forms of praise for itself in order to overcome its doubts It will remain doubtfull as long as you believe in its existence. You who made it cannot trust it, because in your right mind you realize it is not real. The only sane solution is not to try to change reality, which is indeed a fearful attempt, but to accept it as it is. You are part of reality which stands unchanged beyond the reach of your ego but within easy reach of spirit. When you are afraid, be still and know that God is real, and you are His beloved Son in whom He is well pleased. Do not let your ego dispute this, because the ego cannot know what is as far beyond its reach as you are.
9. God is not the author of fear. You are. You have chosen to create unlike Him, and have therefore made fear for yourself. You are not at peace because you are not fulfilling your function. God gave you a very lofty function that you are not meeting. Your ego has chosen to

be afraid instead of meeting it. When you awaken you will not be able to understand this, because it is literally incredible.*Do not believe the incredibile now.* Any attempt to increase its believableness is merely to postpone the inevitable.The word,"inevitable" is fearful to the ego, but joyous to the spirit. God is inevitable and you cannot avoid Him any more than He can avoid you.

10. The ego is afraid of the spirit's joy, because once you have experienced it you will withdraw all protection from the ego, and become totally without investment in fear. Your investment is great now because fear is a witness to the separation, and your ego rejoices when you witness to it. Leave it behind! Do not listen to it and do not preserve it. Listen only to God, who is as incapable of deception as is the spirit He created. Release yourself and release others. Do not present a false and unworthy picture of yourself to others, and do not accept such a picture of them yourself.

11. The ego has built a shabby and unsheltering home for you, because it cannot build otherwise. Do not try to make this impoverished house stand. Its weakness is your strength. Only God could make a home that is worthy of his creations, who have chosen to leave it empty by their own dispossession. Yet his home will stand forever, and is ready for you when you choose to enter it. Of this you can be wholley certain. God is as incapable of creating the imperishable as the ego is of making the eternal.

12. Of your ego you can do nothing to save yourself or others, but of your spirit you can do everything for the salvation of both. Humility is a lesson for the ego, not for the spirit. Spirit is beyond humility, because it recognizes its radiance and gladly sheds its light everywhere. The meek shall inherit the earth because their egos are humble,

and this gives them true perception. The Kingdom of Heaven is the spirit's right, whose beauty and dignity are beyond doubt, beyond perception , and stand forever as the Love of God for His creations, who are wholly worthy of Him and only of Him. Nothing else is sufficiently worthy to be a gift for a creation of God Himself.

13. I will substitute your ego if you wish, but never for your spirit. A father can safely leave a child with an elder brother, who has shown himself responsible, but this involves no confusion about the child's origin. The brother can protect the child's body and his ego, but he does not confuse himself with the father because he does this. I can be entrusted with your body and your ego only because this enables you not to be concerned with them, and lets me teach you their unimportance. I could not understand their importance to you if I had not once been tempted to believe in them myself. Let us undertake to learn this lesson together so we can be free of them together. I need devoted teachers who share my aim of healing the mind. Spirit is far beyond the need of your protection or mine. Remember this:

*In this world you need not have tribulation because I have overcome the world. That is why you should have good cheer.*(T.p56)

## THE UNHEALTHY OBSERVER ACCORDING TO A COURSE IN MIRACLES

*When stress or disappointment is active in the unhealthy observer's life they withdraw from others and become paranoid. They become reclusive and fantasize on the immanent danger to their world, skewing reality to the point of "unreal."*

Dissociation
   An ego defense that seperates the ego from the Holy Spirit- the wrong mind from the right mind-splitting off what seems fearful, which merely reinforces the fear that is the ego's goal;the ego's attempt to separate two conflicting thought systems and keep them both in our minds, so that its thought system of darkness is safe from undoing by the light. (Gloss.P.61)

## MY ATTACK THOUGHTS ARE ATTACKING MY INVULNERABILITY

1. It is surely that if you can be attacked you are not invulnerable.
   You see attack as a real threat. That is because you believe that you can really attack. And what would have effects through you must also have effects on you. It is the law that will ultimately save you, but you are missing it now. You must therefore learn how it can be used for your own best interests, rather than against them.
2. Because your attack thoughts will be projected, you will fear attack. And if you fear attack, you must believe that you are invulnerable. Attack thoughts therefore make you vulnerable in your own mind, which is where the attack thoughts are. Attack thoughts and invulnerability cannot be accepted together. They contradict each other.

3. The idea for today introduces the thought that you always attack yourself first if attack thoughts must entail the belief that you are vulnerable, their effect is to weaken you in your own eyes. Thus, they have attacked your own perception of yourself. And because you believe in them, you can no longer believe in yourself. A false image of yourself has come to take the place of what you are. (W.P.40)

Preoccupations with problems set up to be incapable of solution are favorite ego devices for impeding learning progress. In all these diversionary tactics, however, the one question that is never asked by those who pursue them is;"What for?" This is the question you must learn to ask in connection with everything. What is the purpose? Whatever it is it will direct your efforts automaticly. When you make a decision of purpose, then, you have made a decision about your fixture effort; a decision that will remain in effect unless you change your mind. (T.P.67)

*The cynicism and antagonism of the unhealthy observer isolates them even farther as to "go it alone." Their minds engorge and worsen their distortions of reality. The ideas possess them to the point of schizophrenic insanity.*

## VI. THE REWARDS OF GOD

1. The ego does not recognize the real source of "threat" and if you associate yourself with the ego, you do not understand the situation as it is. Only your allegiance to it gives the ego any power over you. I have spoken

of the ego as if it were a separate thing, acting on its own. This was necessary to persuade you that you cannot dismiss it lightly, and relize how much of your thinking is ego directed. We cannot safely let go at that, however, or you will regard yourself as necessarily conflicted as long as you are here, or as long as you believe you are here. The ego is nothing more than a part of your belief about yourself. Your other life has continued without interruption, and has been and always will be totally unaffected by your attempts to dissociate it. (T.P.67)

7. Judgement is but a toy, a whim, the senseless means by which to play the game of death in your imagination. But vision sets all things right, bringing them gently within the kindly sway of Heaven's laws. What if you recognize this world is a hallucination? What if you really understood you really made it up? What if you realized that those who seem to walk about in it, to sin, to die, attack and murder and destroy themselves are wholley unreal? Could you have faith in what you see, if you accepted this? And would you see it? (T.p.443)

*The schizophrenic insanity of the unhealthy observer plus their very antagonism of everyone and everything isolate them further from their family, friends, and themselves.*

To be alone is to be guilty. For to experience yourself as alone is to deny the oneness of the Father and his Son, and thus to attack reality. (T.p.312)

The illusory space between ousrselves and God, and ourselves and others, brought about by the belief in separation; in this space arise the dreams of sickness and hate, since the projection onto bodies must always follow the mind's belief in separation. (Gloss.P. 79)

And what is limited cannot be heaven. So, it must be hell. (T.p.563) You are enemy indeed to him because you do not know him as yourself. (T.p.556)
Someone must lose his innocence that someone else can take it from him, making it his own. (T.P. 563)

*The Observer's use of "compartmentalization" fragments their personal relationships in their specific utility roles. And , they rather would not confuse or enmesh cross purposes in their personal relationships because they don't wish to be bothered by the excess rationalization it takes to justify a separate reason for the same relationship. Plus, it takes too much effort to "feel" a difference to justify the plurality of the relationship.*

The ego's use of relationships is so fragmented that it frequently goes even further, one part of one aspect, suites its purposes, while it prefers different parts of another aspect. Thus does it assemble reality to its own capricious liking, offering for your seeking a picture whose likeness does not exist. For there is nothing in Heaven or earth that it resembles, and so, however much you seek for it's reality, you cannot find it because it is not real. (T.P.313)

## IV. THE TWO PICTURES

1. God established His relationship with you to make you happy, and nothing you do that does not share His purpose can be real. The purpose God ascribed to anything is its only function. Because of his reason for creating His relationship with you, the function of relationships became forever "to make happy." *And nothing else.* To fulfill this function you relate to your creations as God to His. For nothing God created is apart from happiness, and nothing God created but would extend happiness as its Creator did. Whatever does not fulfill this function cannot be real.

2. In this world it is impossible to create Yet it is possible to make happy. I have said repeatedly that the Holy Spirit would not deprive you of your special relationships, but would transform them. And all that is meant by that is that he will restore to them the function given them by God. The function you have given them is clearly not to make happy. But the holy relationship shares God's purpose, rather than aiming to make a substitute for it. Every special relationship you have made is a substitute for God's Will, and glorifies yours instead of His because of the illusion that they are different.

3. You have made very real relationships even in this world. Yet you do not recognize them because you have raised their substitutes to such predominance that, when truth calls to you, as it does constantly, you answer with a substitute. Every special relationship you have made has, as its fundamental purpose, the aim of occupying your mind so completely that you will not hear the call of truth.

4. In a sense the special relationship was the ego's answer to the creation of the Holy Spirit, who was God's Answer to the separation. For, although the ego did not understand what had been created it was aware of threat. The whole defense system the ego evolved to protect the separation from the Holy Spirit was in response to the gift with which God blessed it, and by his blessing enabled it to be healed. This blessing holds within itself the truth about everything. And the truth is that the Holy Spirit is in close relationship with you, because in Him is your relationship to God restored to you. The relationship with Him has never been broken, because the Holy Spirit has not been separate from anyone since the separation. And through Him have all your holy relationships been carefully preserved, to serve God's purpose for you.
5. The ego is always alert to threat, and part of your mind into which the ego was accepted is very anxious to preserve its reason as it sees it. It does not realize that it is totally insane. And you must realize just what this means if you would be restored to sanity. The insane protect their thought systems, but they do so insanely. And all their defenses are as insane as what they are supposed to protect. The separation has nothing in it, no part, no "reason," and no attribute that is not insane. And, its "protection" is part of it, as insane as the whole. The special relationship, which is it's chief defense, must therefore be insane.
6. You have but little difficulty now in realizing that the thought system the special relationship protects is but a system of delusions. You recognize at least in general terms, that the ego is insane. Yet the special relationship seems to you somehow to be "different." Yet we have looked at it far closer than we have at many other

THE OBSERVER

aspects of the ego's thought system that you have been more willing to let go. While this one remains, you will not let the others go. For this one is not different. Retain this one, and you have retained the whole.

7. It is essential to realize that defenses *do* what they would defend. The underlying basis for their effectiveness is that they offer what they *defend*. *What they defend is placed in them for safe-keeping, and as they* operate they bring them to you. Every defense operates by giving gifts, and the gift is a miniature of the thought system the defense protects, set in a golden frame. The frame is very elaborate, all set with jewels, and deeply carved and polished. Its purpose is to be of value *in itself* and to divert your attention to what it discloses. But the frame without the picture you cannot have. Defenses operate to think you can.

8. The special relationship has the most imposing and deceptive frame of all the defenses the ego uses. Its thought system is offered here, surrounded by a frame so heavy and so elaborate that the picture is almost obliterated by its imposing structure. Into the frame are woven all sorts of fanciful and fragmented illusions of love, set with dreams of sacrifice and self- aggrandizement , and interlaced with gilded threads of self-destruction. The glitter of blood shines like rubies, and the tears are are faceted like diamonds and gleam in the dim light in which the offering is made.

9. Look at the *picture*. Do not let the frame distract you. This gift is given you for your damnation, and if you take it you will believe that you *are* damned. You cannot have

the frame without the picture. What you value is the frame, for there you see no conflict. Yet the frame is only the wrapping for the gift of conflict. The frame is not the gift. Be not deceived by the most superficial aspects of this thought system, for these aspects enclose the whole, complete in every aspect. Death lies in this glittering gift. Let not your gaze dwell on the hypnotic gleaming of the frame. Look at the picture, and realize that death is offered you.

10. That is why the holy instant is so important in defense of the truth. The truth itself needs no defense, but you do need defense against your acceptance of the gift of death. When you, who are truth accept an idea so dangerous to truth, you threaten truth with destruction. And your defense must now be undertaken to keep truth whole. The power of Heaven, the Love of God, the tears of Christ, and the joy of his eternal Spirit are marshalled to defend you from your own attack. For you attack They, being part of Them, and They must save you, for They love Themselves.

11. The holy instant is a miniature of Heaven, sent you *from* Heaven. It is a picture too set in a frame. Yet, if you accept this gift you will not see the frame at all because the gift can only be accepted by your willingness to focus all your attention on the picture. The holy instant is a miniature of eternity. It is a picture of timelessness, set in a frame of time. If you focus on the picture, you will realize that it is only the frame that made you think that it was a picture. Without the frame, the picture is seen as to what it represents. For as the whole thought system of the ego lies in its gifts, so the whole of Heaven lies in

this instant, borrowed from eternity, and set in time for you.(T.p.360)

16. As God ascends into his Rightful place and you to yours, you will experience again the meaning of relationship and know it to be true. Let us ascend in peace together to the Father, by giving Him ascendance in our minds. We will gain everything by giving Him the the power and the glory, and keeping no illusions of where they are. They are in us through his ascendance. What he has given is His. It shines in every part of Him, as in the whole. The whole reality of your relationship with Him lies in our relationship to one another. The holy instant shines alike on all relationships, for in it they *are* one. For here is only healing, already complete and perfect. For here is God, and where He is only the perfect and complete can be. (T.p. 361)

## VIII. THE IMMEDIACY OF SALVATION

1. The one remaining problem that you have is that you see an interval between the time when you forgive, and will receive the benefits of trusting in your brother. This but reflects the little you would keep between you and your brother, that you and he might be a little separate. For time and space are on illusion, which takes different forms. If it has been projected beyond your mind you think of it as time. The nearer it is brought to you where it is, the more you think of it in terms of space.
2. There is a distance you would keep apart from your brother, and this space you perceive as time because

you still believe you are external to him. This makes trust impossible. And you cannot believe that trust would settle every problem now. Thus do you think it safer to remain a little careful and a little watchful of interests perceived as separate. From this perception you cannot conceive of gaining what forgiveness offers *now*. The interval you think lies in between the giving and receiving of the gift seems to be one in which you sacrifice and suffer loss. You see eventual salvation, not immediate results.

3. Salvation is immediate. Unless you so perceive it, you will be afraid of it, believing that the risk of loss is great between the time its purpose is made yours and its effects will come to you In this form is the error still obscured that is the source of fear. Salvation *would* wipe out the space you see between you still, and let you instantly become as one. And it is here you fear the loss would lie. Do not project this fear to time, for time is not the enemy you perceive. Time is as neutral as the body is, except in terms of what you see it for. If you would keep a little space between you and your brother still, you then would want a little time in which forgiveness is withheld a little while. And this but makes the interval between the time in which forgiveness is withheld from you and given seem dangerous, with terror justified.(T.p. 559)

9. Be not content with future happiness. It has no meaning and is not your just reward. For you have cause for freedom *now*. What profits freedom in a prisoner's form? Why should deliverance be disguised as death? Delay is senseless and the "reasoning" that would maintain the effects of present

cause must be delayed until a future time, is merely a denial of the fact that consequence and cause must come as one. Look not to time, but to the little space between you still, to be delivered from. And do not let it be disquised as time, and so preserved because its form is changed and what it is cannot be recognized. The Holy Spirit's purpose now is yours. Should not his happiness be yours as well? (T.p.560)

*The Unhealthy Observer is so fraught with fear from the outside world that the feeling carries over into other aspects of their reality. The sense of paranoia is learned from a very studious perspective. And, because they invested so much doubt and study into these aspects they continue to hold their breath until the ultimate realities present themselves. Thus, they always expect another set of realities to surface after the present" showing" and thus stay in the shadow of the "doubt."*
You who believe that God is fear made but one substitution. It has taken many forms, because it was the substitution of illusion for truth; of fragmentation for wholeness. It has become so splintered and subdivided and divided again, over and over, that it is now about impossible to perceive it once was one, and still is what it was. That one error that brought truth to illusion, infinity to time, and life to death, was all you ever made. Your whole world rests upon it. Everything you see reflects it, and every special relationship that you ever made is a part of it (T.p. 37)

Perception w-m : condemnation, whereby people are separated into those to be hated and those to be "loved", a judgement always based upon the past.
(Gloss. P. 213)
You have paid very dearly for your illusions, and nothing you have paid for brought you peace. Are you not glad that

Heaven cannot be sacrificed, and sacrifice cannot be asked of you. (T.p. 413)

Fear binds the world. Forgiveness sets it free.
1. The ego makes illusions. Truth undoes it's evil dreams by shining them away. Truth never makes attack. It merely is. And by its presence is the mind recalled from fantasies, awakening to the real. Forgiveness bids this presence enter in, and take its rightful place within the mind. Without forgiveness is the mind in chains, believing in its own futility. Yet with forgiveness does the light shine through the dream of darkness, offering it hope, and giving it the means to realize the freedom that is its inheritance (W.p. 468)

Sickness
    A conflict in the mind(guilt) displaced unto the body; the ego's attempt to defend *itself* against the truth,(spirit) by focusing attention on the body; a sick body is the effect of a sick or split mind that is its cause representing the ego's desire to make others guilty by sacrificing ones self projecting responsibility for the attack unto them. (T.p. 188)

Dissociation is not a solution; it is a delusion. The delusional believe that truth will assail them, and they do not recognize it because they prefer the delusion. (T.p. 146)

## I THE ATTRACTION OF PAIN

9. Your little part is but to give the Holy Spirit the whole idea of sacrifice. And, to accept the peace He gives instead,

without the limits that would hold its extension back, and so would limit your awareness of it. For what he gives must be extended if you would have its limitless power, and use it for the Son of God's release. It is not this you would be rid of, and having it you cannot limit it. If peace is homeless, so are you and so am I. And He Who is our home is homeless with us. Is this your wish? Wold you forever be a wanderer in search of peace? Would you invest your hope of peace and happiness in what must fail?

10. Faith in the eternal is always justified, for the eternal is forever kind, infinite in its patience and wholly loving. It will accept you wholley, and give you peace. Yet it can unite only with what already is at peace in you, immortal as itself. The body can bring you neither peace nor turmoil; neither joy nor pain. It is a means and not an end. It has no purpose of itself, but what is given to it. The body will seem to be whatever is the means for reaching the goal that you assign to it. Only the mind can set a purpose, and only the mind can see the means for its accomplishment, and justify its use. Peace and guilt are both conditions of the mind, to be attained. And these conditions are home of the emotion that calls them forth, and therefore is compatible with them.

11. But think you which it is that is compatible with you. Here is your choice, and it is free. But all that lies in it will come with it, and what you think you are can never be a part from it. The body is the great seeming betrayer of faith. In it lies disillusionment and the seeds of faithlessness, but only if you ask of it what it cannot give. Can your mistake be reasonable grounds for depression and disillusionment, and for retaliative attack on what you think has failed you? Use not your error as the justification for your faithlessness.

You have not sinned, but you have been mistaken in what is faithful. And the correction of your mistake will give you the grounds for faith.

12. It is impossible to seek for pleasure through the body and not find pain. It is essential that this relationship be understood, for it is one that the ego sees as proof of sin. It is not really punitive at all. It is but the inevitable result of equating yourself with the body which is the invitation to pain. For it invites fear to enter and become your purpose. The attraction of guilt must enter with it and whatever fear directs the body to do is therefore painful. It will share the pain of all illusions, and the illusion of pleasure will be the same as pain.

13. Is not this inevitable? Under fear's orders the body will pursue guilt, serving its master whose attraction to guilt maintains the whole illusion to its existence This then is the attraction of pain. Ruled by this perception the body becomes the servant of pain, seeking it dutifully and obeying the idea that pain is pleasure. It is this idea that underlies all of the ego's heavy investment in the body. And it is this insane relationship that it keeps hidden, and yet feeds upon. To you it teaches that the body's pleasure is happiness. Yet, to itself it whispers, "It is death."

14. Why should the body be anything to you? Certainly what it is made of is not precious. And just as certainly it has no feeling. It transmits to you the feeling that you want. Like any communication medium the body receives and sends the messages that it is given. It has no feeling for them. All of the feeling with which they are invested is given by the sender and the receiver. The ego and the Holy Spirit both recognize this. And both recognize that here the sender

and the receiver are the same. The Holy Spirit tells you this with joy. The ego hides it, for it would keep you unaware of it. Who would send messages of hatred and attack if he but understood he sends them to himself? Who would accuse, make guilty, and condemn himself?

15. The ego's messages are always sent away from you, in the belief that for your message of attack and guilt will someone other than yourself suffer. And even if you suffer, yet someone else will suffer more. The great deceiver recognizes that this is not so, but as the" enemy" of peace, it urges you to send out all your messages of hate and free yourself. And to convince you that this is possible, it bids the body search for pain in attack upon another, calling it pleasure and offering it to you as freedom *from* attack.

16. Hear not its madness, and believe not the impossible is true. Forget not that the ego has dedicated the body to the goal of sin, and places in it all its faith continually , in solomn celebration of the ego's rule. Not one but must believe that yielding to the attraction of guilt is the escape from pain. Not one but must regard the body as himself, without which he would die, and yet within which is his death equally inevitable

17. It is not given to the ego's disciples to realize that they have dedicated themselves to death. Freedom is offered them but they have not accepted it, The Holy Spirit too, is a communication medium, receiving from the Father and offering His messages unto the Son. Like the ego, the Holy Spirit is both the sender and the receiver. For what is sent through Him returns to *Him, seeking itself along the way, and finding what it seeks. So does the* ego find the death *it* seeks, returning it to you.

## C. THE THIRD OBSTACLE: THE ATTRACTION OF DEATH

1. To you and your brother, in whose special relationship the Holy Spirit entered, it is given to release and be released from the dedication to death. For it was offered you, and you accepted. Yet you must learn still more about this strange devotion, for it contains the third obstacle that peace must flow across. No one can die unless he chooses death. What seems to be the fear of death is really its attraction. Guilt, too is feared and fearful. Yet it could have no hold at all except on those who are attracted to it and seek it out. And so it is with death. Made by the ego, its dark shadow falls across all living things because the ego is the *enemy* of life.
2. And yet a shadow cannot kill. What is a shadow to the living? They but walk past and it is gone. But what of those whose dedication is not to live; the black- draped "sinners", the ego's mournful chorus, plodding so heavily from life, dragging their chains, and marching in the slow procession that honors their grim master, lord of death? Touch any one of them with the gentle hands of forgiveness, and watch the chains fall away, along with yours. See him throw aside the black robe he was wearing to his funeral, and hear him laugh at death. The sentence sin would lay upon him he can escape through your forgiveness. This is no arrogance. It is the will of God. What is impossible to you who choose His Will as yours? What is death to you? Your dedication is not to death, nor to its master.When you accepted the Holy Spirit's purpose in place of the ego's you renounced death, exchanging it for life. We know that an idea leaves not its source.

And death is the result of the thought we call the ego, as surely as life is the result of the Thought of God.

## LESSON 320 (GROWTH LINE)

1. The Son of God is limitless. There are no limits on his strength, his peace, his joy, nor any attributes his Father gave in his creation. What he wills with his Creator and Redeemer must be done. His holy will can never be denied, because his father shines upon his Heaven. I am he to whome all this is given. I am he in whom the power of my Father's Will abides.
*Your will can do all things in me, and then extend to all the world as well through me. There is no limit on Your Will. And so all power has been given to Your Son.*

## LESSON 261 (DEMA1TERIALIZATION LINE)

1. I will identify with what I think is refuge and security. I will behold myself where I perceive my strength, and think I live within the citadel where I am safe and cannot be attacked. Let me today seek not security in danger, nor attempt to find my peace in murderous attack. I live in God. In him I find my refuge and my strength. In him is my identity. In Him is everlasting peace. And only there will I remember Who I really am.
*Let me not seek for idols. I would come, my Father, home ,to hem peace will come to everyone. Christ*

*is our eyes today. And his sigh whom You created as my Self.*

## LESSON 269 (ARCHETYPE)

1. *Father, Christ's vision is Your gift to me, and it has power to translate all that the body's eyes behold into the sight of a forgiven world. How glorious and gracious is the world! Yet how much more will I perceive in it than sight can give. The world forgiven signifies Your Son acknowledges his Father, lets his dreams be brought to truth, and waits expectantly the one remaining instant more of time which ends forever, as Your memory returns to him. And now his will is onewith Yours. His function now is but Your Own,and every thought except Your own is gone.*
2. The quiet of today will bless our hearts, and through them peace will come to everyone. Christ is our eyes today. And through His sight we offer healing to the world through him, the holy Son whom God created whole; the holy Son whom God created one.

## CHAPTER 6
# THE QUESTIONER

"Perfect love casts out fear. If fear exists, then there is not perfect love."

(T.12/147 ACIM)

## World:
### Level I

tThe effect of the ego's belief in separation, which is it's cause; the thought of separation and attack on God given form; being the expression of the belief in time and space, it was not created by God, who transcends time and space entirely; unless specifically referring to the world of knowledge, refers only to perception, the post-separation domain of the ego.

### Level II

w--m: a prism of separation which reinforces the ego's belief in sin and guilt, perpetuating the seeming existence of this world.

# A HEALTHY TROOPER-QUESTIONER ACCORDING TO A COURSE IN MIRACLES

*Reliable, hardworking Healthy Trooper-Questioners are trustworthy and efficient. They know themselves and extend trust to others.*

*The Trooper-Questioners are endearing and evoke loyalty from others. Their cooperation is extended as an equal; however, there is a sense of independence about them. They engage completely in their work and play by the rules.*

## III. TOLERANCE

1. God's teachers do not judge. To judge is to be dishonest, for to judge is to assume a position you do not have. Judgment without self-deception is impossible. Judgment implies that you have been deceived in yourself. Judgment implies a lack of trust, and trust remains the bedrock of the teacher of God's whole thought system. Let this be lost, and all his learning goes. Without

> r--m: a classroom wherein we learn our lessons of forgiveness, the Holy Spirit's teaching devicse to help us transcend the world; thus the purpose of the world is to teach us that there is no world. (Gloss., p. 226).
>
> **Real world:** the state of mind in which, through total forgiveness, the world of separation is released from the projections of guilt we had placed upon it; thus, it is the mind that has changed, not the world, and we see through the vision of Christ which blesses rather than condemns; tThe Holy Spirit's happy dream; the end of the Aatonement, undoing our thoughts of separation, and allowing God to take the last step. (Gloss., p. 173).

judgment are all things equally acceptable, for who could judge otherwise? Without judgment are all men brothers, for who is there who stands apart? Judgment destroys honesty and shatters trust. No teacher of God can judge and hope to learn (Manual, p. 12).

*Healthy Trooper-Questioners are apprised of the reality of forgiveness in their spiritual repertoire of skills. It is only after numerous insults to their sensibilities that they forget they ever forgave, and the sense of fear and repressed foreboding stay with them.*

# LESSON 325

*All things I think I see reflect ideas.*

1. This is salvation's keynote: what I see reflects a process in my mind, which starts with my idea of what I want. From there, the mind makes up an image of the mind desires, judges valuable, and therefore seeks to find. These images are then projected outward, looked upon, esteemed as real, and guarded as one's own. From insane

wishes comes an insane world. From judgment comes a world condemned. And from forgiving thoughts a gentle world comes forth, with mercy for the Holy Son of God, to offer him a kindly home where he can rest a while before he journeys on, and help his brothers walk ahead with him, and find the way to Heaven and to God.

2. *Our Father, Your ideas reflect the truth, and mine apart from Yours but make up dreams. Let me behold what only Yours reflect, for Yours and Yours alone establish truth (W.p.464).*

## VIII. THE LITTLE GARDEN

1. It is only the awareness of the body that makes love seem limited. For the body is a limit on love. The belief in limited love was its origin, and it was made to limit the unlimited. Think not that this is merely allegorical, for it was made to limit you. Can you who see yourself within a body know yourself as an idea? Everything you recognize you identify with externals, something outside itself. You cannot even think of God without a body, or in some form you think you recognize.

2. The body cannot know, and while you limit your awareness to its tiny senses, you will not see the grandeur that surrounds you. God cannot come into a body, nor can you join Him there. Limits on love will always seem to shut Him out, and keep you apart from Him. The body is a tiny fence around a little part of a glorious and complete idea. It draws a circle, infinitely small, around a very little segment of Heaven, splintered from the whole, proclaiming that within it is your kingdom, where God can enter not.

3. Within this kingdom the ego rules, and cruelly: and to defend this little speck of dust it bids you fight against the universe. This fragment of your mind is such a tiny part of it that, could you but appreciate the whole, you would see instantly that it is like the smallest sunbeam to the sun, or like the faintest ripple on the

surface of the ocean. In its amazing arrogance, this tiny sunbeam has decided it is the sun; this almost imperceptible ripple hails itself as the ocean. Think how alone and frightened is this little thought, this infinitesimal illusion, holding itself apart against the universe. The sun becomes the sunbeam's "enemy," which would devour it, and the ocean terrifies the little ripple and "wants" to swallow it.

4. Yet neither sun nor ocean is even aware of all this strange and meaningless activity. They merely continue, unaware that they are feared and hated by a tiny segment of themselves. Even that segment is not lost to them, for it could not survive apart from them; and what it thinks it is in no way changes its total dependence on them for its being. Its whole existence still remains in them. Without the sun, the sunbeam would be gone; the ripple without the ocean is inconceivable.

5. Such is the strange position in which those in a world inhabited by bodies seem to be. Each body seems to house a separate mind, a disconnected thought, living alone and in no way joined to the thought by which it was created. Each tiny fragment seems to be self-contained, needing another for some things, but by no means totally dependent on its one Creator for everything; needing the whole to give it any meaning, for by itself it does mean nothing. Nor has it any life apart and by itself.

6. Like the sun and ocean your Self continues, unmindful that this tiny part regards itself as you. It is not missing; it could not exist if it were separate, nor would the whole be whole without it. It is not a separate kingdom, ruled by an idea of separation from the rest. Nor does a fence surround it, preventing it from joining with the rest, and keeping it apart from its Creator. This little aspect is no different from the whole, being continuous with it and at one with it. It leads no separate life, because its life is the oneness in which its being was created .

7. Do not accept this little, fenced-off aspect as yourself. The sun and ocean are as nothing, beside what you are. The sunbeam

sparkles only in the sunlight, and the ripple dances as it rests upon the ocean. Yet in neither sun nor ocean is the power that rests in you. Would you remain within your tiny kingdom? Arched high above it and surrounding it with love is the glorious whole, which offers all its happiness and deep content to every part. The little aspect that you think you set apart is no exception.

8. Love knows no bodies, and reaches to everything created like itself. Its total lack of limit is its meaning. It is completely impartial in its giving, encompassing only to preserve and keep complete what it would give. In your tiny kingdom you have so little! Should it not, then, be there that you would call on love to enter? Look at the desert—dry and unproductive, scorched and joyless—that makes up your little kingdom; and realize the life and joy that love would bring to it from where it comes, and where it would return with you.

9. The thought of God surrounds your little kingdom, waiting at the barrier you built, to come inside and shine upon the barren ground. See how life springs up everywhere! The desert becomes a garden, green and deep and quiet, offering rest to those who lost their way and wander in the dust. Give them a place of refuge, prepared by love for them where once a desert was. Everyone you welcome will bring love with him from Heaven for you. They enter one by one into this holy place, but they will not depart as they had come, alone. The love they brought with them will stay with them, as it will stay with you. Under its beneficence, your little garden will expand, and reach out to everyone who thirsts for living water, but has grown too weary to go on alone.

10. Go out and find them, for they bring your Self with them; and lead them gently to your quiet garden, and receive their blessing there. So will it grow and stretch across the desert, leaving no lonely little kingdoms locked away from love, and leaving you inside. You will recognize yourself, and see your little garden gently transformed into the Kingdom of Heaven, with all the love of its Creator shining upon it.

11. The holy instant is your invitation to love, to enter into your bleak and joyless kingdom, and to transform it into a garden of peace and welcome. Love's answer is inevitable. It will come because you came without the body, and interposed no barriers to interfere with its glad coming. In the holy instant you ask of love only what it offers everyone, neither less nor more. Asking for everything, you will receive it. Your shining Self will lift the tiny aspect that you tried to hide from Heaven, straight to Heaven. No part of love calls on the whole in vain. No Son of God remains outside His Fatherhood (T.p.392).

12. Be sure of this; love has entered your special relationship, and entered fully at your weak request. You do not yet let go of all the barriers you hold against your brother. You and he will not be able to give love welcome separately. You could no more know God alone than He knows you without your brother, but together you could no more be unaware of love than love could know you not, or fail to recognize itself in you.

13. You have reached the end of an ancient journey, not realizing yet that it is over. You are still worn and tired, and the desert dust still seems to cloud your eyes and keep you sightless. Yet He whom you welcomed has come to you, and would welcome you. He has waited long to give you this. Receiving it now of Him, for he would have you know Him. Only a little wall of dust still stands between you and your brother. Blow on it lightly and with happy laughter, and it will fall away. Walk into the garden love has prepared for both of you (T.p.393).

## THE AVERAGE TROOPER-QUESTIONER ACCORDING TO A COURSE IN MIRACLES

*Average Trooper Questioners become very safeguarding and are successful in their work. They are self-affirming through their loyalty and*

**Defenses:**

w--m: the dynamics we use to "protect" ourselves from guilt, fear, and seeaming attack fromof others, the most important of which are denial and projection; by their very nature '"defenses do what they would defend,", as they reinforce the belief in our own vulnerability which merely increases our fear and belief that we need defense.

r--m: reinterpreted as the means to free us from feart; e.g., denial denies the denial of truth and projecting our guilt enables us to be aware of what we have denied, so that we may truly forgive it (Gloss., p. 37).

---

in their identification with authority figures. They always wish to be affirmed that they are on the same page and wearing the same colors as the authority figure.

6. Forgiveness is the great release from time. It is the key to learning that the past is over. Madness speaks no more. There is no other teacher and no other way. For what has been undone no longer is. Who can stand upon a distant shore, and dream himself across an ocean, to a place and time that have long since gone by? How real a hindrance can this dream be to where he really is? For this is fact and does not change whatever dreams he has. Yet can he still imagine he is elsewhere, and in another time. In the extreme, he can delude himself that this is true, and pass from mere imagining into belief and into madness, quite convinced that where he would prefer to be, he is.

7. Is this a hindrance to the place whereon he stands? Is any echo from the past that he may hear a fact in what is there to

hear where he is now? How much can his own illusions about time and place effect a change in where he really is?

8. The unforgiven is a voice that calls from out a past forever more gone by. Everything that points to it as real is but a wish that what is gone could be made real again and seem as here and now, in place of what is really now and here. Is this a hindrance to the truth the past is gone, and cannot be returned to you? Do you want that fearful instant kept, when Heaven seemed to disappear and God was feared and made a symbol of your hate? (T.p.551).

*When Average Trooper-Questioners are disillusioned they become fearful and angry, and then they "stall." The obedience to the authority figure then becomes rebellious and compromised. The tactics of becoming passive-aggressive and ambivalent are presented by the disappointed questioner.*

### B. To Have Peace, Teach Peace to Learn It.

1. All who believe in separation have a basic fear of retaliation and abandonment. They believe in attack and rejection, so that is what they perceive and teach and learn. These insane ideas are clearly the result of dissociation and projection. What you teach you are, but it is quite apparent that you can teach wrongly, and can therefore teach yourself wrong. Many thought I was attacking them, even though it was apparent that I was not. An insane learner learns strange lessons. What you must recognize is that when you do not share a thought system, you are weakening it. Those who believe in it therefore perceive this as an attack on them. This is because everyone identifies himself with his thought system, and every thought system centers on what you believe you are. If the center of the thought system is true, only truth extends from it; but if a lie is at its center, only deception proceeds from it (T.p.106).

## THE QUESTIONER

*Trooper-Questioners always bear grudges of unforgivingness from the past and thus are mentally sarcastic, always seeing things with the emotionally expectant sense that this is not true. When aspects of reality trigger their lack of consistent expectations, even to their own surprise, they become unpredictably volatile and uncooperative. They become "counterphobic" and show anger rather than a "tail-between-their-legs" fear. They will be the tough persona of "in your face" even if they have to be politely exclusionary to make the statement.*

3. You have probably reacted for years as if you were being crucified. This is a marked tendency of the separated, who always refuse to consider what they have done to themselves. Projection means anger, anger fosters assault, and assault promotes fear. The real meaning of crucifixion lies in the apparent intensity of the assault of some of the Sons of God upon another. This, of course, is impossible. Otherwise I cannot serve as a model for learning (T.p.92).

6. If you react as if you were persecuted, you are teaching persecution. This is not a lesson a Son of God should want to teach if He is to realize His own salvation (T.p.93).

1. Doubts about being must not enter your mind, or you cannot know what you are with certainty. Certainty is of God for you. Vigilance is not necessary for truth, but it is necessary against illusions (T.p.111).

2. Everything outside the kingdom is illusion. When you threw truth away you saw yourself as if you were without it. By making another kingdom that you valued, you did not keep only the Kingdom of God in your mind, and thus placed part of your mind outside it. What you have made has imprisoned your will and given you a sick mind that must be healed. Your vigilance against this sickness is the way to heal it (T.p.111#8sub7, #9sub2).

## III. THE UNREALITY OF SIN

1. The attraction of guilt is found in sin, not error. Sin will be repeated because of this attraction. Fear can become so acute that the sin is denied the acting out, but while the guilt remains attractive the mind will suffer, and not let go of the idea of sin. For guilt still calls to it, and the mind hears it and yearns for it, making itself a willing captive to its sick appeal. Sin is an idea of evil that cannot be corrected, and yet will be forever desirable. As an essential part of what the ego thinks you are, you will always want it, and only an avenger, with a mind unlike your own, could stamp it out through fear.

2. The ego does not think it is possible that love, not fear, is really called upon by sin, and always answers. For the ego brings sin to fear, demanding punishment. Yet punishment is but another form of guilt's protection, for what is deserving punishment must have been really done. Punishment is always the great preserver of sin, treating it with respect and honoring its enormity. What must be punished must be true, and what is true must be eternal, and will be repeated endlessly. For what you think is real you want, and will not let go.

3. An error, on the other hand, is not attractive. What you see clearly as a mistake you want corrected. Sometimes a sin can be repeated over and over, with obviously distressing results, but without the loss of its appeal. Suddenly, you change its status from a sin to a mistake. Now you will not repeat it; you will merely stop and let it go, unless the guilt remains. For then you will but change the form of sin, granting that it was an error, but keeping it uncorrectable. This is not really a change in your perception, for it is sin that calls for punishment, not error. (T.p.404)

4. The Holy Spirit cannot punish sin. Mistakes He recognizes, and would correct them all as God entrusted Him to do; but sin He knows not, nor can He recognize mistakes that cannot be corrected. For a mistake that cannot be corrected is meaningless to Him.

Mistakes are for correction, and they call for nothing else. What calls for punishment must call for nothing. Every mistake must be a call for love. What then is sin? What could it be but a mistake you would keep hidden; a call for help that you would keep unheard and thus unanswered?

5. In time, the Holy Spirit clearly sees the Son of God can make mistakes. On this you share His vision. Yet you do not share His recognition of the difference between time and eternity, and when correction is completed, time is eternity. The Holy Spirit can teach you how to look on time differently and see beyond it, but not while you believe in sin. In error, yes, for this can be corrected by the mind, but sin is the belief that your perception is unchangeable, and that the mind must accept as true what it is told through it. If it does not obey, the mind is judged insane. The only power that could change perception is thus kept impotent, held to the body by the fear of changed perception, which its teacher, who is one with it, would bring.

6. When you are tempted to believe that sin is real, remember this: If sin is real, both God and you are not. If creation is extension, the Creator must have extended Himself, and it is impossible that what is part of Him is totally unlike the rest. If sin is real, God must be at war with Himself. He must be split, and torn between good and evil; partly sane and partially insane: for He must have created what wills to destroy Him, and has the power to do so. Is it not easier to believe that you have been mistaken than to believe that you have been mistaken than to believe in this?

7. While you believe that your reality or your brother's is bounded by a body, you will believe in sin. While you believe that bodies can unite, you will find guilt attractive and believe that sin is precious. For the belief that bodies limit the mind leads to a perception of the world in which the proof of separation seems to be everywhere. God and His creation seem to be split apart and overthrown, for sin would prove what God created holy could not prevail against it, nor remain itself before the power of sin. Sin is perceived as

mightier than God, before which God Himself must bow, and offer His creation to its conqueror. Is this humility or madness?

8. If sin is real, it must forever be beyond the hope of healing. For there would be a power beyond God's, capable of making another will that could attack His Will and overcome it; and give His Son a will apart from His, and in eternal opposition to Him and to each other. Your holy relationship has, as its purpose now, the goal of proving this is impossible. Heaven has smiled upon it, and the belief in sin has been uprooted in its smile of love. You see it still, because you do not realize that its foundation has gone. Its source has been removed, and so it can be cherished but a little while before it vanishes. Only the habit of looking for it still remains.

9. And yet you look with Heaven's smile upon your lips, and Heaven's blessing on your sight. You will not see sin long. For in the new perception the mind corrects it when it seems to be seen, and it becomes invisible. Errors are quickly recognized and quickly given to correction, to be healed, not hidden. You will be healed of sin and all its ravages the instant that you give it no power over your brother; and you will help him overcome mistakes by joyously releasing him from the belief in sin.

10. In the holy instant, you will see the smile of Heaven shining on both you and your brother, and you will shine upon Him in glad acknowledgment of the grace that has been given you. For sin will not prevail against a union Heaven has smiled upon. Your perception was healed in the holy instant Heaven gave you. Forget what you have seen, and raise your eyes in faith to what you now can see. The barriers to Heaven will disappear before your holy sight, for you who were sightless have been given vision, and you can see. Look not for what has been removed, but for the glory that has been restored for you to see.

11. Look upon your Redeemer, and behold what He would show you in your brother, and let not sin arise again to blind your eyes. For sin would keep you separate from him, but your Redeemer would

have you look upon your brother as yourself. Your relationship is now a temple of healing, a place where all the weary ones can come and rest. Here is the rest that waits for all after the journey, and it is brought nearer to all by your relationship. (T.p.406)

*Trooper-Questioners also attempt to assuage their fears by expressing blaming and scapegoating. When things go smoothly they are the model "organization people"—the corporate loyalists who are dutiful and diligent to their tasks. When things go astray, they get authoritarian and highly opinioned in their partnerships.*

## VIII. THE HOLY MEETING PLACE

1. In the darkness you have obscured the glory God gave you, and the power He bestowed upon His guiltless Son. All this lies hidden in every darkened place, shrouded in guilt and in the dark denial of innocence. Behind the dark doors you have closed lies nothing, because nothing can obscure the gift of God. It is the closing of the doors that interferes with recognition of the Power of God that shines in you. (T.p.289)

5. Before you make any decisions for yourself, remember that you have decided against your function in Heaven, and then consider carefully whether you want to make decisions here. Your function here is only to decide against deciding what you want in recognition that you do not know. (T.p.280)

7. The problem is not one of concentration; it is the belief that no one, including yourself, is worth consistent effort. Side with me consistently against this deception, and do not permit this shabby belief to pull you back. The disheartened are useless to themselves and to me, but only the ego can be disheartened. (T.p.63-34#7sub2-4)

## IV. SEEKING AND FINDING

1. The ego is certain that love is dangerous, and this is always its central teaching. It never puts it this way; on the contrary, everyone who believes that the ego is salvation seems to be intensely engaged in the search for love. Yet the ego, though encouraging the search for love very actively, makes one provision: do not find it. Its dictates, then, can be summed up simply as: "Seek and do not find." This is the one promise it will keep. For the ego pursues its goal with fanatic insistence, and its judgment, though severely impaired, is completely consistent. (T.p.223)

2. The search the ego undertakes is therefore bound to be defeated, and since it also teaches that it is your identification, its guidance leads you to a journey which must end in perceived self-defeat; for the ego cannot love, and in its frantic search for love it is seeking what it is afraid to find. The search is inevitable because the ego is part of your mind, and because of its source the ego is not wholly split off, or it could not be believed at all; for it is your mind that believes in it and gives existence to it. Yet it is also your mind that has the power to deny the ego's existence, and you will surely do so when you realize exactly what the journey is on which the ego sets you.

3. It is surely obvious that no one wants to find what would utterly defeat him. Being unable to love, the ego would be totally inadequate in love's presence, for it could not respond at all. Then, you would have to abandon the ego's guidance, for it would be quite apparent that it had not taught you the response you need. The ego will therefore distort love, and teach you that love really calls forth the responses the ego can teach. Follow its teaching, then, and you will search for love, but will not recognize it.

4. Do you realize that the ego must set you on a journey which cannot but lead to a sense of futility and depression? To seek and not to find is hardly joyous. Is this the promise you would keep?

The Holy Spirit offers you another promise, and one that will lead to joy; for His promise is always, "Seek and you will find," and under His guidance you cannot be defeated. His is the journey to accomplishment, and the goal He sets before you He will give you. He will never deceive God's Son, whom He loves with the love of the Father.

5. You will undertake a journey because you are not at home in this world; and you will search for your home whether you realize where it is or not. If you believe it is outside you the search will be futile, for you will be seeking it where it is not. You do not remember how to look within, for you do not believe your home is there. Yet the Holy Spirit remembers it for you, and He will guide you to your home because that is His mission. As He fulfills His mission, He will teach you yours, for your mission is the same as His. By guiding your brothers home, you are but following Him. (T.p.224)

6. Behold the guide your Father gave you, that you might learn you have eternal life; for death is not your Father's will nor yours, and whatever is true is the will of the Father. You pay no price for life, for that was given you, but you do pay a price for death, and a very heavy one. If death is your treasure, you will sell everything else to purchase it. You will believe that you have purchased it, because you have sold everything else. Yet you cannot sell the Kingdom of Heaven. Your inheritance can neither be bought nor sold. There can be no disinherited parts of the Sonship, for God is whole and all His extensions are like Him.

7. The Atonement is not the price of your wholeness, but it is the price of your awareness of your wholeness; for what you chose to "sell" had to be kept for you, since you could not "buy" it back. Yet you must invest in it, not with money but with spirit; for spirit is will, and will is the "price" of the Kingdom. Your inheritance awaits only the recognition that you have been redeemed. The Holy Spirit guides you into life eternal, but you must relinquish your investment in death, or you will not see life, though it is all around you.

All fear is ultimately reducible to the basic misperception that you have the ability to usurp the power of God. Of course you neither can nor have been able to do this. Here is the real basis for your escape from fear. His escape is brought about by your acceptance of the Atonement, which enables you to realize that your errors never really occurred. (T.p.18#4)

## THE UNHEALTHY TROOPER-QUESTIONER ACCORDING TO A COURSE IN MIRACLES

*Unhealthy Trooper-Questioners concentrate on their fears to the point of over reacting. They become extremely anxious to the point of paranoia.*

## VII. THE LAST UNANSWERED QUESTION

1. Do you not see that all your misery comes from the strange belief that you are powerless? Being helpless is the cost of sin. Helplessness is sin's condition, the one requirement that it demands to be believed. Only the helpless could believe in it. Enormity has no appeal save to the little, and only those who first believe that they are little could see attraction there. Treachery to the Son of God is the defense of those who do not identify with him. You are for Him or against Him; either you love Him or attack Him, protect his unity or see Him shattered and slain by your attack.

2. No one believes the Son of God is powerless, and those who see themselves as helpless must believe that they are not the Son of God. What can they be except his enemy? and what can they do but envy him his power, and by their envy make themselves afraid of it? These are the dark ones, silent and afraid, alone and

not communicating, fearful the power of the Son of God will strike them dead, and raising up their helplessness against Him. They join the army of the powerless, to wage their war of vengeance, bitterness, and spite on him, to make him one with them. Because they do not know that they are one with Him, they know not whom they hate. They are indeed a sorry army, each one as likely to attack his brother or turn upon himself as to remember that they thought they had a common cause.

3. Frantic and loud and strong, the dark ones seem to be. Yet they know not their "enemy," except they hate him. In hatred they have come together, but have not joined each other; for had they done so, hatred would be impossible. The army of the powerless must be disbanded in the presence of strength. Those who are strong are never treacherous, because they have no need to dream of power and to act out their dream. How would an army act in dreams? Any way at all. It could be seen attacking anyone with anything. Dreams have no reason in them. A flower turns into a poisoned spear, a child becomes a giant, and a mouse roars like a lion. Love is turned to hate as easily. This is no army, but a madhouse. What seems to be a planned attack is bedlam. (T.p.461–462)

*Is this what I would see? Do I want this?*

9. This is your one decision; this is the condition for what occurs. It is irrelevant to how it happens, but not to why. You have control of this, and if you choose to see a world without an enemy, in which you are not helpless, the means to see it will be given you.

10. Why is the final question so important? Reason will tell you why. It is the same as are the other three, except in time. The others are decisions that can be made, and then unmade and made again; but truth is constant, and implies a state where vacillations are impossible. You can desire a world you rule, that rules you not, and change your mind. You can desire to exchange your helplessness for

power, and lose this same desire as a little glint of sin attracts you. You can want to see a sinless world, and let an "enemy" tempt you to use the body's eyes and change what you desire.

11. In content all the questions are the same; for each one asks if you are willing to exchange the world of sin for what the Holy Spirit sees, since it is this the world of sin denies. Therefore those who look on sin are seeing the denial of the real world. Yet the last question adds the wish for constancy in your desire to see the real world, so the desire becomes the only one you have. By answering the final question "yes," you add sincerity to the decisions you have already made to all the rest; for only then have you renounced the option to change your mind again. When it is this you do not want, the rest are wholly answered.

12. Why do you think you are unsure the others have been answered? Could it be necessary they be asked so often, if they had? Until the last decision has been made, the answer is both "yes" and "no;" for you have answered "yes" without perceiving that "yes" must mean "not no." No one decides against his happiness, but he may do so if he does not see he does it. And, if he sees his happiness as ever-changing, now this, now that, and now an elusive shadow attached to nothing, he does decide against it.

13. Elusive happiness, or happiness in changing form that shifts with time and place, is an illusion that has no meaning. Happiness must be constant, because it is attained by giving up the wish for the inconstant. Joy cannot be perceived except through constant vision, and constant vision can be given only those who wish for constancy. The power of the Son of God's desire...(T.p.464)

## VI. FROM VIGILANCE TO PEACE

1. Although you can love the Sonship only as one, you can perceive it as fragmented. It is impossible, however, to see something

in part of it that you will not attribute to all of it. That is why attack is never discrete, and why it must be relinquished at all. Fear and love make or create, depending on whether the ego or the Holy Spirit begets or inspires them, but they will return to the mind of the thinker and they will affect his total perception. That includes his concept of God, of His creations, and of His own. He will not appreciate any of them if He regards them fearfully. He will appreciate all of them if He regards them with love.

2. The mind that accepts attack cannot love. That is because it believes it can destroy love, and therefore does not understand what love is. If it does not understand what love is, it cannot perceive itself as loving. This loses the awareness of being, induces feelings of unreality, and results in utter confusion. Your thinking has done this because of its power, but your thinking can also save you from this because its power is not of your making. Your ability to direct your thinking as you choose is part of its power. If you do not believe you can do this you have denied the power of your thought, and thus rendered it powerless in your belief.

3. The ingeniousness of the ego to preserve itself is enormous, but it stems from the very power of the mind the ego denies. This means that the ego attacks what is preserving it, which must result in extreme anxiety. That is why the ego never recognizes what it is doing. It is perfectly logical but clearly insane. The ego draws upon the one source that is totally inimical to its existence for its existence. Fearful of perceiving the power of this source, it is forced to depreciate it. This threatens its own existence, a state which it finds intolerable. Remaining logical but still insane, the ego resolves this completely insane dilemma in a completely insane way. It does not perceive its existence as threatened by projecting the threat onto you, and perceiving your being as nonexistent. This ensures its continuance if you side with it, by guaranteeing that you will not know your own safety. (T.p.124)

4. The ego cannot afford to know anything. Knowledge is total, and the ego does not believe in totality. This unbelief is its own

origin, and while the ego does not love you it is faithful to its own antecedents, begetting as it was begotten. Mind always reproduces as it was produced. Produced by fear, the ego reproduces fear. This is its allegiance, and this allegiance makes it treacherous to love because you are love. Love is your power, which the ego must deny. It must also deny everything this power gives you because it gives you everything; no one who has everything wants the ego. Its own maker, then, does not want it. Rejection is therefore the only decision the ego could possibly encounter, if the mind that made it knew itself; and if it recognized any part of the Sonship, it would know itself.

5. The ego therefore opposes all appreciation, all recognition, all sane perception, and all knowledge. It perceives their threat as total, because it senses that all commitments the mind makes are total. Forced, therefore, to detach itself from you, it is willing to attach itself to anything else; but there is nothing else. The mind can, however, make up illusions, and if it does so it will believe in them, because that is how it made them.

6. The Holy Spirit undoes illusions without attacking them, because He cannot perceive them at all. They therefore do not exist for Him. He resolves the apparent conflict; He wants you to realize that, because conflict is meaningless, it is not understandable. As I have already said, understanding brings appreciation and appreciation brings love. Nothing else can be understood, because nothing else is real and therefore nothing else has meaning.

7. If you will keep in mind what the Holy Spirit offers you, you cannot be vigilant for anything but God and His Kingdom. The only reason you may find this hard to accept is because you may still think there is something else. Belief does not require vigilance unless it is conflicted. If it is, there are conflicting components within it that have led to a state of war, and vigilance has therefore become essential. Vigilance has no place in peace. It is necessary against beliefs that are not true, and would never have been called upon by

the Holy Spirit if you had not believed the untrue. When you believe something, you have made it true for you. When you believe what God does not know, your thought seems to contradict His, and this makes it appear as if you are attacking Him. (T.p.124)

8. I have repeatedly emphasized that the ego does believe it can attack God, and tries to persuade you that you have done this. If the mind cannot attack, the ego proceeds perfectly logically to the belief that you must be a body. By not seeing you as you are, it can see itself as it wants to be. Aware of its weakness, the ego wants your allegiance, but not as you really are. The ego therefore wants to engage your mind in its own delusional system, because otherwise the light of your understanding would dispel it. It wants no part of truth, because the ego itself is not true. If truth is total, the untrue cannot exist. Commitment to either must be total; they cannot coexist in your mind without splitting it. If they cannot coexist in peace, and if you want peace, you must give up the idea of conflict entirely and for all time. This requires vigilance only as long as you do not recognize what is true. While you believe that two totally contradictory thought systems share truth, your need for vigilance is apparent.

9. Your mind is dividing its allegiance between two kingdoms, and you are totally committed to neither. Your identification with the Kingdom is totally beyond question except by you, when you are thinking insanely: What you are is not established by your perception, and is not influenced by it at all. Perceived problems in identification at any level are not problems of fact. They are problems of understanding, since their presence implies a belief that what you are is up to you to decide. The ego believes this totally, being fully committed to it. It is not true. The ego therefore is totally committed to untruth, perceiving in total contradiction to the Holy Spirit and to the knowledge of God.

10. You can be perceived with meaning only by the Holy Spirit because your being is the knowledge of God. Any belief you accept

apart from this will obscure God's voice in you, and will therefore obscure God to you. Unless you perceive His creation truly you cannot know the Creator, since God and His creation is your wholeness, your sanity, and your limitless power. This limitless power is God's gift to you, because it is what you are. If you dissociate your mind from it you are perceiving the most powerful force in the universe as if it were weak, because you do not believe you are part of it. (T.p.125)

11. Perceived without your part in it, God's creation is seen as weak, and those who see themselves as weakened do attack. The attack must be blind, however, because there is nothing to attack. Therefore, they make up images, perceive them as unworthy, and attack them for their unworthiness. That is all the world of the ego is: nothing. It has no meaning. It does not exist. Do not try to understand it because if you do, you are believing that it can be understood and is therefore capable of being appreciated and loved. That would justify its existence, which cannot be justified. You cannot make the meaningless meaningful. This can only be an insane attempt.

12. Allowing insanity to enter your mind means that you have not judged sanity as wholly desirable. If you want something else you will make something else, but because it is something else, it will attack your thought system and divide your intelligence. You cannot create in this divided state, and you must be vigilant against this divided state because only peace can be extended. Your divided mind is blocking the extension of the Kingdom, and its extension is your joy. If you do not extend the Kingdom, you are not thinking with your Creator and creating as He created.

13. In this depressing state, the Holy Spirit reminds you gently that you are sad because you are not fulfilling your function as co-creator with God, and are therefore depriving yourself of joy. This is not God's choice, but yours. If your mind could be out of accord with God's, you would be willing without meaning. Yet because God's will is unchangeable, no conflict of will is possible. This is the

Holy Spirit's perfectly consistent teaching. Creation, not separation, is your will because it is God's, and nothing that opposes this means anything at all. Being a perfect accomplishment, the Sonship can only accomplish perfectly, extending the joy in which it was created, and identifying itself with both its Creator and its creations, knowing they are One. (T.p.126)

6. It is extremely hard for those who still believe sin meaningful to understand the Holy Spirit's justice. They must believe He shares their own confusion, and cannot avoid the vengeance that their own belief in justice must entail; and so they fear the Holy Spirit, and perceive the "wrath" of God in Him. Nor can they trust Him not to strike them dead with lightning bolts torn from the "fires" of Heaven by God's own angry hand. They do believe that Heaven is Hell and are afraid of love; and deep suspicion and the chill of fear come over them when they are told that they have never sinned. Their world depends on sin's stability; and they perceive the "threat" of what ten wants God knows as justice to be more destructive to themselves and to their world than Be rescued from

2. The unhealed cannot pardon, for they are the witnesses that pardon is unfair..They would retain the consequences of the guilt they overlook. Yet no one can forgive a sin that he believes is real; and what has consequences must be real, because what it has done is there to see. (TP.568)

*Unhealthy Trooper-Questioners may succumb to a variety of anxiety disorders to the point of depression. Thus they can be insecure, doubting or "questioning" everything, clingy, feeling inferior, and self-effacing to the point they wish to be rescued.*

Sickness
A conflict in the mind(guilt) displaced onto the body; the ego's attempt to defend itself against truth(spirit) by focusing attention on

a body; a sick body is the effect of the sick or split mind that is it's cause, representing the ego's desire to make others guilty by sacrificing ones self, projecting responsibility for the attack onto them. (Glossary P. 188)
Wrong Mindedness

The part of our separated and split minds that contain the ego – the voice of sin, guilt, fear, and attack; we are repeatedly asked to choose right-mindedness, which imprisons us still further in the world of separation (Glossary P. 288)

*The Trooper-Questioner often wants to be rescued from the consequences of their own decisions. They play the "coward" quite often and "quit." Their masochistic tendencies sentence themselves to a nihilistic philosophy that combines with schizophrenia. They just plain give up.*

Projection
The fundamental law of mind; projection makes perception – what we see inwardly determines what we see outside our minds. (Glossary P.170)

## I. RIGHT TEACHING AND RIGHT LEARNING

1. A good teacher clarifies his own ideas and strengthens them by teaching them. Teacher and pupil are alike in the learning process. They are in the same order of learning, and unless they share their lessons conviction will be lacking. A good teacher must believe in the ideas he teaches, but he must meet another condition: he must believe in the students to whom he offers the ideas.

2. Many stand guard over their ideas because they want to protect their thought systems as they are, and learning means change. Change is always fearful to the separated, because the separation was their first experience of change. You believe that if you allow no change to enter into your ego you will find peace. This profound confusion is possible only if you maintain that the same thought system can stand on two foundations. Nothing can reach spirit from the ego, and nothing can reach the ego from spirit. Spirit can neither strengthen the ego nor reduce the conflict within it. The ego cannot know. They are therefore not in communication and can never be in communication. Nevertheless, the ego can learn, even though its maker can be misguided. He cannot, however, make the totally lifeless out of the life-given.

3. Spirit need not be taught, but the ego must be. Learning is ultimately perceived as frightening because it leads to the relinquishment, not the destruction, of the ego to the light of spirit. This is the change the ego must fear, because it does not share my charity. My lesson was like yours, and because I learned it I can teach it. I will never attack your ego, but I am trying to teach you how its thought system arose. When I remind you of your true creation, your ego cannot but respond with fear.

4. Teaching and learning are your greatest strengths now, because they enable you to change your mind and help others to change theirs. Refusing to change your mind will not prove that the separation has not occurred. The dreamer who doubts the reality of his dream while he is still dreaming is not really healing his split mind. You dream of a separated ego and believe in a world that rests upon it. This is very real to you. You can undo it by not changing your mind about it. If you are willing, renounce the role of guardian of your thought system and open to me; I will correct it very gently and lead you back to God. (T.p.53)

5. Every good teacher hopes to give his students so much of his own learning that they will one day no longer need him. This is the

one true goal of the teacher. It is impossible to convince the ego of this, because it goes against all of its own laws; but remember that laws are set up to protect the continuity of the system in which the lawmaker believes. It is natural for the ego to try to protect itself once you have made it, but it is not natural for you to want to obey its laws unless you believe them. The ego cannot make this choice because of the nature of its origin. You can, because of the nature of yours.

6. Egos can clash in any situation, but spirit cannot clash at all. If you perceive a teacher as merely "a larger ego" you will be afraid, because to enlarge an ego would be to increase anxiety about separation. I will teach with you and live with you if you if you will think with me, but my goal will always be to absolve you finally from the need for a teacher. This is the opposite of the ego-oriented teacher's goal. He is concerned with the effect of his ego on other egos, and therefore interprets their interaction as a means of ego preservation. I would not be able to devote myself to teaching if I believed this, and you will not be a devoted teacher as long as you believe it. I am constantly being perceived as a teacher either to be exalted or rejected, but I do not accept either perception for myself.

7. Your worth is not established by teaching or learning. Your worth is established by God. As long as you dispute this, everything you do will be fearful, particularly any situation that lends itself to the belief in superiority and inferiority. Teachers must be patient and repeat their lessons until they are learned. I am willing to do this, because I have no right to set your learning limits for you. Again, nothing you do or think or wish or make is necessary to establish your worth. This point is not debatable except in delusions. Your ego is never at stake because God did not create it. Your spirit is never at stake because He did. Any confusion on this point is delusional, and no form of devotion is possible as long as this delusion lasts.

8. The ego tries to exploit all situations into forms of praise for itself in order to overcome its doubts. It will remain doubtful as long as you believe in its existence. You who made it cannot trust it, because in your right mind you realize it is not real. The only sane solution is not to try to change reality, which is indeed a fearful attempt, but to accept it as it is. You are part of reality, which stands unchanged beyond the reach of your ego, but within easy reach of spirit. When you are afraid, be still and know that God is real, and you are His beloved Son in whom He is well pleased. Do not let your ego dispute this, because the ego cannot know what is as far beyond its reach as you are. (T.p.54)

9. God is not the author of fear; you are. You have chosen to create unlike Him, and have therefore made fear for yourself. You are not at peace because you are not fulfilling your function. God gave you a very lofty function that you are not meeting. Your ego has chosen to be afraid instead of meeting it. When you awaken you will not be able to understand this, because it is literally incredible. Do not believe the incredible now. Any attempt to increase its believableness is merely to postpone the inevitable. The word "inevitable" is fearful to the ego, but joyous to the spirit. God is inevitable, and you cannot avoid Him any more than He can avoid you.

10. The ego is afraid of the spirit's joy, because once you have experienced it you will withdraw all protection from the ego, and become totally without investment in fear. Your investment is great now because fear is a witness to it. Leave it behind! Do not listen to it and do not preserve it. Listen only to God, who is as incapable of deception as is the spirit He created. Release yourself and release others. Do not present a false and unworthy picture of yourself to others, and do not accept such a picture of them yourself.

11. The ego has built a shabby and unsheltering home for you, because it cannot build otherwise. Do not try to make this

impoverished house stand. Its weakness is your strength. Only God could make a home that is worthy of His creations, who have chosen to leave it empty by their own dispossession. Yet His home will stand forever, and is ready for you when you choose to enter it. Of this you can be wholly certain. God is as incapable of creating the perishable as the ego is of making the eternal.

12. Of your ego you can do nothing to save yourself or others, but of your spirit you can do everything for the salvation of both. Humility is a lesson for the ego, not for the spirit.
Spirit is beyond humility, because it recognizes radiance and gladly sheds its light everywhere. The meek shall inherit the Earth because their egos are humble, and this gives them truer perception. The Kingdom of Heaven is the spirit's right, whose beauty and dignity are far beyond doubt, beyond perception, and stand forever as the mark of the love of God for His creations, who are wholly worthy of Him and only of Him. Nothing else is sufficiently worthy to be a gift for a creation of God Himself. (T.p.55)

13. I will substitute for your ego if you wish, but never for your spirit. A father can safely leave a child with an elder brother who has shown himself responsible, but this involves no confusion about the child's origin. The brother can protect the child's body and his ego, but he does not confuse himself with the father because he does this. I can be entrusted with your body and your ego only because this enables you not to be concerned with them, and lets me teach you their unimportance. I could not understand their importance to you if I had not once been tempted to believe in them myself. Let us undertake to learn this lesson together so we can be free of them together. I need devoted teachers who share my aim of healing the mind. Spirit is far beyond the need of your protection or mine. Remember this:

*"In this world you need not have tribulation because I have overcome the world." That is why you should have good cheer.* (T.p.56)

## XL. THE TEST OF TRUTH

1. Yet the essential thing is learning that you do not know. Knowledge is power, and all power is of God. You who have tried to keep power for yourself have "lost" it. You still have the power, but you have interposed so much between it and your awareness of it that you cannot use it. Everything you have taught yourself has made your power more and more obscure to you. You know not what it is, nor where. You have made a semblance of power and a show of strength so pitiful that it must fail you; for power is not a seeming strength, and truth is beyond semblance of any kind. Yet all that stands between you and the power of God in you is but your learning of the false, and your attempts to undo the true.

2. Be willing, then, for all of it to be undone, and be glad that you are not bound to it forever; for you have taught yourself how to imprison the Son of God, a lesson so unthinkable that only the insane, in deepest sleep, could even dream of it. Can God learn how not to be God? Can His Son, given all power by Him, learn to be powerless? What have you taught yourself that you can possibly prefer to keep, in place of what you have and what you are?

3. Atonement teaches you how to escape forever from everything that you have taught yourself in the past, by showing you only what you are now. Learning has been accomplished before its effects are manifest. Learning is therefore in the past, but its influence determines the present by giving it whatever meaning it holds for you. Your learning gives the present no meaning at all. Nothing you have ever learned can help you understand the present, or teach you how to undo the past. Your past is what you have taught yourself. Let it all go. Do not attempt to understand any event or anything or anyone in its "light," for the darkness in which you try to see can only obscure. Put no confidence at all in darkness to illuminate your understanding, for if you do you contradict the light, and thereby think you see the darkness. Yet darkness cannot

be seen, for it is nothing more than a condition in which seeing becomes impossible. (T.p.296)

4. You who have not yet brought all of the darkness you have taught yourself into the light in you, can hardly judge the truth and value of this course. Yet God did not abandon you, and so you have another lesson sent from Him, already learned for every child of light by him to whom God gave it. This lesson shines with God's glory, for in it lies His power, which He shares so gladly with His Son. Learn of His happiness, which is yours, but to accomplish this, all your dark lessons must be brought willingly to truth, and joyously laid down by hands open to receive, not closed to take. Every dark lesson that you bring to Him who teaches light, He will accept from You, because You do not want it; and He will gladly exchange each one for the bright lesson He has learned for you. Never believe that any lesson you have learned apart from Him means anything.

5. You have one test, as sure as God, by which to recognize if what you learned is true. If you are wholly free of fear of any kind, and if all those who meet or even think of you share in your perfect peace, then you can be sure that you have learned God's lesson, and not your own. Unless all this is true, there are dark lessons in your mind that hurt and hinder you, and everyone around you. The absence of perfect peace means but one thing: you think you do not will for God's Son what His Father wills for him. Every dark lesson teaches this, in one form or another; and each bright lesson with which the Holy Spirit will replace the dark ones you do not accept, teaches you that you will with the Father and His Son.

6. Do not be concerned about how you can learn a lesson so completely different from everything you have taught yourself. How would you know? Your part is very simple. You need only recognize that everything you learned you do not want. Ask to be taught, and do not use your experiences to confirm what you have learned. When your peace is threatened or disturbed in any way, say to yourself:

## THE QUESTIONER

*I do not know what anything, including this, means; and so I do not know how to respond to it. I will not use my own past learning as the light to guide me now.*

By this refusal to attempt to teach yourself what you do not know, the guide whom God has given you will speak to you. He will take His rightful place in your awareness the instant you abandon it, and offer it to Him. (T.p.297)

7. You cannot be your guide to miracles, for it is you who made them necessary; and because you did, the means on which you can depend for miracles has been provided for you. God's Son can make no needs His Father will not meet, if He but turn to him ever so little. Yet He cannot change Himself, for your identity is changeless by seeing His Son as He always was, and not as He would make Himself. The miracle brings the effects that only guiltlessness can bring, and thus establishes the fact that guiltlessness must be.

8. How can you, so firmly bound to guilt and committed so to remain, establish for yourself your guiltlessness? That is impossible; but be sure that you are willing to acknowledge that it is impossible. It is only because you think that you can run some little part, or deal with certain aspects of your life alone, that the guidance of the Holy Spirit is limited. Thus would you make Him undependable? Use this fancied undependability as an excuse for keeping certain dark lessons from Him; and by so limiting the guidance that you would accept you are unable to depend on miracles to answer all your problems for you.

9. Do you think that what the Holy Spirit would have you give, He would withhold from you? You have no problems that He cannot solve by offering you a miracle. Miracles are for you; and every fear or pain or trial you have has been undone. He has brought all of them to light, having accepted them instead of you, and recognized they never were. There are no dark lessons He has not already lightened for you. The lessons you would teach yourself He

has corrected already. They do not exist in His mind at all; for the past binds Him not, and therefore binds not you. He does not see time as you do, and each miracle He offers you corrects your use of time, and makes it His. (T.p.298)

10. He who has freed you from the past would teach you, you are free of it. He would accept His accomplishments as yours, because He did them for you; and because He did, they are yours. He has made you free of what you made. You can deny Him, but you cannot call on Him in vain. He always gives His gifts in place of yours. He would establish his bright teaching so firmly in your mind that no dark lesson of guilt can abide in what He has established as holy by His presence. Thank God that He is there and works through you, and all his works are yours. He offers you a miracle with every one you let him do through you.

11. God's Son will always be indivisible. As we are held as one in God, so do we learn as one in Him. God's teacher is as like to His Creator as is His Son, and through His teacher does God proclaim His oneness and His Son's. Listen in silence, and do not raise your voice against Him; for He teaches the miracle of oneness, and before His lesson division disappears. Teach like Him here, and you will remember that you have always created like your Father. The miracle of creation has never ceased, having the holy stamp of immortality upon it. This is the will of God for all creation, and all creation joins in willing this.

12. Those who remember always that they know nothing, and who have become willing to learn everything, will learn it; but whenever they trust themselves, they will not learn. They have destroyed their motivation for learning by thinking they already know. Think not you understand anything until you pass the test of perfect peace, for peace and understanding go together and never can be found alone. Each brings the other with it, for it is the law of God they be not separate. They are cause and effect, each to the other, so where one is absent the other cannot be.

13. Only those who recognize they cannot know unless the effects of understanding are with them, can really learn at all; for this it must be peace they want, and nothing else. Whenever you think you know, peace will depart from you, because you have abandoned the Teacher of Peace. Whenever you fully realize that you know not, peace will return, for you will have invited Him to do so by abandoning the ego on behalf of Him. Call not upon the ego for anything; it is only this that you need do. The Holy Spirit will, of Himself, fill every mind that so makes room for Him.

14. If you want peace, you must abandon the teacher of attack. The Teacher of Peace will never abandon you. You can desert Him, but He will never reciprocate, for His faith in you is His understanding. It is as firm as is His faith in His Creator, and He knows that faith in His Creator must encompass faith in His creation. In this consistency lies His Holiness which He cannot abandon, for it is not His will to do so. With your perfection ever in His sight, He gives the gift of peace to everyone who perceives the need for peace, and who would have it. Make way for peace, and it will come; for understanding is in you, and from it peace must come. (T.p.299)

15. The power of God, from which they both arise, is yours as surely as it is His. You think you know Him not, only because, alone, it is impossible to know Him. Yet see the mighty works that He will do through you, and you must be convinced you did them through Him. It is impossible to deny the source of effects so powerful they could not be of you. Leave room for Him, and you will find yourself so filled with power that nothing will prevail against your peace; and this will be the test by which you recognize that you have understood. (T.p.300)

## III. THE FEAR OF REDEMPTION

1. You may wonder why it is so crucial that you look upon your hatred and realize its full extent. You may also think that it would

be easy enough for the Holy Spirit to show it to you, and to dispel it without the need for you to raise it to awareness yourself. Yet there is one more obstacle you have interposed between yourself and the Atonement. We have said that no one will countenance fear if he recognizes it. Yet in your disordered state of mind you are not afraid of fear. You do not like it, but it is not your desire to attack that really frightens you. You are not seriously disturbed by your hostility. You keep it hidden because you are more afraid of what it covers. You could look even upon the ego's darkest cornerstone without fear if you did not believe that, without the ego, you would find within yourself something you fear even more. You are not really afraid of crucifixion. Your real terror is of redemption.

2. Under the ego's dark foundation is the memory of God, and it is of this that you are really afraid; for this memory would instantly restore you to your proper place, and it is this place that you have sought to leave. Your fear of attack is nothing compared to your fear of love. You would be willing to look even upon your savage wish to kill God's Son, if you did not believe that it saves you from love; for this wish caused the separation, and you have protected it because you do not want the separation healed. You realize that, by removing the dark cloud that obscures it, your love for your Father would impel you to answer His call and leap into Heaven. You believe that attack is salvation because it would prevent you from this; for still deeper than the ego's foundation, and much stronger than it will ever be, is your intense and burning love of God, and His for you. This is what you really want to hide.

3. In honesty, is it not harder for you to say "I love" than "I hate"? You associate love with weakness and hatred with strength, and your own real power seems to you as your real weakness. You could not control your joyous response to the call of love if you heard it, and the whole world you thought you made would vanish. The Holy Spirit, then, seems to be attacking your fortress, for you would shut out God, and He does not will to be excluded. (T.p.242)

4. You have built your whole insane belief system because you think you would be helpless in God's presence, and you would save yourself from His love because you think it would crush you into nothingness. You are afraid it would sweep you away from yourself and make you little. Because you believe that magnitude lies in defiance, and that attack is grandeur, you think you have made a world God would destroy; and by loving him, which you do, you would throw this world away, which you would. Therefore, you have used the world to cover your love, and the deeper you go into the blackness of the ego's foundation the closer you come to the love that is hidden there, and it is this that frightens you.

5. You can accept insanity because you made it, but you cannot accept love because you did not. You would rather be a slave of the crucifixion than a Son of God in redemption. Your individual death seems more valuable than your living oneness, for what is given you is not so dear as what you made. You are more afraid of God than of the ego, and love cannot enter where it is not welcome; but hatred can, for it enters of its own volition and cares not for yours.

6. You must look upon your illusions and not keep them hidden, because they do not rest on their own foundation. In concealment they appear to do so, and thus they seem to be self-sustained. This is the fundamental illusion on which the others rest; for beneath them, and concealed as long as they are hidden, is the loving mind that thought it made them in anger; and the pain in this mind is so apparent, when it is uncovered, that its need of healing cannot be denied. Not all the tricks and games you offer it can heal it, for here is the real crucifixion of God's Son.

7. Yet He is not crucified. Here is both His pain and His healing, for the Holy Spirit's vision is merciful and His remedy is quick. Do not hide suffering from His sight, but bring it gladly to Him. Lay before His eternal sanity all your hurt, and let Him heal you. Do not leave any spot of pain hidden from His light, and search your mind carefully for any thoughts you may fear to uncover; for He will heal

every little thought you have kept to hurt you and cleanse it of its littleness, restoring it to the magnitude of God.

8. Beneath all the grandiosity you hold so dear is your real call for help; for you call for love to your Father as your Father calls you to Himself. In that place which you have hidden, you will only to unite with the Father, in loving remembrance of Him. You will find this place of truth as you see it in your brothers, for though they may deceive themselves, like you they long for the grandeur that is in them; and perceiving it you will welcome it and it will be yours. Grandeur is the right of God's Son, and no illusions can satisfy Him or save Him from what He is. Only His love is real, and He will be content only with his reality. (T.p.243)

9. Save him from his illusions that you may accept the magnitude of your Father in peace and joy, but exempt no one from your love, or you will be hiding a dark place in your mind where the Holy Spirit is not welcome. Thus you will exempt yourself from His healing power, for by not offering total love you will not be healed completely. Healing must be as complete as fear, for love cannot enter where there is one spot of fear to mar its welcome.

10. You who prefer separation to sanity cannot obtain it in your mind. You were at peace until you asked for special favor, and God did not give it for the request was alien to Him, and you could not ask this of a Father who truly loved His Son. Therefore you made of Him an unloving father, demanding of Him what only such a father could give. The peace of God's Son was shattered, for he no longer understood His Father. He feared what He had made, but still more did he fear his real Father, having attacked His own glorious equality with Him.

11. In peace we needed nothing and asked for nothing. In war he demanded everything and found nothing; for how could the gentleness of love respond to his demands, except by departing in peace and returning to the Father? If the Son did not wish to remain in peace, He could not remain at all; for a darkened mind cannot

live in the light, and it must seek a place of darkness where it can believe it is where it is not. God did not allow this to happen. Yet you demanded that it happen and therefore believed that it was so.

12. To "single out" is to "make alone" and thus make lonely. God did not do this to you. Could He set you apart, knowing that your peace lies in His oneness? He denied you only your request for pain, for suffering is not of His creations. Having given you creation, He could not take it from you. He could but answer your insane request with a sane answer that would abide with you in your insanity; and this He did. No one who hears His answer but will give up insanity; for His answer is the reference point beyond illusions, from which you can look back on them and see them as insane; but seek this place and you will find it, for love is in you and will lead you there. (T.p.244–245)

## VI. WAKING TO REDEMPTION

1. It is impossible not to believe what you see, but it is equally impossible to see what you do not believe. Perceptions are built upon the basis of experience, and experience leads to beliefs. It is not until beliefs are fixed that perceptions stabilize. In effect, then, what you believe, you do see. That is what I meant when I said, "Blessed are ye who have not seen and still believe," for those who believe in the resurrection will see it. The resurrection is the complete triumph of Christ over the ego, not by attack but by transcendence, for Christ does rise above the ego and all its works, and ascends to the Father of His Kingdom.

2. Would you join in the resurrection or the crucifixion? Would you condemn your brothers or free them? Would you transcend your prison and ascend to the Father? These questions are all the same, and are answered together. There has been much confusion about what perception means because the word is used both for

awareness and for the interpretation of awareness. Yet you cannot be aware without interpretation, for what you perceive is your interpretation.

3. This course is perfectly clear. If you do not see it clearly, it is because you are interpreting against it and therefore do not believe it; and since belief determines perception, you do not perceive what it means and therefore do not accept it. Yet different experiences lead to different beliefs, and with them different perceptions; for perceptions are learned with beliefs, and experience does teach. I am leading you to a new kind of experience that you will become less and less willing to deny. Learning of Christ is easy, for to perceive with him involves no strain at all. His perceptions are your natural awareness, and it is only the distortions you introduce that tire you. Let the Christ in you interpret for you, and do not try to limit what you see by narrow little beliefs that are unworthy of God's Son; for until Christ comes into His own, the Son of God will see Himself as Fatherless. (T.p.207)

4. I am your resurrection and your life. You live in me because you live in God, and everyone lives in you as you live in everyone. Can you, then, perceive unworthiness in a brother and not perceive it in yourself? Can you perceive it in yourself and not perceive it in God? Believe in the resurrection because it has been accomplished in you. This is as true now as it will ever be, for the resurrection is the will of God, which knows no time and no exceptions. Make no exceptions yourself, or you will not perceive what has been accomplished for you; for we ascend unto the Father together, as it was in the beginning, is now, and ever shall be, for such is the nature of God's Son as His Father created Him.

5. Do not underestimate the power of the devotion of God's Son, nor the power of the God He worships over Him; for He places Himself at the altar of His God whether it be the god He made or the God who created Him. That is why his slavery is as complete as his freedom, for he will obey only the god he accepts. The God

THE QUESTIONER

of crucifixion demands that he crucify, and his worshipers obey. In His name they crucify themselves, believing that the power of the Son of God is born of sacrifice and pain. The God of resurrection demands nothing, for He does not will to take away. He does not require obedience, for obedience implies submission. He would only have you learn your will and follow it, not in the spirit of sacrifice and submission, but in the gladness of freedom.

6. Resurrection must compel your allegiance gladly, because it is the symbol of joy. Its whole compelling power lies in the fact that it represents what you want to be. The freedom to leave behind everything that hurts you and humbles you and frightens you cannot be thrust upon you, but it can be offered you through the grace of God. And you can accept it by his grace, for God is gracious to His Son, accepting Him without question as His own. Who, then, is your own? The Father has given you all that He is, and He Himself is yours with them. Guard them in their resurrection, for otherwise you will not awake in God, safely surrounded by what is yours forever.

7. You will not find peace until you have removed the nails from the hands of God's Son, and taken the last thorn from His forehead. The love of God surrounds His Son whom the god of crucifixion condemns. Teach not that I died in vain. Teach rather that I did not die by demonstrating that I live in you; for undoing the crucifixion of God's Son is the work of the redemption, in which everyone has a part of equal value. God does not judge His guiltless Son. Having given Himself to Him, how could it be otherwise? (T.p.208)

8. You have nailed yourself to a cross, and placed a crown of thorns upon your own head.Yet you cannot crucify God's Son for the will of God cannot die.3His Son has been redeemed from his own crucifiction and you cannot assign to death whom God has given eternal life. The dream of crucifixion still lies heavy on your eyes, but what you see in dreams is not reality. While you perceive the Son of God as crucified, you are asleep; and as long as you

believe that you can crucify him, you are only having nightmares. You who are beginning to wake are still aware of dreams, and have not yet forgotten them. The forgetting of dreams and the awareness of Christ come with the awakening of others to share your redemption.

9. You will awaken to your own call, for the call to awake is within you. If I live in you, you are awake, but you must see the works I do through you, or you will not perceive that I have done them unto you. Do not set limits on what you believe? I can do through you, or you will not accept what I do for you. Yet it is done already, and unless you give all that you have received you will not know that your Redeemer liveth, and that you have awakened with him. Redemption is recognized only by sharing it.

10. God's Son is saved. Bring only this awareness to the Sonship and you will have a part in the redemption as valuable as mine; for your part must be like mine if you learn it of me. If you believe that yours is limited, you are limiting mine. There is no order of difficulty in miracles because all of God's Sons are of equal value, and their equality is their oneness. The whole power of God is in every part of Him and nothing contradictory to His will is either great or small. What does not exist has no size and no measure. To God all things are possible, and to Christ is given to be like the Father. (T.p.209)

## VII. THE TOTALITY OF THE KINGDOM

1. Whenever you deny a blessing to a brother you will feel deprived, because denial is as total as love. It is as impossible to deny part of the Sonship as it is to love it in part. Nor is it possible to love it totally at times. You cannot be totally committed sometimes. Denial has no power in itself, but you can give it the power of your mind, whose power is without limit. If you use it to deny reality, reality is gone for you. Reality cannot be partly appreciated. That

is why denying any part of it means you have lost the awareness of all of it. Yet denial is a defense, and so it is capable of being used positively as well as negatively. Used negatively it will be destructive, because it will be used for attack, but in the service of the Holy Spirit, it can help you recognize part of reality, and thus appreciate all of it. Mind is too powerful to be subject to exclusion. You will never be able to exclude yourself from your thoughts.

2. When a brother acts insanely he is offering you an opportunity to bless him. His need is yours; you need the blessing you can offer him. There is no way for you to have it except by giving it. This is the law of God, and it has no exceptions. What you deny you lack, not because it is lacking, but because you have denied it in another and are therefore not aware of it in yourself. Every response you make is determined by what you think you are, and what you want to be is what you think you are. What you want to be, then, must determine every response you make.

3. You do not need God's blessing, because that you have forever, but you do need yours. The ego's picture of you is deprived, unloving, and vulnerable. You cannot love this, yet you can very easily escape from this image by leaving it behind. You are not there, and that is not you. Do not see this picture in anyone, or you have accepted it as you. All illusions about the Sonship are dispelled together as they were made together. Teach no one that he is what you would not want to be. Your brother is the mirror in which you see the image of yourself as long as perception lasts; and perception will last until the Sonship knows itself as whole. You made perception and it must last as long as you want it. Illusions are investments. They will last as long as you value them. Values are relative, but they are powerful because they are mental judgments.

4. The only way to dispel illusions is to withdraw all investment from them, and they will have no life for you because you will have put them out of your mind. While you include them in it, you are giving life to them, except there is nothing there to receive your gift. (T.p.127)

5. The gift of life is yours to give, because it was given you. You are unaware of your gift because you do not give it. You cannot make nothing live, since nothing cannot be enlivened. Therefore you are not extending the gift you both have and are, and so you do not know your being. All confusion comes from not extending life, because that is not the will of your Creator. You can do nothing apart from Him, and you do nothing apart from Him. Keep His way to remember yourself and teach His way lest you forget yourself. Give only honor to the Sons of the living God, and count yourself among them gladly.

6. Only honor is a fitting gift for those whom God Himself created worthy of honor, and whom He honors. Give them the appreciation God accords them always, because they are His beloved Sons in whom He is well pleased. You cannot be apart from them because you are not apart from Him. Rest in His love and protect your rest by loving, but love everything He created, of which you are a part, or you cannot learn of His peace and accept His gifts for yourself and as yourself. You cannot know your own perfection until you have honored all those who were created like you.

7. One child of God is the only teacher sufficiently worthy to teach another. One teacher is in all minds and he teaches the same lesson to all. He always teaches you the inestimable worth of every Son of God, teaching it with infinite patience born of the infinite love for which He speaks. Every attack is a call for His patience, since His patience can translate attack into blessing. Those who attack do not know they are blessed. They attack because they believe they are deprived. Give, therefore, of your abundance, and teach your brothers theirs. Do not share their illusions of scarcity, or you will perceive yourself as lacking.

8. Attack could never promote attack unless you perceived it as a means of depriving you of something you want. Yet you cannot lose anything unless you do not value it, and therefore do not want

it. This makes you feel deprived of it, and by projecting your own rejection you then believe that others are taking it from you. You must be fearful if you believe that your brother is attacking you to tear the Kingdom of Heaven from you. This is the ultimate basis for all the ego's projection. (T.p.128)

9. Being the part of your mind that does not believe it is responsible for itself, and being without allegiance to God, the ego is incapable of trust. Projecting its insane belief that you have been treacherous to your Creator, it believes that your brothers, who are as incapable of this as you are, are out to take God from you. Whenever a brother attacks another, that is what he believes; projection always sees your wishes in others. If you choose to separate yourself from God, that is what you will think others are doing to you.

10. You are the will of God. Do not accept anything else as your will, or you are denying what you are. Deny this and you will attack, believing you have been attacked; but see the love of God in you, and you will see it everywhere because it is everywhere. See His abundance in everyone, and you will know that you are in Him with them. They are part of you, as you are part of God. You are as lonely without understanding this as God Himself is lonely when His Sons do not know Him. The peace of God is understanding this. There is only one way out of the world's thinking, just as there was only one way into it. Understand totally by understanding totality.

11. Perceive any part of the ego's thought system as wholly insane, wholly delusional, and wholly desirable, and you have correctly evaluated all of it. This correction enables you to perceive any part of Creation as wholly real, wholly perfect, and wholly desirable. Wanting this only, you will have this only, and giving this only, you will be only this. The gifts you offer to the ego are always experienced as sacrifices, but the gifts you offer to the Kingdom are gifts to you. They will always be treasured by God because they belong

to his beloved Sons, who belong to Him. All power and glory are yours because the Kingdom is His. (T.p.129)

## LESSON 317   (GROWTH LINE)
*I follow in the way appointed me.*

1. I have a special place to fill: a role for me alone. Salvation waits until I take this part as what I choose to do. Until I make this choice, I am the slave of time and human destiny; but when I willingly and gladly go the way my Father's plan appointed me to go, then will I recognize salvation is already here, already given all my brothers and already mine as well.

2. Father, your way is what I choose today. Where it would lead me do I choose to go; what would it have me do I choose to do. Your way is certain and the end secure. The memory of You awaits me there, and all my sorrows end in your embrace, which You have promised to Your Son, who thought mistakenly that he had wandered from the sure protection of Your loving arms.

## LESSON 297   (ARCHETYPE)
*Forgiveness is the only gift I give.*

1. Forgiveness is the only gift I give, because it is the only gift I want: and everything I give, I give myself. This is salvation's simple formula. I, who would be saved, would make it mine to be the way I live within a world that needs salvation, and that will be saved as I accept Atonement for myself.

2. Father, how certain are Your ways: how sure their final outcome, and how faithfully is every step in my salvation set already, and accomplished by Your grace. Thanks be to You for Your eternal gifts, and thanks to You for my identity.

# LESSON 332 (DEMATERIALIZATION LINE)
*Fear binds the world. Forgiveness sets it free.*

1. The ego makes illusions. Truth undoes its evil dreams by shining them away. Truth never makes attack. It merely is. And its presence is by the mind recalled from fantasies, awaking to real. Forgiveness bids this presence enter in, and take its right place within the mind. Without forgiveness is the mind in chains, believing in its own futility. Yet with forgiveness does light shine through the dream of darkness, offering it hope, giving it the means to realize the freedom that is its inheritance.

2. We would not bind the world today. Fear holds it prisoner. And yet Your love has given us the means to set it free. Father, we would release it now. For as we offer freedom, it is given us, and we would not remain as prisoners, while You are holding freedom out to us.

**CHAPTER 7**
# THE EPICUREAN

"Health is a result of relinquishing all attempts
to use the body lovelessly."
(T.146/157 ACIM)  Joyful    Multitalented    Debauched

# THE HEALTHY EPICUREAN "7" ACCORDING TO A COURSE IN MIRACLES

*Healthy Epicureans are enthusiastic, vivacious, and multitalented. They are highly excited for new sought-after experiences, and they become dilettantes of many different disciplines. They are often called the hard-working and hard-playing generalists. Epicureans work hard to play hard.*

## I. THE HOLY ENCOUNTER

1. Glory to God in the highest, and to you because He has so willed it. Ask and it shall be given to you, because it has already been given. Ask for light and learn that you are light. If you want understanding and enlightenment you will learn it, because your decision to learn it is the decision to listen to the Teacher who knows of light and can therefore teach it to you. There is no limit on your learning because there is no limit on your mind. There is no limit on His teaching because He was created to teach. Understanding His function perfectly He fulfills it perfectly, because that is His joy and yours.

2. To fulfill the will of God perfectly is the only joy and peace that can be fully known, because it is the only function that can be fully experienced. When this is accomplished, then, there is no other experience. Yet the wish for other experience will block its accomplishment, because God's will cannot be forced upon you, being an experience of total willingness. The Holy Spirit understands how to teach this, but you do not. That is why you need Him, and why God gave Him to you. Only His teaching will release your will to God's, uniting it with His power and glory and establishing them as yours. You share them as God shares them, because this is the natural outcome of their being. (T.p.142)

3. The will of the Father and of the Son are one, by their extension. Their extension is the result of their oneness, holding their unity together by extending their joint will. This is perfect creation by the perfectly created, in union with the perfect Creator. The Father must give fatherhood to His Son, because His own Fatherhood must be extended outward. You who belong in God have the holy function of extending His Fatherhood by placing no limits upon it. Let the Holy Spirit teach you how to do this, for you can know what it means only of God Himself.

4. When you meet anyone, remember it is a holy encounter. As you see him, you will see yourself. As you treat him, you will treat yourself. As you think of him, you will think of yourself. Never forget this, for in him you will find yourself or lose yourself. Whenever two Sons of God meet, they are given another chance at salvation. Do not leave anyone without giving salvation to him and receiving it yourself; for I am always there with you, in remembrance of you.

5. The goal of the curriculum, regardless of the teacher you choose, is "Know thyself." There is nothing else to seek. Everyone is looking for himself and for the power and glory he thinks he has lost. Whenever you are with anyone, you have another opportunity to find them. Your power and glory are in him because they are yours. The ego tries to find them in yourself alone, because it does not know where to look. The Holy Spirit teaches you that if you look only at yourself you cannot find yourself, because that is not what you are. Whenever you are with a brother, you are learning what you are, because you are teaching what you are. He will respond either with pain or with joy, depending on which teacher you are following. He will be imprisoned or released according to your decision, and so will you. Never forget your responsibility to him, because it is your responsibility to yourself. Give him his place in the Kingdom and you will have yours. (T.p.142)

6. The Kingdom cannot be found alone, and you who are the Kingdom cannot find yourself alone. To achieve the goal of the curriculum, then, you cannot listen to the ego, whose purpose is to defeat its own goal. The ego does not know anything; but you can know it, and you will know it if you are willing to look at what the ego would make of you. This is your responsibility, because once you have really looked at it you will accept the Atonement for yourself. What other choice could you make? Having made this choice you will understand why you once believed that, when you met someone else, you thought he was someone else; and every holy encounter in which you enter fully will teach you this is not so.

7. You can encounter only part of yourself because you are part of God, who is everything. His power and glory are everywhere, and you cannot be excluded from them. The ego teaches that your strength is in you alone. The Holy Spirit teaches that all strength is in God and therefore in you. God wills no one suffer. He does not will anyone to suffer for the wrong decision, including you. That is why he has given you the means for undoing it. Through his power and glory all your wrong decisions are undone completely, releasing you and your brother from every imprisoning thought any part of the Sonship holds. Wrong decisions have no power, because they are not true. The imprisonment they seem to produce is no more true than they are.

8. Power and glory belong to God alone. So do you. God gives whatever belongs to him because He gives of Himself, and everything belongs to Him. Giving of yourself is the function He gave you. Fulfilling it perfectly will let you remember what you have of Him, and by this you will remember also what you are in Him. You cannot be powerless to do this, because this is your power. Glory is God's gift to you, because that is what He is: glory everywhere to remember what you are. (T.p.143)

*Healthy Epicureans "thrill" at the chance to do something they always wanted to do. The terms "responsive" and "enthusiastic" are most appropriate in their vivacious, ecstatic joy.*

But it is pride that argues you have come into a world quite separate from yourself, impervious to what you think, and quite apart from what you chance to think it is. There is no world. This is the central thought the Course attempts to teach. Not everyone is ready to accept it, and each one must go as far as he can let himself be led along the road to truth. He will return and go still further, or perhaps step back a while and return again. (T.p.243#6)

*Healthy Epicureans are practical and willing learners who ultimately become accomplished achievers. They are then the most appreciative of life for the wonder and the awesomeness of nature.*

## THE AVERAGE EPICUREAN

*Average Epicureans endeavor to be world travelers and sophisticates, knowing the best places to eat and scheduling the finest entertainment for their meals. They enjoy culturing the "in" crowd. Their materialism knows no bounds. They will want everything within their means and then some. It would be normal for them to have two or three of everything, and if it were offered to upgrade to the larger more powerful grade of object, then that would be the choice. They enjoy being the "bon vivant" effortless connoisseurs of the finest of everything the world has to offer for their consumption. They obsess with constant amusement of new and different "things." They'll try anything once. They become doers of too many things at once. Their management style is to have numerous things going on at once, where they do not finish a project only to start another one.*

## VII. THE CONSISTENCY OF MEANS AND END

1. We have said much about discrepancies of means and end, and how these must be brought in line before your holy relationship can bring you only joy; but we have also said the means to meet the Holy Spirit's goal will come from the same source as does His purpose. Being so simple and direct, this course has nothing in it that is not consistent. The seeming inconsistencies, or parts you find more difficult than others, are merely indications of areas where means and end are still discrepant. This produces great discomfort. This need not be. This course requires almost nothing of you. It is impossible to imagine one that asks so little, or could offer more.

2. The period of discomfort that follows the sudden change in a relationship from sin to holiness may now be almost over. To the extent you still experience it, you are refusing to leave the means to Him who changed the purpose. You recognize you want the goal, and are you not also willing to accept the means? If you are not, let us admit that you are inconsistent. A purpose is attained by means, and if you want a purpose you must want the means as well. How can one be sincere and say, "I want this above all else, and yet I do not want to learn the means to get it?" (T.p.439)

3. To obtain the goal the Holy Spirit indeed asks little. He asks no more to give the means as well. The means are second to the goal; and when you hesitate, it is because the purpose frightens you, and not the means. Remember this, for otherwise you will make the error of believing the means are difficult. Yet how can they be difficult if they are merely given you? They guarantee the goal, and they are perfectly in line with it. Before we look at them a little closer, remember that if you think they are impossible, your wanting of the purpose has been shaken; for if a goal is possible to reach, the means to do so must be possible as well.

4. It is impossible to see your brother as sinless and yet to look upon him as a body. Is this not perfectly consistent with the goal of

holiness? For holiness is merely the result of letting the effects of sin be lifted, so what was always true is recognized. To see a sinless body is impossible, for holiness is positive and the body is merely neutral. It is not sinful, but neither is it sinless. As nothing, which it is, the body cannot meaningfully be invested with attributes of Christ or of the ego. Either must be an error, for both would place the attributes where they cannot be, and both must be undone for the purposes of truth.

5. The body is the means by which the ego tries to make the unholy relationship seem real. The unholy instant is the time of bodies, but the purpose here is sin. It cannot be attained but in illusion, and so the illusion of a brother as a body is quite in keeping with the purpose of unholiness. Because of this consistency, the means remain unquestioned while the end is cherished. Seeing adapts to wish, for sight is always is always secondary to desire; and if you see the body, you have chosen judgment and not vision, for vision, like relationships, has no order. You either see it or not.

6. Who sees a brother's body has laid a judgment on him, and sees him not. He does not really see him as sinful; he does not see him at all. In the darkness of sin he is invisible. He can but be imagined in the darkness, and it is here that the illusions you hold about him are not held up to his reality. Here are illusions and reality kept separated. Here are illusions never brought to truth, and always hidden from it; and here in darkness, is your brother's reality imagined as a body, in unholy relationships with other bodies, serving the cause of sin an instant before he dies. (T.p.440)

7. There is indeed a difference between this vain imagining and vision. The difference lies not in them, but in their purpose. Both are but means, each one appropriate to the end for which it is employed. Neither can serve the purpose of the other, for each one is a choice of purpose, employed on its behalf. Either is

meaningless without the end for which it was intended, nor is it valued as a separate thing apart from the intentions. The means seem real because the goal is valued; and judgment has not value unless the goal is sin.

8. The body cannot be looked upon except through judgment. To see the body is the sign that you lack vision, and have denied the means the Holy Spirit offers you to serve his purpose. How can a holy relationship achieve its purpose through the means of sin? Judgment you taught yourself; vision is learned from Him. Who would undo your teaching? His vision cannot see the body because it cannot look on sin; thus it leads you to reality. Your holy brother, sight of whom is your release, is no illusion. Attempt to see him not in darkness, for your imaginings about him will seem real there. You closed your eyes to shut him out. Such was your purpose, and while this purpose seems to have a meaning, the means for its attainment will be evaluated as worth the seeing, and so you will not see.

9. Your question should not be, "How can I see my brother without the body?" Ask only, "Do I really wish to see him sinless?" As you ask, forget not that his sinlessness is your escape from fear. Salvation is the Holy Spirit's goal. The means is vision; for what the seeing look upon is sinless. No one who loves can judge, and what he sees is free of condemnation; and what he sees he did not make, for it was given him to see, as was the vision that made his seeing possible. (T.p.441)

*Average Epicureans eventually learn to use the "bait and poison" strategy to keep everyone controlled and within the sevens' mental gamesmanship advantage for able one-upmanship. When they are put upon wrongly, at least in their own eyes, they act like martyrs and make sure you know it…always trying to place the guilt everywhere and anywhere or on anyone except themselves.*

3. You have probably reacted for years as if you were being crucified. This is a marked tendency of the separated, who always refuse to consider what they have done to themselves. Projection means anger, anger fosters assault, and assault promotes fear. The real meaning of the crucifixion lies in the apparent intensity of the assault of some of the Sons of God upon another. This, of course, is impossible, and must be fully understood as impossible. Otherwise, I cannot serve as a model for learning. (T.p.92)

## II. THE GUILTLESS SON OF GOD

1. The ultimate purpose of projection is always to get rid of guilt. Yet, characteristically, the ego attempts to get rid of guilt from its viewpoint only. For much as the ego wants to retain guilt, you find it intolerable, since guilt stands in the way of you remembering God, whose pull is so strong that you cannot resist it. On this issue, then, the deepest split of all occurs, for if you are to retain guilt, as the ego insists, you cannot be you. Only by persuading you that it is you, could the ego possibly induce you to project guilt, and thereby keep it in your mind.

2. Yet consider how strange a solution the ego's arrangement it. You project guilt to get rid of it, but you are actually merely concealing it. You do experience the guilt, but you have no idea why. On the contrary, you associate it with a weird assortment of "ego ideals," which the ego claims you have failed. Yet you have no idea that you are failing the Son of God by seeing him as guilty. Believing you are no longer you, you do not realize that you are failing yourself.

3. The darkest of your hidden cornerstones holds your belief in guilt from your awareness; for in that dark and secret place is the realization that you have betrayed God's Son by condemning him to death. You do not even suspect this murderous but insane idea lies hidden there, for the ego's destructive urge is so intense that

## THE EPICUREAN

nothing short of the crucifixion of God's Son can ultimately satisfy it. It does not know who the Son of God is, because it is blind. Yet let it perceive guiltlessness anywhere, and it will try to destroy it because it is afraid.

4. Much of the ego's strange behavior is directly attributable to its definition of guilt. To the ego, the guiltless are guilty. Those who do not attack are its "enemies" because, by not valuing its interpretation of salvation, they are in an excellent position to let it go. They have approached the darkest and deepest cornerstone in the ego's foundation, and while the ego can withstand your raising all else to question, it guards this one secret with its life, for its existence depends on keeping this secret. So it is this secret that we must look upon, for the ego cannot protect you against truth, and in its presence the ego is dispelled. (T.p.239)

5. In the calm light of truth, let us recognize that you believe you have crucified God's Son. You have not admitted to this "terrible" secret because you would still wish to crucify Him if you could find Him. Yet the wish has hidden Him from you because it is very fearful, and so you are afraid to find Him. You have handled this wish to kill yourself by not knowing who you are and identifying with something else. You have projected guilt blindly and indiscriminately, but you have not uncovered its source. For the ego does not want to kill you, and if you identify with it you must believe its goal is yours.

6. I have said that the crucifixion is the symbol of the ego. When it was confronted with the real guiltlessness of God's Son it did attempt to kill Him, and the reason it gave was that guiltlessness is blasphemous to God. To the ego, the ego is God, and guiltlessness must be interpreted as the final guilt that fully justifies murder. You do not yet understand that any fear you may experience in connection with this course stems ultimately from this interpretation, but if you will consider your reactions to it you will become increasingly convinced that this is so.

7. This course has explicitly stated that its goal for you is happiness and peace. Yet you are afraid of it. You have been told again and again that it will set you free, yet you sometimes react as if it is trying to imprison you. You often dismiss it more readily than you dismiss the ego's thought system. To some extent, then, you must believe that by not learning the course you are protecting yourself; and you do not realize that it is only your guiltlessness that can protect you.

8. The Atonement has always been interpreted as the release from guilt, and this is correct if it is understood. Yet even when I interpret it for you, you may reject it and do not accept it for yourself. You have perhaps recognized the futility of the ego and its offerings, but though you do not want them, you may not yet look upon the alternative with gladness. In the extreme, you are afraid of redemption and you believe it will kill you. Make no mistake about the depth of this fear; for you believe that, in the presence of truth, you might turn on yourself and destroy yourself. (T.p.241)

9. Little child, this is not so. Your "guilty secret" is nothing, and if you will bring it to the light, the light will dispel it; and then no dark cloud will remain between you and the remembrance of your Father, for you will remember His guiltless Son, who did not die because he is immortal. You will see that you were redeemed with Him, and have never been separated from Him. In this understanding lies your remembering, for it is the recognition of love without fear. There will be great joy in Heaven on your homecoming, and the joy will be yours; for the redeemed son of man is the guiltless Son of God, and to recognize Him is your redemption.

*Average Epicureans become a jaded doers and self-centered, overinflated egocentrics who become demanding, as well as anal-retentive poor thinkers with no consideration for other people's true feelings. They become "empty human doings." Their souls get sucked into "solipsism."*

THE EPICUREAN

# I. THE HOLY INSTANT AND ATTRACTION OF GOD

1. As the ego would limit your perception of your brothers to the body, so would the Holy Spirit release your vision and let you see the Great Rays shining from them, so unlimited that they reach to God. It is this shift in vision that is accomplished in the holy instant. Yet it is needful for you to learn just what this shift entails, so you will become willing to make it permanent. Given this willingness it will not leave you, for it is permanent. Once you have accepted it as the only perception you want, it is translated into knowledge by the part that God Himself plays in the Atonement, for it is the only step in it He understands. Therefore, in this there will be no delay when you are ready for it. God is ready now, but you are not.

2. Our task is but to continue, as fast as possible, the necessary process of looking straight at all the interference and seeing it exactly as it is; for it is impossible to recognize as wholly without gratification what you think you want. The body is the symbol of the ego, as the ego is the symbol of the separation; and both are nothing more than attempts to limit communication, and thereby to make it impossible. Communication must be unlimited in order to have meaning, and deprived of meaning, it will not satisfy you completely. Yet it remains the only means by which you can establish real relationships, which have no limits, having been established by God. (T.p.322)

3. In the holy instant, where the Great Rays replace the body in awareness, the recognition of relationships without limits is given you; but in order to see this, it is necessary to give up every use the ego has for the body, and to accept the fact that the ego has no purpose you would share with it. For the ego would limit everyone to a body for its own purposes, and while you think it has a purpose, you will choose to utilize the means by which it tries to turn its purpose into accomplishment. This will never be accomplished. Yet you have surely recognized that the ego, whose goals are altogether

unattainable, will strive for them with all its might, and will do so with the strength that you have given it.

4. It is impossible to divide your strength between Heaven and Hell, God and the ego, and release your power to creation, which is the only purpose for which it was given to you. Love would always give increase. Limits are demanded by the ego, and represents its demands to make little and ineffectual. Limit your sight of a brother to his body, which you will do as long as you would not release him from it, and you have denied His gift to you. His body cannot give it; and seek it not through yours. Yet your minds are already continuous, and their union need only be accepted and the loneliness in Heaven is gone.

5. If you would but let the Holy Spirit tell you of the Love of God for you, and the need your creations have to be with you forever, you would experience the attraction of the eternal. No one can hear Him speak of this and long remain willing to linger here; for it is your will to be in Heaven, where you are complete and quiet, in such sure and loving relationships that any limit is impossible. Would you not exchange your little relationships for this? The body is little and limited, and only those whom you would see without the limits the ego would impose on them can offer you the gift of freedom. (T.p.323)

6. You have no conception of the limits you have placed on your perception, and no idea of all the loveliness that you could see; but this you must remember: the attraction of guilt opposes the attraction of God. His attraction for you remains unlimited, but because your power, being His, is as great as His, you can turn away from love. What you invest in guilt you withdraw from God . 5 And your sight grows weak and dim and limited, for you have attempted to separate the Father from the Son, and limit their communication. Seek not atonement in further separation. And limit not your vision of God's Son to what interferes with his release, and what the Holy Spirit must undo to set Him free; for his belief in limits has imprisoned him.

*Average Epicureans develop guilt-ridden associates to make themselves appear good and guiltless. This especially happens to those in marriage relationships where their love is insidiously replaced with codependence and a sense of one-upmanship wherein the mates feel beholden to the Epicureans to perform as they have in the past.*

## VII. THE NEEDLESS SACRIFICE

1. Beyond the poor attraction of the special love relationship, and always obscured by it, is the powerful attraction of the Father for His Son. There is no other love that can satisfy you, because there is no other love. This is the only love that is fully given and fully returned. Being complete, it asks nothing. Being wholly pure, everyone joined in it has everything. This is not the basis for any relationship in which the ego enters; for every relationship on which the ego embarks is special.

2. The ego establishes relationships only to get something; and it would keep the giver bound to itself through guilt. It is impossible for the ego to enter into any relationship without anger, for the ego believes that anger makes friends. This is not its statement, but it is its purpose; for the ego really believes that it can get and keep by making guilty. This is its one attraction, an attraction so weak that it would have no hold at all, except that no one recognizes it. For the ego always seems to attract through love, and has no attraction at all to anyone who perceives that it attracts through guilt.

3. The sick attraction of guilt must be recognized for what it is; for having been made real to you it is essential to look at it clearly, and by withdrawing your investment in it, to learn to let it go. No one would choose to let go what he believes has value. Yet the attraction of guilt has value to you only because you have not looked at what it is, and have judged it as valuable completely in the dark. As we bring it to light, your only question will be why it was you

ever wanted it. You have nothing to lose by looking open-eyed at this, for ugliness such as this belongs not in your holy mind. This host of God can have no investment here.

4. We said before that the ego attempts to maintain and increase guilt, but in such a way that you do not recognize what it would do to you; for it is the ego's fundamental doctrine that what you do to others you have escaped. The ego wishes no one well, yet its survival depends on your belief that you are exempt from its evil intentions. It counsels, therefore, that if you are host to it, it will enable you to direct its anger outward, thus protecting you; and thus it embarks on an endless, unrewarding chain of special relationships, forged out of anger and dedicated to but one insane belief: that the more anger you invest outside yourself, the safer you become (T.p.317).

5. It is this chain that binds the Son of God to guilt, and it is this chain the Holy Spirit would remove from His holy mind; for the chain of savagery belongs not around the chosen host of God, who cannot make himself host to the ego. In the name of His release, and in the name of Him who would release Him, let us look more closely at the relationships the ego contrives, and let the Holy Spirit judge them truly; for it is certain that if you will look at them, you will offer them gladly to Him. What he can make of them you do not know, but you will become willing to find out, if you are willing first to perceive what you have made of them.

6. In one way or another, every relationship the ego makes is based on the idea that by sacrificing itself, it becomes bigger. The "sacrifice," which it regards as purification, is actually the root of its bitter resentment; for it would prefer to attack directly, and avoid delaying what it really wants. Yet the ego acknowledges "reality" as it sees it, and recognizes that no one could interpret direct attack as love. Yet to make guilty is direct attack, although it does not seem to be; for the guilty expect attack and having asked for it, they are attracted to it.

7. In such insane relationships, the attraction of what you do not want seems to be much stronger than the attraction of what you do want; for each one thinks that he has sacrificed something to the other, and hates him for it. Yet this is what he thinks he wants. He is not in love with the other at all. He merely believes he is in love with sacrifice; and for this sacrifice, which he demands of himself, he demands that the other accept the guilt and sacrifice himself as well. Forgiveness becomes impossible, for the ego believes that to forgive another is to lose him. It is only by attack without forgiveness that the ego can ensure the guilt that holds all its relationships together.

8. Yet they only seem to be together; for relationships, to the ego, mean only that bodies are together. It is always this that the ego demands, and it does not object where the mind goes or what it thinks, for this seems unimportant. As long as the body is there to receive its sacrifice, it is content. To the ego, the mind is private, and only the body can be shared. Ideas are basically of no concern except as they bring the body of another closer or farther; and it is in these terms that it evaluates ideas as good or bad. What makes another guilty and holds him through the guilt is "good." What releases him from guilt is "bad," because he would no longer believe that bodies communicate, and so he would be "gone" (T.p.318).

9. Suffering and sacrifice are the gifts with which the ego would "bless" all unions; and those who are united at its altar accept suffering and sacrifice as the price of union. In their angry alliances, born of the fear of loneliness, each seeks relief from guilt by increasing it in the other; for each believes that this decreases guilt in him. The other seems always to be attacking and wounding him, perhaps in little ways, perhaps "unconsciously," yet never without demand of sacrifice. The fury of those joined at the ego's altar far exceeds your awareness of it; for what the ego really wants you do not realize.

10. Whenever you are angry, you can be sure that you have formed a special relationship which the ego has "blessed," for anger is its blessing. Anger takes many *forms*, but it cannot long deceive

those who will learn that love brings no guilt at all, and what brings guilt cannot be love and must be anger. All anger is nothing more than an attempt to make someone feel guilty, and this attempt is the only basis the ego accepts for special relationships. Guilt is the only need the ego has, and as long as you identify with it, guilt will remain attractive to you. Yet remember this: to be with a body is not communication, and if you think it is, you will feel guilty about communication and will be afraid to hear the Holy Spirit, recognizing in His voice your own need to communicate.

11. The Holy Spirit cannot teach through fear. How can He communicate with you, while you believe that to communicate is to make yourself alone? It is clearly insane to believe that by communicating you will be abandoned, and yet many do believe it. For they think their minds must be kept private or they will lose them, but if their bodies are together their minds remain their own. The union of the bodies thus becomes the way in which they would keep minds apart; for bodies cannot forgive. They can only do as the mind directs.

12. The illusion of the autonomy of the body and its ability to overcome loneliness is but the working of the ego's plan to establish its own autonomy. As long as you believe that to be with a body is companionship, you will be compelled to attempt to keep your brother in his body, held there by guilt; and you will see safety in guilt and danger in communication. The ego will always teach that loneliness is solved by guilt, and that communication is the cause of loneliness; and despite the evident insanity of this lesson, many have learned it.

13. Forgiveness lies in communication as surely as damnation lies in guilt. It is the Holy Spirit's teaching function to instruct those who believe communication to be damnation, that communication is salvation; and He will do so, for the power of God in Him and you is joined in a real relationship so holy and so strong, that it can overcome even this without fear.

14. It is through the holy instant that what seems impossible is accomplished, making it evident that it is not impossible. In the holy instant guilt holds no attraction, since communication has been restored; and guilt, whose only purpose is to disrupt communication, has no function here. Here there is no concealment, and no private thoughts. The willingness to communicate attracts communication to it, and overcomes loneliness completely. There is complete forgiveness here, for there is no desire to exclude anyone from your completion, in sudden recognition of the value of his part in it. In the protection of your wholeness, all are invited and made welcome; and you understand that your completion is God's, whose only need is to have you be complete. Your completion makes you His in your awareness; and here it is that you experience yourself as you were created and as you are (T.p.30).

## Chapter 26
## TRANSITION

### I. THE "SACRIFICE" OF ONENESS

1. In the "dynamics" of attack is sacrifice a key idea. It is the pivot upon which all compromise, all desperate attempts to strike a bargain, and all conflicts achieve a seeming balance. It is the symbol of the central theme that somebody must lose. Its focus on the body is apparent, for it is always an attempt to limit loss. The body is itself a sacrifice, a giving up of power in the name of saving just a little for yourself. To see a brother in another body, separate from yours, is the expression of a wish to see a little part of him and sacrifice the rest. Look at the world, and you will see nothing attached to anything beyond itself. All seeming entities can come a little nearer, or go a little farther off, but cannot join.

2. The world you see is based on "sacrifice" of oneness. It is a picture of complete disunity and total lack of joining. Around each

entity is built a wall so seeming solid that it looks as if what is inside can never reach without, and what is out can never reach and join with what is locked away within the wall. Each part must sacrifice the other part to keep itself complete, for if they joined each one would lose its own identity, and by their separation are their selves maintained.

3. The little that the body fences off becomes the self, preserved through sacrifice of all the rest; and all the rest must lose this little part, remaining incomplete to keep its own identity intact. In misperception of yourself the body's loss would be a sacrifice indeed. For sight of bodies becomes the sign that sacrifice is limited, and something still remains for you alone. For this little to belong to you are limits placed on everything outside, just as they are on everything you think is yours; for giving and receiving are the same. To accept the limits of a body is to impose these limits on each brother whom you see, for you must see him as you see yourself.

4. The body is a loss, and can be made to sacrifice; and while you see your brother as a body, apart from you and separate in his cell, you are demanding sacrifice of him and you. What greater sacrifice could be demanded than that God's Son perceive Himself without His Father; and His Father be without His Son? Yet every sacrifice demands that they be separate and without the other. The memory of God must be denied if any sacrifice is asked of anyone. What witness to the wholeness of God's Son is seen within a world of separate bodies, however much he witnesses to truth? He is invisible in such a world; nor can his song of union and of love be heard at all; yet is it given him to make the world recede before his song and the sight of him replace the body's eyes (T.p.542).

5. Those who would see the witnesses to truth instead of to illusion merely ask that they might see a purpose in the world that gives it sense and makes it meaningful. Without your special function has this world no meaning for you. Yet it can become a treasure house as rich and limitless as Heaven itself. No instant passes here

in which your brother's holiness cannot be seen, to add a limitless supply to every meager scrap and tiny crumb of happiness that you allot yourself.

6. You can lose sight of oneness, but cannot make sacrifice of its reality; nor can you lose what you would sacrifice, nor keep the Holy Spirit from His task of showing you that it has not been lost. Hear, then, the song your brother sings to you, and let the world recede, and take the rest his witness offers on behalf of peace; but judge him not, for you will hear no song of liberation for yourself, nor see what it is given him to witness to, that you may see it and rejoice with him. Make not his holiness a sacrifice to your belief in sin. You sacrifice your innocence with his and die each time you see in him a sin deserving death.

7. Yet every instant can you be reborn, and given life again. His holiness gives life to you, who cannot die because his sinlessness is known to God, and can no more be sacrificed by you than can the light in you be blotted out because he sees it not. You who would make a sacrifice of life, and make your eyes and ears bear witness to the death of God and of His Holy Son, think not that you have power to make of Them what God willed not They be. In Heaven, God's Son is not imprisoned in a body, nor is sacrificed in solitude to sin; and as He is in Heaven, so must He be eternally and everywhere: He is the same forever. Born again each instant, untouched by time, and far beyond the reach of any sacrifice of life or death; for neither did He make, and only one was given Him by one who knows His gifts can never suffer sacrifice and loss (T.p.543).

## (EXCERPT FROM: V. THE EGO BODY ILLUSION [T.P.65])

4. The body is the ego's home by its own election. It is the only identification with which the ego feels safe, since the body's

vulnerability is its own best argument that you cannot be of God. This is the belief that the ego sponsors eagerly. Yet the ego hates the body because it cannot accept it as good enough to be its home. Here is where the mind becomes actually dazed. Being told by the ego that it is really part of the body and that the body is its protector, the mind is also told that the body cannot protect it. Therefore, the mind asks, "Where can I go for protection?" to which the ego replies, "Turn to me." The mind, and not without cause, reminds the ego that it has itself insisted that it is identified with the body, so there is no point in turning to it for protection. The ego has no real answer to this because there is none, but it does have a typical solution. It obliterates the question from the mind's awareness. Once out of awareness the question can and does produce uneasiness, but it cannot be answered because it cannot be asked.

5. This is the question that must be asked: "Where can I go for protection?" "Seek and ye shall find" does not mean that you should seek blindly and desperately for something you would not recognize. Meaningful seeking is consciously directed. The goal must be formulated clearly and kept in mind. Learning and wanting to learn are inseparable. You learn best when you believe what you are trying to learn is of value to you; however, not everything you may want to learn has lasting value. Indeed, many of the things you want to learn may be chosen because their value will not last.

6. The ego thinks it is an advantage not to commit itself to anything that is eternal, because the eternal must come from God. Eternalness is the one function the ego has tried to develop, but has systematically failed to achieve. The ego compromises with the issue of the eternal, just as it does with all issues touching on the real question in any way. By becoming involved with tangential issues, it hopes to hide the real question and keep it out of mind. The ego's characteristic busyness with nonessentials is for precisely that purpose. Preoccupations with problems set up to be incapable of solution are favorite ego devices for impeding learning progress. In all

these diversionary tactics, however, the one question that is never asked by those who pursue them is, "What for?" This is the question that you must learn to ask in connection with everything. What is the purpose? Whatever it is, it will direct your efforts automatically. When you make a decision of purpose, then you have made a decision about your future effort, a decision that will remain in effect unless you change your mind (T.pp.65–67).

## II. THE ALTERNATIVE TO PROJECTION

1. Any split in mind must involve a rejection of part of it, and this is the belief in separation. The wholeness of God, which is His peace, cannot be appreciated except by a whole mind that recognizes the wholeness of God's creation. By this recognition it knows its Creator. Exclusion and separation are synonymous, as are separation and dissociation. We have said before that the separation was and is dissociation and that once it occurs, projection becomes its main defense, or the device that keeps it going. The reason, however, may not be so obvious as you think.

2. What you project you disown, and therefore do not believe is yours. You are excluding yourself by the very judgment that you are different from the one on whom you project. Since you have also judged against what you project, you continue to attack it because you continue to keep it separated from them. The ego justifies this on the grounds that it makes you seem "better" than they are, and thus you imagine that you have made yourself safe.

3. Yet projection will always hurt you. It reinforces your belief in your own split mind, and its only purpose is to keep the separation going. It is solely a device of the ego to make you feel different from your brothers and separated from them. The ego justifies this on the grounds that it makes you seem better seem "better" than they are, thus obscuring your equality with them still further.

Projection and attack are inevitably related, because projection is always a means of justifying attack. Anger without projection is impossible. The ego uses projection only to destroy your perception of both yourself and your brothers. The process begins by excluding something that exists in you but which you do not want, and leads directly to excluding you from your brothers.

4. We have learned, however, that there is an alternative to projection. Every ability of the ego has a better use, because its abilities are directed by the mind, which has a better voice. The Holy Spirit extends and the ego projects. As their goals are opposed, so is the result.

5. The Holy Spirit begins by perceiving you as perfect. Knowing this perfection is shared He recognizes it in others, thus strengthening it in both. Instead of anger this arouses love for both, because it establishes inclusion. Perceiving equality, the Holy Spirit perceives equal needs. This invites Atonement automatically, because Atonement is the one need in this world that is universal. To perceive yourself this way is the only way in which you can find happiness in the world. That is because it is the acknowledgment that you are in this world, for the world is unhappy.

6. How else can you find joy in a joyless place except by realizing that you are not there? You cannot be anywhere God did not put you, and God created you as part of Him. That is both where you are and what you are. It is completely unalterable. It is total inclusion. You cannot change it now or ever. It is not a belief but a fact. Anything that God created is as true as He is. Its truth lies only in its perfect inclusion in Him who alone is perfect. To deny this is to deny yourself and Him, since it is impossible to accept one without the other.

7. The perfect equality of the Holy Spirit's perception is the reflection of the perfect equality of God's knowing. The ego's perception has no counterpart in God, but the Holy Spirit remains the Bridge between perception and knowledge. By enabling you to use perception in a way that reflects knowledge, you will ultimately remember

it. The ego would prefer to believe that this memory is impossible, yet it is your perception in a way that reflects knowledge, and you will ultimately remember it. The ego would prefer to believe that this memory is impossible, yet it is your perception the Holy Spirit guides. Your perception will end where it began. Everything meets in God, because everything was created by Him and in Him.

8. God created His Sons by extending His thought, and retaining the extensions of His thought in His mind. All his thoughts are thus perfectly united within themselves and with each other. The Holy Spirit enables you to perceive this wholeness now. God created you to create. You cannot extend His Kingdom until you know of its wholeness.

9. Thoughts begin in the mind of the thinker, from which they reach outward. This is as true of God's thinking as it is of yours. Because your mind is split, you can perceive as well as think. Yet perception cannot escape the basic laws of mind. You perceive from your mind and project your perceptions outward. Although perception of any kind is unreal, you made it and the Holy Spirit can therefore use it well. He can inspire perception and lead it toward God. This convergence seems to be far in the future only because your mind is not in perfect alignment with the idea, and therefore does not want it now (T.p.98).

11. The ego can accept the idea that return is necessary because it can so easily make the idea seem difficult. Yet the Holy Spirit tells you that even return is unnecessary, because what never happened cannot be difficult. However, you can make the idea of return both necessary and difficult. Yet it is surely clear that the perfect need nothing, and you cannot experience perfection as a difficult accomplishment, because that is what you are. This is the way in which you must perceive God's creations, bringing all of your perceptions into the one line the Holy Spirit sees. This line is the direct line of communication with God, and lets your mind converge with His. There is no conflict anywhere in this perception because it means

that all perception is guided by the Holy Spirit, whose mind is fixed on God. Only the Holy Spirit can resolve conflict, because only the Holy Spirit is conflict-free. He perceives only what is true in your mind, and extends outward only to what is true in other minds.

12. The difference between the ego's projection and the Holy Spirit's extension is very simple. The ego projects to exclude, and therefore to deceive. The Holy Spirit extends by recognizing Himself in every mind, and thus perceives them as one. Nothing conflicts in this perception, because what the Holy Spirit perceives is all the same. Whenever He looks He sees Himself, and because He is united He offers the whole Kingdom always (T.p.98).

3. This is the one message God gave to Him and for which He must speak, because that is what He is. The peace of God lies in that message, and so the peace of God lies in you. The great peace of the Kingdom shines in your mind forever, but it must shine outward to make you aware of it. The Holy Spirit was given you with perfect impartiality, and only by recognizing Him impartially can you recognize Him at all. The ego is legion, but the Holy Spirit is one. No darkness abides anywhere in the Kingdom, but your part is only to allow no darkness to abide in your own mind. This alignment with light is unlimited, because it is in alignment with the light of the world. Each of us is the light of the world, and by joining our minds in this light we proclaim the Kingdom of God together and as one (T.p.99).

## THE GIFTS OF THE KINGDOM

*Average Epicureans greedily get into conspicuous consumption, albeit gluttony or excessiveness of anything. They may think that bigger is* better or three of something is better than just one. They become hyperactive and yet codedependent as they do for others wanting a return favor. They invest for a return. They never feel they have enough or that they have ever done enough. They become addicted to things and events, being seen as event junkies. In effect, with all their activities and consumption, they stay high to keep from getting high. Eventually they become jaded doers and self-centered, overinflated egocentrics who become demanding, as well as anal-retentive poor thinkers with no consideration for other people's true feelings. They become "empty human doings." Their souls gets sucked into "solipsism." They become insensitive to their true original feelings and seared from those subtle considerations of everyone around them.

## THE UNHEALTHY EPICUREAN

Unhealthy Epicureans have committed too many sins, to the point that their guilt defeats them and they become anal-retentive on everyone around them. It is they who have gone too far, and in their attempt to control themselves they become anal-retentive of "religious" in their demands on everyone around them to "do as they do."

Remember all temptation is but this: a mad belief that God's insanity would make you sane and give you what you want, that either God or you must lose to madness because your aims cannot be resolved. Death demands life, but life is not maintained at any cost. No one can suffer for the will of God to be fulfilled. Salvation is His will because you share it; not for you alone, but for the self that is the Son of God. He cannot lose, for if He could, the loss would be his Father's and in Him no less is possible; and this is the same because it is the truth (T.p.54).

*Unhealthy Epicureans' self-respect has dissipated into fear and self-recrimination, to appear to everyone as though they have done nothing "amiss."*

*Unhealthy Epicureans want to sell a bill of goods: themselves. They are the masters of deceit, believing their own lies. They are the compulsive liars and the pedophiles and sexual experimenters approaching the vilest behavior, all the while fantasizing their participation in the most perverse circumstances.*

*Unhealthy Epicureans use religion as a tool to convince themselves they aren't guilty (to no avail). They use religion to rationalize their unacceptable behaviors, almost to hallow their behaviors.*

## THE ACCEPTANCE OF REALITY

1. Fear of the will of God is one of the strangest beliefs the human mind has ever made. It could not possibly occurred unless the mind were already profoundly split, making it possible for it to be afraid of what it really is. Reality cannot "threaten" anything accept illusions, since reality can only uphold truth. (T.P. 160)

*Unhealthy Epicureans ultimately spin out of control acting out their anxiety. They act crudely offensive and are insensitive regarding other people's legitimate wants or needs.*
*They become obnoxious in their going after what they want. They become manic-depressive psychotics at low end and develop "hysterical" panic disorders as they near their end.*

## LESSON 213 (ARCHETYPE)
**I am not a body.**
**I am free.**
**I am still as God created me.**

1. (193) *All things are lessons God would have me learn.*
*A lesson is a miracle which God offers to me, in place of thoughts I made that hurt me. What I learn of Him becomes the way I am set free. And so I choose to learn His lessons and forget my own.*
**I am not a body. I am free.**
**For I am still as God created me.**

## LESSON 274 (GROWTH LINE)
**Today belongs to love. Let me not fear.**

1. *Father, today I would let all things be as You created them, and give your Son the honor due his sinnlessness; the love of brother to his brother and his Friend. Through this I am redeemed. Through this as well the truth will enter where illusions were, light will replace all darkness, and your Son will know he is as You created him.*

2. *A speciel blessing comes to us today, from Him Who is our Father. Give this day to him, and there will be no fear today, because the day is given unto love.*

## LESSON 251 (DEMATERIALIZATION LINE)
**I am in need of nothing but the truth.**

1. I sought for many things, and found despair. Now do I seek but one, for in that one is all I need, and only what

I need. All that I sought before I needed not, and did not even want. My only need I did not recognize. But now I see that I only need truth. In that all needs are satisfied, all cravings end, all hopes are finally fulfilled and dreams are gone. Now have I everything that I could need. Now have I everything that I could want. And now at last I find myself at peace.

2. *And for that peace, our Father we give thanks. What we denied ourselves You have restored, and only that is what we really want.*

## CHAPTER 8
# THE CONTROLLER

"Beware the temptation to perceive yourself unfairly treated."
(T.523/563 ACIM)

**Invulnerability:** our natural state as a Son of God; our true being spirit and not the body, nothing of the ego's world can harm us; recognizing our invulnerability becomes the basis of our defenselessness, the conditions for forgiveness (Gloss., p. 116).

# A HEALTHY CONTROLLER ACCORDING TO A COURSE IN MIRACLES

*Honorable natural leaders are protective and helpful in maintaining courage and direction to all within their influence. They are magnanimous in their promotion of individuals and organizations they care to safeguard.*

## II. THE VOICE FOR GOD

1. Healing is not creating; it is reparation. The Holy Spirit promotes healing by looking beyond it to what the children of God were before healing was needed, and will be when they have been healed. This alteration of the time sequence should be quite familiar, because it is very similar to the shift in the perception of time that the miracle introduces. The Holy Spirit is the motivation for miracle-mindedness; it is the decision to heal the separation by letting it go. Your will is still in you because God placed it in your mind, and although you can keep it asleep you cannot obliterate it.

God Himself keeps your will alive by transmitting it from His mind to yours as long as there is time. The miracle itself is a reflection of this union of will between Father and Son.

2. The Holy Spirit is the spirit of joy. He is the call to return, with which God blessed the minds of His separated Sons. This is the vocation of the mind. The mind had no calling until the separation, because before that it had only being, and would not have understood the call to right thinking. The Holy Spirit is God's answer to the separation: the means by which the Atonement heals until the whole mind returns to creating.

3. The principle of Atonement and the separation began at the same time. When the ego was made, God placed in the mind the call to Joy. This call is so strong that the ego always dissolves at its sound. That is why you must choose to hear one of two voices within you. One you made yourself, and that one is not of God, but the other is given you by God, who asks you only to listen to it. The Holy Spirit is in you in a very literal sense. His is the voice that calls you back to where you were before and will be again. It is possible even in this world to hear only that voice and no other. It takes effort and great willingness to learn. It is the final lesson that I learned, and God's Sons are as equal as learners as they are Sons.

4. You are the Kingdom of Heaven, but you have let the belief in darkness enter your mind and so you need a new light. The Holy Spirit is the radiance that you must let banish the idea of darkness. His is the glory before which dissociation falls away, and the Kingdom of Heaven breaks through into its own. Before the separation you did not need guidance. You knew as you will know again, but as you do not know now.

5. God does not guide, because He can share only perfect knowledge. Guidance is evaluative, because it implies there is a right way and also a wrong way, one to be chosen and the other to be avoided. By choosing one you give up the other. The choice for the Holy Spirit is the choice of God. God is not in you in a literal

## THE CONTROLLER

sense; you are part of Him. When you chose to leave Him, He gave you a voice to speak for Him because He could no longer share His knowledge with you without hindrance. Direct communication was broken because you had made another voice.

6. The Holy Spirit calls you both to remember and to forget. You have chosen to be in a state of opposition in which opposites are possible. As a result there are choices you must make. In the holy state the will is free, so that its creative power is unlimited and choice is meaningless. Freedom to choose is the same power as freedom to create, but its application is different. Choosing depends on a split mind. The Holy Spirit is one way of choosing. God did not leave His children comfortless, even though they chose to leave Him. The voice they put in their minds was not the voice for His will, for which the Holy Spirit speaks (T.pp.75–76).

7. The voice of the Holy Spirit does not command, because it is incapable of arrogance. It does not demand, because it does not seek control. It does not overcome, because it does not attack. It merely reminds. It is compelling only because of what it reminds you of. It brings to your mind the other way, remaining quiet even in the midst of the turmoil you may make. The voice for God is always quiet because it speaks of peace. Peace is stronger than war because it heals. War is division, not increase. No one gains from strife. "What profiteth it a man if he gain the whole world and lose his own soul?" If you listen to the wrong voice you have lost sight of your soul. You cannot lose it, but you cannot know it. It is therefore "lost" to you until you choose right.

8. The Holy Spirit is your guide in choosing. He is in the part of your mind that always speaks for the right choice, because He speaks for God. He is your remaining communication with God, which you can interrupt but cannot destroy. The Holy Spirit is the way in which God's will is done on Earth as it is in Heaven. Both Heaven and Earth are in you, because the call of both is in your mind. The voice for God comes from your own altars to Him. These altars are not things; they

are devotions. Yet you have other devotions now. Your divided devotion has given you the two voices, and you must choose at which altar you want to serve. The call you answer now is an evaluation because it is a decision. The decision is very simple. It is made on the basis of which call is worth more to you.

9. My mind will always be like yours, because we were created as equals. It was only my decision that gave me all power in Heaven and Earth. My only gift to you is to help you make the same decision. This decision is the choice to share it, because the decision itself is the decision to share. It is made by giving, and is therefore the one choice that resembles true creation. I am your model for decision. By deciding for God I showed you that this decision can be made, and that you can make it.

10. I have assured you that the Mind that decided for me is also in you, and that you can let it change you just as it changed me. This mind is unequivocal, because it hears only one voice and answers in only one way. You are the light of the world with me. Rest does not come from sleeping but from waking. The Holy Spirit is the call to awaken and be glad. The world is very tired, because it is the idea of weariness. Our task is the joyous one of waking it to the call for God. Everyone will answer me the call of the Holy Spirit, or the Sonship cannot be as one. What better vocation could there be for any part of the Kingdom than to restore it to the perfect integration that can make it whole? Hear only this through the Holy Spirit within you, and teach your brothers to listen as I am teaching you (T.p.76-77).

11. When you are tempted by the wrong voice, call on me to remind you how to heal by sharing my decision and making it stronger. As we share this goal, we increase its power to attract the whole Sonship, and to bring it back into the oneness in which it was created. Remember that "yoke" means "join together," and "burden" means "message." Let us restate "My yoke is easy and my burden light" in this way: "Let us join together, for my message is light" (T.p.77).

## II. HONESTY

1. All other traits of God's teachers rest on trust. Once that has been achieved, the others cannot fail to follow. Only the trusting can afford honesty, for only they can see its value. Honesty does not apply only to what you say. The term actually means consistency. There is nothing you say that contradicts what you think or do; no thought opposes any other thought; no act belies your word; and no word lacks agreement with another. Such are the truly honest. At no level are they in conflict with themselves. Therefore it is impossible for them to be in conflict with anyone or anything (M.p.11).

2. The peace of mind which the advanced teachers of God experience is largely due to their perfect honesty. It is only the wish to deceive that makes for war. No one at one with himself can even conceive of conflict. Conflict is the inevitable result of self-deception, and self-deception is dishonesty. There is no challenge to a teacher of God. Challenge implies doubt, and the trust on which God's teachers rest secure makes doubt impossible; therefore, they can only succeed. In this, as in all things, they are honest. They can only succeed, because they never do their will alone. They choose for all mankind, for all the world and all things in it, for the unchanging and unchangeable beyond appearances, and for the Son of God and His Creator. How could they not succeed? They choose in perfect honesty, sure of their choice as of themselves (Mt.pp.11–12).

## VIII  THE LITTLE GARDEN

1. It is only the awareness of the body that makes love seem limited. For the body is a limit on love. The belief in limited love was its origin, and it was made to limit the unlimited. Think not that this is merely allegorical, for it was made to limit you. Can you who see yourself within a body know yourself as an idea? Everything

you recognize you identify with externals, something outside itself. You cannot even think of God without a body, or in some form you think you recognize.

2. The body cannot know, and while you limit your awareness to its tiny senses, you will not see the grandeur that surrounds you. God cannot come into a body, nor can you join Him there. Limits on love will always seem to shut Him out, and keep you apart from Him. The body is a tiny fence around a little part of a glorious and complete idea. It draws a circle, infinitely small around a very little segment of Heaven, splintered from the whole, proclaiming that within it is your kingdom where God can enter not.

3. Within this kingdom the ego rules, and cruelly; and to defend this little speck of dust it bids you fight against the universe. This fragment of your mind is such a tiny part of it that, could you but appreciate the whole, you would see instantly that it is like the smallest sunbeam to the sun, or like the faintest ripple on the surface of the ocean. In its amazing arrogance, this tiny sunbeam has decided it is the sun; this almost imperceptible ripple hails itself as the ocean. Think how alone and frightened is this little thought, this infinitesimal illusion, holding itself apart against the universe. The sun becomes the sunbeam's "enemy" that would devour it, and the ocean terrifies the little ripple and wants to swallow it.

4. Yet neither sun nor ocean is even aware of all this strange and meaningless activity. They merely continue, unaware that they are feared and hated by a tiny segment of themselves. Even that segment is not lost to them, for it could not survive apart from them; and what it thinks it is in no way changes its total dependence on them for its being. Its whole existence still remains in them. Without the sun, the sunbeam would be gone; the ripple without the ocean is inconceivable (T.pp.390–391).

5. Such is the strange position in which those in a world inhabited by bodies seem to be. Each body seems to house a separate mind, a disconnected thought, living alone and in no way joined

to the thought by which it was created. Each tiny fragment seems to be self-contained, needing another for some things, but by no means totally dependent on its one Creator for everything; needing the whole to give it any meaning, for by itself it does mean nothing, nor has it any life apart and by itself.

6. Like the sun and ocean your Self continues, unmindful that this tiny part regards itself as you. It is not missing; it could not exist if it were separate, nor would the whole be whole without it. It is not a separate kingdom, ruled by an idea of separation from the rest. Nor does a fence surround it, preventing it from joining with the rest, and keeping it apart from its Creator. This little aspect is no different from the whole, being continuous with it and at one with it. It leads no separate life, because its life is the oneness in which its being was created.

7. Do not accept this little, fenced-off aspect as yourself. The sun and ocean are as nothing beside what you are. The sunbeam sparkles only in the sunlight, and the ripple dances as it rests upon the ocean. Yet in neither sun nor ocean is the power that rests in you. Would you remain within your tiny kingdom a sorry king, a bitter ruler of all that he surveys, who looks to nothing yet who would still die to defend it? This little self is not your kingdom. Arched high above it and surrounding it with love is the glorious whole, which offers all its happiness and deep content to every part. The little aspect that you think you set apart is no exception.

8. Love knows no bodies, and reaches to everything created like itself. Its total lack of limit is its meaning. It is completely impartial in its giving, encompassing only to preserve and keep complete what it would give. In your tiny kingdom you have so little! Should it not, then, be there that you would call on love to enter? Look at the desert—dry and unproductive, scorched and joyless— that makes up your little kingdom, and realize the life and joy that love would bring to it from where it comes, and where it would return with you.

9. The thought of God surrounds your little kingdom, waiting at the barrier you built, to come inside and shine upon the barren ground. See how life springs up everywhere! The desert becomes a garden, green and deep and quiet, offering rest to those who lost their way and wander in the dust. Give them a place of refuge, prepared by love for them where once a desert was, and everyone you welcome will bring love with him from Heaven for you. They enter one by one into this holy place, but they will not depart as they had come, alone. The love they brought with them will stay with them, as it will stay with you, and under its beneficence your little garden will expand, and reach out to everyone who thirsts for living water, but has grown too weary to go on alone (T.p.392).

10. Go out and find them, for they bring your Self with them; and lead them gently to your quiet garden, and receive their blessing there. So will it grow and stretch across the desert, leaving no lonely little kingdoms locked away from love, and leaving you outside. You will recognize yourself, and see your little garden gently transformed into the Kingdom of Heaven, with all the love of its Creator shining upon it.

11. The holy instant is your invitation to love, to enter into your bleak and joyless kingdom, and to transform it into a garden of peace and welcome. Love's answer is inevitable. It will come because you came without the body, and interposed no barriers to interfere with its glad coming. In the holy instant, you ask of love only what it offers everyone, neither less nor more. Asking for everything, you will receive it, and your shining Self will lift the tiny aspect that you tried to hide from Heaven, straight to Heaven. No part of love calls on the whole in vain. No Son of God remains outside His Fatherhood.

12. Be sure of this; love has entered your special relationship, and entered fully at your weak request. You do not recognize that love has come, because you have not yet let go of all the barriers you

# THE CONTROLLER

**Not to make error real:** one of the key elements in the Hholy Spirit's plan of forgiveness, correcting the ego's plan to make sin real which inevitably leads us either to erect defenses against it out of fear, or to forgive it falsely; true forgiveness, on the other hand, recognizes the error as a call for love and correction; making the error real, as when we falsely empathize with one another, or magically hope to solve an external problem roots us still further in the ego's thought system, while seeing all problems or forms of suffering as external reflections of internal guilt allows the true healing of the mind to occur. (Gloss., p.157).

**Child:** metaphor to describe the "little wisdom" of the

hold against your brother; and you and he will not be able to give love welcome separately. You could no more know God alone than He knows you without your brother; but together you could no more be unaware of love than love could know you not, or fail to recognize itself in you.

13. You have reached the end of an ancient journey, not realizing yet that it is over. You are still worn and tired, and the desert's dust still seems to cloud your eyes and keep you sightless. Yet He whom you welcomed has come to you, and would welcome you. He has waited long to give you this. Receive it now of Him, for He would have you know Him. Only a little wall of dust still stands between you and your brother. Blow on it lightly and with happy laughter, and it will fall away; and walk into the garden love has prepared for both of you (T.pp.392–393).

*Healthy Controllers are strong willed, assertive, and wily. They are decisive and commanding. They champion people and stand behind* them through thick and thin. They become self-confident heroes of worthy causes, going beyond the call of duty.

## THE AVERAGE ENNEATYPE "8" ACCORDING TO A COURSE IN MIRACLES

*Average Controllers are rugged individualist who intimidate others to get their way. They are the power brokers who make waves to expand the empire in their wheeler-dealer fashion.*

*Average Eights become more self-centered and conceited in their unswerving deference to their own well-being. They are often entrepreneurs, pursuing their own interests. They are not easily cooperative team players and not too concerned about the welfare of others unless others contribute to their estate. They dominate their environments to get their way, even if it means creating adversarial relationships.*

---

separated Sons, who are like little children who do not understand the world, and therefore need to be taught by their elder brother Jesus to distinguish what is true from what is false, the world of reality from the world of fantasy; if we were spiritually advanced adults we would not need the help that A Course in Miracles provides. (Gloss., p.44).

**Dissociation**: an ego defense that separates the ego from the Holy Spirit—the wrong mind from the right mind—splitting off what seems fearful, which merely reinforces the fear that is the ego's goal: the ego's attempt to separate two conflicting thought systems and keep them both in our minds, so that its thought system of darkness is safe from undoing by the light. (Gloss., .p. 133).

> **Projection:** the fundamental law of mind:; projection makes perception—what we see inwardly determines what we see outside our minds.
>
> w--m reinforces guilt by displacing it onto someone else, attacking it there and denying its presence in ourselves; an attempt to shift responsibility for separation from ourselves to others (Gloss., p. 170).

*Average Controllers become combative and willful to an irrational degree of belligerence. They become unscrupulous and are "con men." They play with danger and place themselves in harm's way for the "high" of recovering and coming through it. They embody unreasonableness and become high-risk event junkies ready for any "dare."*

## V. THE UNHEALED HEALER

1. The ego's plan for forgiveness is far more widely used than God's. This is because it is undertaken by unhealed healers, and is therefore of the ego. Let us consider the unhealed healer more carefully now. By definition, he is trying to give what he has not received. If an unhealed healer is a theologian, for example, he may begin with the premise, "I am a miserable sinner, and so are you." If he is a psychotherapist, he is more likely to start with the equally incredible belief that attack is real for both himself and the patient, but that it does not matter for either of them.

2. I have repeatedly said that beliefs of the ego cannot be shared, and this is why they are unreal. How, then, can "uncovering" them make them real? Every healer who searches fantasies for truth must be unhealed, because he does not know where to look for truth, and therefore does not have the answer to the problem of healing.

3. There is an advantage to bringing nightmares into awareness, but only to teach that they are not real, and that anything they contain is meaningless. The unhealed healer cannot do this because he does not believe it. All unhealed healers follow the ego's plan for forgiveness in one form or another. If they are theologians, they are likely to condemn themselves, teach condemnation, and advocate a fearful solution. Projecting condemnation onto God, they make Him appear retaliative, and fear His retribution. What they have done is merely to identify with the ego, and by perceiving what it does, condemn themselves because of this confusion. It is understandable that there have been revolts against this concept, but to revolt against it is still to believe in it.

4. Some newer forms of the ego's plan are as unhelpful as the older ones, because form does not matter and the content has not changed. In one of the newer forms, for example, a psychotherapist may interpret the ego's symbols in a nightmare, and then use them to prove that the nightmare is real. Having made it real, he then attempts to dispel its effects by depreciating the importance of the dreamer. This would be a healing approach if the dreamer were also identified as unreal. Yet if the dreamer is equated with the mind, the mind's corrective power through the Holy Spirit is denied. This is a contradiction even in the ego's terms, and one which it usually notes even in its confusion (T.p.171).

## VIII. GRANDEUR VERSUS GRANDIOSITY

1. Grandeur is of God, and only of Him. Therefore, it is in you. Whenever you become aware of it, however dimly, you abandon the

ego automatically, because in the presence of the grandeur of God the meaninglessness of the ego becomes perfectly apparent. When this occurs, even though it does not understand it, the ego believes that its "enemy" has struck, and attempts to offer gifts to induce you to return to its "protection." Self-inflation is the only offering it can make. The grandiosity of the ego is its alternative to the grandeur of God. Which will you choose?

2. Grandiosity is always a cover for despair. It is without hope because it is not real. It is an attempt to counteract your littleness, based on the belief that the littleness is real. Without this belief, grandiosity is meaningless, and you could not possibly want it. The essence of grandiosity is competiveness, because it always involves attack. It is a delusional attempt to outdo, but not to undo. We said before that the ego vacillates between suspiciousness and viciousness. It remains suspicious as long as you despair yourself. It shifts to viciousness when you decide not to tolerate self-abasement, and seek relief. Then it offers you the illusion of attack as a solution.

3. The ego does not understand the difference between grandeur and grandiosity, because it sees no difference between miracle impulses and ego-alien beliefs of its own. I told you that the ego is aware of threat to its existence, but makes no distinctions between these two very different kinds of threat. Its profound sense of vulnerability renders it incapable of judgment except in terms of attack. When the ego experiences threat, its only decision is whether to attack now or to withdraw to attack later. If you accept its offer of grandiosity it will attack immediately. If you do not, it will wait (T.pp.177–178).

9. Can your grandeur be arrogant when God himself witnesses to it? What can be real that has no witnesses? What good can come of it? If no good can come of it, then the Holy Spirit cannot

use it. What he cannot transform to the will of God does not exist at all. Grandiosity is delusional because it is used to replace your grandeur. Yet what God has created cannot be replaced. God is incomplete without you because His grandeur is total, and you cannot be missing from it.

10. You are altogether irreplaceable in the Mind of God. No one else can fill your part in it, and while you leave your part of it empty, your eternal place waits for your return. God, through His voice, reminds you of it, and God Himself keeps your extensions safe within it. Yet you do not know them until you return to them. You cannot replace the Kingdom, and you cannot replace yourself. God, who knows your value, would not have it so. Your value is in God's mind, and therefore not in yours alone. To accept yourself as God created you cannot be arrogance, because it is the denial of arrogance. To accept your littleness is arrogant, because it means that you believe your evaluation of yourself is truer than God's.

11. Yet if truth is indivisible, your evaluation of yourself must be God's. You did not establish your value and it needs no defense. Nothing can attack it nor prevail over it. It does not vary. It merely is. Ask the Holy Spirit what it is and He will tell you, but do not be afraid of His answer, because it comes from God. It is an exalted answer because of its Source, but the Source is true and so is its answer. Listen and do not question what you hear, for God does not deceive. He would have you replace the ego's belief in littleness with His own exalted answer to what you are, so that you can cease to question it and know it for what it is.

## V. BEYOND PERCEPTION

1. I have said that the abilities you possess are only shadows of your real strength, and that perception, which is inherently judgmental, was introduced only after the separation. No one has

> **Sacrifice:** a central belief in the ego's thought system:; someone must lose if another is to gain; the principle of giving up in order to receive (giving to get); e.g., in order to receive God's love we must pay a price, usually in the form of suffering to expiate our guilt (sin); in order to receive another's love, we must pay for it though the special love bargains; the reversal of the principle of salvation or justice: no one loses and everyone gains. (Gloss., p. 179).

been sure of anything since. I have also made it clear that the resurrection was the means for the return to knowledge, which was accomplished by the union of my will with the Father's. We can now establish a distinction that will clarify some of our subsequent statements.

2. Since the separation, the words "create" and "make" have become confused. When you make something, you do so out of a specific sense of lack or need. Anything made for a specific purpose has no true generalizability. When you make something to fill a perceived lack, you are tacitly implying that you believe in the separation. The ego has invented many ingenious thought systems for this purpose. None of them is creative; inventiveness is wasted effort even in its most ingenious form. The highly specific nature of invention is not worthy of the abstract creativity of God's creations.

3. Knowing, as we have already observed, does not lead to doing. The confusion between your real creation and what you have made of yourself is so profound that it has become literally

impossible for you to know anything. Knowledge is always stable, and it is quite evident that you are not. Nevertheless, you are perfectly stable as God created you. In this sense, when your behavior is unstable, you are disagreeing with God's idea of your creation. You can do this if you choose, but you would hardly want to do it if you were in your right mind.

4. The fundamental question you continually ask yourself cannot properly be directed to yourself at all. You keep asking what it is you are. This implies that the answer is not only one you know, but is also one that is up to you to supply. Yet you cannot perceive yourself correctly. You have no image to be perceived. The word "image" is always perception-related, and not a part of knowledge. Images are symbolic and stand for something else. The idea of "changing your image" recognizes the power of perception but also implies that there is nothing stable to know (T.p.44).

5. Knowing is not open to interpretation. You may try to "interpret" meaning, but this is always open to error because it refers to the perception of meaning. Such incongruities are the result of attempts to regard yourself as separated and unseparated at the same time. It is impossible to make so fundamental a confusion without increasing your overall confusion still further. Your mind may have become very ingenious, but as always happens when method and content are separated, it is utilized in a futile attempt to escape from an inescapable impasse, and ingenuity is totally divorced from knowledge, because knowledge does not require ingenuity. Ingenious thinking is not the truth that shall set you free, but you are free of the need to engage in it when you are willing to let it go.

6. Prayer is a way of asking for something. It is the medium of miracles, but the only meaningful prayer is for forgiveness, because those who have been forgiven have everything. Once forgiveness has been accepted, prayer in the usual sense becomes utterly meaningless. The prayer for forgiveness is nothing more than a request that you may be able to recognize what you already have. In electing

perception instead of knowledge, you placed yourself in a position where you could resemble your Father only by perceiving miraculously. You have lost the knowledge that you yourself are a miracle of God. Creation is your Source and your only real function.

7. The statement "God created man in his own image and likeness" needs reinterpretation. "Image" can be understood as "thought" and "likeness" as "of a like quality." God did create Spirit in His own thought and of a quality like to His own. There is nothing else. Perception, on the other hand, is impossible without a belief in "more" and "less." At every level it involves selectivity. Perception is a continual process of accepting and rejecting, organizing and reorganizing, and shifting and changing. Evaluation is an essential part of perception, because judgments are necessary in order to select.

8. What happens to perceptions if there are no judgments and nothing but perfect equality? Perception becomes impossible (T.p.45).

# THE UNHEALTHY ENNEATYPE CONTROLLER ACCORDING TO A COURSE IN MIRACLES

*Unhealthy Controllers are callous to the feelings and concerns of others. They up the ante to develop megalomaniacal delusions of grandeur of themselves and become impulsively tyrannical, bullying, and willfully ruthless.*

## Chapter 9
## THE ACCEPTANCE OF THE ATONEMENT

### I. THE ACCEPTANCE OF REALITY

1. Fear of the will of God is one of the strangest beliefs the human mind has ever made. It could not possibly have occurred unless the mind were already profoundly split, making it possible for it to be afraid of what it really is. Reality cannot "threaten" anything except illusions, since reality can only uphold truth. The very fact that the will of God, which is what you are, is perceived as fearful, demonstrates that you are afraid of what you are. It is not, then, the will of God of which you are afraid, but yours.

2. Your will is not the ego's, and that is why the ego is against you. What seems to be the fear of God is really the fear of your own reality. It is impossible to learn anything consistently in a state of panic. If the purpose of this course is to help you remember what you are, and if you believe that what you are is fearful, then it must follow that you will not learn this course. Yet the reason for the course is that you do not know what you are.

3. If you do not know what your reality is, why would you be so sure that it is fearful? The association of truth and fear, which would be highly artificial at the most, is particularly inappropriate

in the minds of those who do not know what truth is. All this could mean is that you are arbitrarily associating something beyond your awareness with something you do not want. It is evident, then, that you are judging something of which you are totally unaware. You have set up this strange situation so that it is impossible to escape from it without a guide who does know what your reality is. The purpose of this guide is merely to remind you of what you want. He is not attempting to force an alien will upon you. He is merely making every possible effort; within the limits you impose on Him, to reestablish your own will in your awareness.

4. You have imprisoned your will beyond your own awareness, where it remains, but cannot help you. When I said that the Holy Spirit's function is to sort out the true from the false in your mind, I meant that he has the power to look into what you have (T.p.160).In the Unhealthy Controllers' relentless aggression, they can brutally destroy everything that does not conform to their will or way of thinking. They feel invulnerable while playing out their violence in murderousness.

6. Egos can clash in any situation, but spirits cannot clash at all. If you perceive a teacher as merely "a larger ego" you will be afraid, because to enlarge an ego would be to increase anxiety about separation. I will teach with you and live with you if you will think with me, but my goal will always be to absolve you finally from the need for a teacher. This is the opposite of the ego-oriented teacher's goal. He is concerned with the effect of his ego on other egos, and therefore interprets their interaction as a means of ego preservation. I would not be able to devote myself to teaching if I believed this, and you will not be a devoted teacher as long as you believe it. I am constantly being perceived as a teacher to be exalted or rejected, but I do not accept either perception for myself.

7. Your worth is not established by teaching or learning; your worth is established by God. As long as you dispute this, everything

you do will be fearful, particularly any situation that lends itself to the belief in superiority and inferiority. Teachers must be patient and repeat their lessons until they are learned. I am willing to do this, because I have no right to set your learning limits for you. Again, nothing you do or think or wish or make is necessary to establish your worth. This point is not debatable except in delusions. Your ego is never at stake because God did not create it. Your spirit is never at stake because He did. Any confusion on this point is delusional, and no form of devotion is possible as long as this delusion lasts.

8. The ego tries to exploit all situations into forms of praise for itself in order to overcome its doubts. It will remain doubtful as long as you believe in its existence. You who made it cannot trust it, because in your right mind you realize it is not real. The only sane solution is not to try to change reality, which is indeed a fearful attempt, but to accept it as it is. You are part of reality, which stands unchanged beyond the reach of your ego but within easy reach of spirit. When you are afraid, be still and know that God is real, and you are His beloved Son in whom he is well pleased. Do not let your ego dispute this, because the ego cannot know what is as far beyond its reach as you are (T.p.54).

9. God is not the author of fear. You are. You have chosen to create unlike Him, and have therefore made fear for yourself. You are not at peace because you are not fulfilling your function. God gave you a very lofty function that you are not meeting. Your ego has chosen to be afraid instead of meeting it. When you awaken you will not be able to understand this, because it is literally incredible. Do not believe the incredible now. Any attempt to increase its believableness is merely to postpone the inevitable. The word "inevitable" is fearful to the ego, but joyous to the spirit. God is inevitable, and you cannot avoid Him any more than He can avoid you.

10. The ego is afraid of the spirit's joy, because once you have experienced it you will withdraw all protection from the ego, and

become totally without investment in fear. Your investment is great now because fear is a witness to the separation, and your ego rejoices when you witness to it. Leave it behind! Do not listen to it and do not preserve it. Listen only to God, who is as incapable of deception as is the spirit He created. Release yourself and release others. Do not present a false and unworthy picture of yourself to others, and do not accept such a picture of them yourself.

11. The ego has built a shabby and unsheltering home for you, because it cannot build otherwise. Do not try to make this impoverished house stand. Its weakness is your strength. Only God could make a home that is worthy of His creations, who have chosen to leave it empty by their own dispossession. Yet His home will stand forever, and is ready for you when you choose to enter it. Of this you can be wholly certain. God is as incapable of creating the perishable as the ego is of making the eternal.

## Chapter 4
## *THE ILLUSIONS OF THE EGO*

...of your spirit you can do everything for the salvation of both. Humility is a lesson for the ego, not for the spirit. Spirit is beyond humility, because it recognizes its radiance and gladly sheds its light everywhere. The meek shall inherit the Earth because their egos are humble, and this gives them truer perception. The Kingdom of Heaven is the spirit's right, whose beauty and dignity are far beyond doubt, beyond perception, and stand forever as the mark of the love of God for His creations, who are wholly worthy of Him and only of Him. Nothing else is sufficiently worthy to be a gift for a creation of God Himself.

13. I will substitute for your ego if you wish, but never for your spirit. A father can safely leave a child with an elder brother who has shown himself responsible, but this involves no confusion about

the child's origin. The brother can protect the child's body and his ego, but he does not confuse himself with the father because he does this. I can be entrusted with your body and your ego only because this enables you not to be concerned with them, and lets me teach you their unimportance. I could not understand their importance to you if I had not once been tempted to believe in them myself. Let us undertake to learn this lesson together so we can be free of them together. I need devoted teachers who share my aim of healing the mind. Spirit is far beyond the need of your protection or mine. Remember this:

In this world you need not have tribulation because I have overcome the world. That is why you should be of good cheer (T.p.56).

9. Myths and magic are closely associated, since myths are usually related to ego origins, and magic to the powers the ego ascribes to itself. Mythological systems generally include some account of "the creation" and associate this with its particular form of magic. The so-called "battle for survival" is only the ego's struggle to preserve itself, and its interpretation of its own beginning. This beginning is usually associated with physical birth, because it is hard to maintain that the ego existed before that point in time. The more "religiously" ego-oriented may believe that the soul existed before, and will continue to exist after a temporary lapse into ego life. Some even believe that the soul will be punished for this lapse. However, salvation does not apply to spirit, which is not in danger and does not need to be salvaged.

10. Salvation is nothing more than "right-mindedness," which is not the one-mindedness of the Holy Spirit, but which must be achieved before one-mindedness is restored. Right-mindedness leads to the next step automatically, because right perception is uniformly without attack, and therefore wrong-mindedness is obliterated. The ego cannot survive without judgment, and is laid aside accordingly. The mind then has only one direction in which it can

move. Its direction is always automatic, because it cannot but be dictated by the thought system to which it adheres.

11. It cannot be emphasized too often that correcting perception is merely a temporary expedient. It is necessary only because misperception is a block to knowledge, while accurate perception is a stepping stone toward it. The whole value of right perception lies in the inevitable realization that all perception is unnecessary. This removes the block entirely. You may ask how this is possible as long as you appear to be living in this world. That is a reasonable question. You must be careful, however, that you really understand it. Who is the "you" who are living in this world? Spirit is immortal, and immortality is a constant state. It is as true now as it ever was or ever will be, because it implies no change at all. It is not a continuum, nor is it understood by being compared to an opposite. Knowledge never involves comparisons. That is its main difference from everything else the mind can grasp (T.pp.59–60).

2. There have been many healers who did not heal themselves. They have not moved mountains by their faith because their faith was not whole. Some of them have healed the sick at times, but they have not raised the dead. Unless the healer heals himself, he cannot believe that there is no order of difficulty in miracles. He has not learned that every mind God created is equally worthy of being healed because God created it whole. You are merely asked to return to God the mind as He created it. He asks you only for what He gave, knowing that this giving will heal you. Sanity is wholeness, and the sanity of your brothers is yours.

3. Why should you listen to the endless insane calls you think are made upon you, when you can know the voice of God is in you? God commended His spirit to you, and asks that you commend yours to Him. He wills to keep it in perfect peace, because you are of one mind and in spirit with Him. Excluding yourself from the Atonement is the ego's last-ditch defense of its own existence. It

reflects both the ego's need to separate, and your willingness to side with its separateness. This willingness means that you do not want to be healed.

4. But the time is now. You have not been asked to work out the plan of salvation yourself because, as I told you before, the remedy could not be of your making. God Himself gave you the perfect correction for everything you made that is not in accord with His holy will. I am making His plan perfectly explicit to you, and will also tell you of your part in it, and how urgent it is to fulfill it. God weeps at the "sacrifice" of His children who believe they are lost to Him.

5. Whenever you are not wholly joyous, it is because you have reacted with a lack of love to one of God's creations. Perceiving this as "sin," you become defensive because you expect attack. The decision to react in this way is yours, and can therefore be undone . (T.p.89).It can not be undone by repentance in the usual sense

... because this implies guilt. If you allow yourself to feel guilty, you will reinforce the error rather than allow it to be undone for you.

6. Decision cannot be difficult. This is obvious, if you realize that you must already have decided not to be wholly joyous if that is how you feel. Therefore, the first step in the undoing is to recognize that you actively decided wrongly, but can as actively decide otherwise. Be very firm with yourself in this, and keep yourself fully aware that the undoing process, which does not come from you, is nevertheless within you because God placed it there. Your part is merely to return your thinking to the point at which the error was made, and give it over to the Atonement in peace. Say this to yourself as sincerely as you can, remembering that the Holy Spirit will respond fully to your slightest invitation:

"I must have decided wrongly, because I am not at peace. I made the decision myself, but I can also decide otherwise, because I want to be at peace. I do not feel guilty, because the Holy Spirit will undo all the consequences of my wrong decision if I will let Him. I choose to let Him, by allowing Him to decide for God for me" (T.p.90).

*Unhealthy Controllers are the sociopaths of the world who litigiously break people with the law unlawfully. They are the sociopaths who inhabit the prisons of the world. Often when they wind up in prison or in jail, they commit suicide because they cannot stand being "out of control." Control is their only currency of reality.*

3.. The "evil" past has nothing to do with God. He did not create it and He does not maintain it. God does not believe in retribution. His mind does not create that way. He does not hold your "evil" deeds against you. Is it likely that He would hold them against you? Is it likely that He would hold them against me? Be very sure that you recognize how utterly impossible this assumption is, and how entirely it arises from projection. This kind of error is responsible for a host of related errors, including the belief that God rejected Adam and forced him out of the Garden of Eden. It is also why you may believe from time to time that I am misdirecting you. I have made every effort to use words that are almost impossible to distort, but it is always possible to twist symbols around if you wish.

4. Sacrifice is a notion totally unknown to God. It arises solely from fear, and frightened people can be vicious. Sacrificing in any way is a violation of my injunction that you should be merciful even as your Father in Heaven is merciful. It has been hard for many Christians to realize that this applies to themselves. Good teachers never terrorize their students. To terrorize is to attack, and this results in rejection of what the teacher offers. The result is learning failure.

5. I have been correctly referred to as "the Lamb of God who taketh away the sins of the world," but those who represent the

lamb as bloodstained do not understand the meaning of the symbol. Correctly understood, it is a very simple symbol that speaks of my innocence. The lion and the lamb lying down together symbolize that strength and innocence are not in conflict, but naturally live in peace. "Blessed are the pure in heart, for they shall see God" is another way of saying the same thing. A pure mind knows the truth and this is its strength. It does not confuse destruction with innocence because it associates innocence with strength, not with weakness.

6. Innocence is incapable of sacrificing anything, because the innocent mind has everything and strives only to protect its wholeness. It cannot project. It can only honor other minds, because honor is the natural greeting of the truly loved to others who are like them. The lamb "taketh away the sins of the world" in the sense that the state of innocence, or grace, is one in which the meaning of the Atonement is perfectly apparent.


8. The Atonement is entirely unambiguous. It is perfectly clear because it exists in light. Only the attempts to shroud it in darkness have made it inaccessible to those who do not choose to see (T.p.36).


7. The statement "God created man in his own image and likeness" needs reinterpretation. "Image" can be understood a "thought" and "likeness" as "of a like quality." God did create Spirit in His own thought and of a quality like to His own. There is nothing else. Perception, on the other hand, is impossible without a belief in "more" and "less." At every level it involves selectivity. Perception is a continual process of accepting and rejecting, organizing and reorganizing, and shifting and changing. Evaluation is

an essential part of perception, because judgments are necessary in order to select.

8. What happens to perceptions if there are no judgments and there is nothing but perfect equality? Perception becomes impossible (T.p.45).

7. I love you for the truth in you, as God does. Your deceptions may deceive you, but they cannot deceive me. Knowing what you are, I cannot doubt you. I hear only the Holy Spirit in you, who speaks to me through you. You will be answered as you hear the answer in everyone. Do not listen to anything else or you will not hear truly.

8. Believe in your brothers because I believe in you, and you will learn that my belief in you is justified. Believe in me by believing in them, for the sake of what God gave them. They will answer you if you learn to ask only truth of them. Do not ask for blessings without blessing them, for only in this way can you learn how blessed you are. By following this way, you are seeking the truth in you. This is not going beyond yourself, but toward yourself. Hear only God's answer in His Sons, and you are answered.

9. To disbelieve is to side against or to attack. To believe is to accept, and to side with. To believe is not to be credulous, but to accept and appreciate. What you do not believe you do not appreciate, and you cannot be grateful for what you do not value. There is a price you will pay for judgment, because judgment is the setting of a price, and as you set it you will pay it.

10. If paying is equated with getting, you will set the price low but demand a high return. You will have forgotten, however, that to price is to value, so that your return is in proportion to your judgment of worth. If paying is associated with giving, it cannot be

perceived as loss, and the reciprocal relationship of giving and receiving will be recognized. The price will then be set high, because of the value of the return. The price for getting is to lose sight of value, making it inevitable that you will not value what you receive. Valuing it little, you will not appreciate it and you will not want it.

11. Never forget, then, that you set the value on what you receive (T.p.165).

6. The children of light cannot abide in darkness, for darkness is not in them. Do not be deceived by the dark comforters, and never let them enter the mind of God's Son, for they have no place in His temple. When you are tempted to deny Him, remember that there are no other gods that you can place before him, and accept His will for you in peace. For you cannot accept it otherwise.

7. Only God's Comforter can comfort you. In the quiet of His temple, He waits to give you the peace that is yours. Give His peace that you may enter the temple and find it waiting for you, but be holy in the presence of God, or you will not know that you are there. For what is unlike God cannot enter His mind, because it was not His thought and therefore does not belong to Him. Your mind must be as pure as His, if you would know what belongs to you. Guard carefully His temple, for He Himself dwells there and abides in peace. You cannot enter God's presence with the dark companions beside you, but you also cannot enter alone. All your brothers must enter with you, for until you have accepted them you cannot enter; for you cannot understand wholeness unless you are whole, and no part of the Son can be excluded if he would know the wholeness of His Father.

8. In your mind you can accept the whole Sonship and bless it with the light your Father gave it. Then you will be worthy to dwell in the temple with Him, because it is your will not to be alone. God blessed His Son forever. If you will bless Him in time, you will be in

eternity. Time cannot separate you from God if you use it on behalf of the eternal (T.p.200).

## LESSON 304 (ARCHETYPE 304)
*Let not my world obscure the sight of Christ.*

1. I can obscure my holy sight, if I intrude my world upon it. Nor can I behold the holy sights Christ looks upon, unless it is His vision that I use. Perception is a mirror, not a fact; and what I look on is my state of mind, reflected outward. I would bless the world by looking on it through the eyes of Christ, and I will look upon the certain signs that all my sins have been forgiven me.

2. You lead me from the darkness to the light; from sin to holiness. Let me forgive and thus receive salvation for the world. It is Your gift, my Father, given me to offer Your Holy Son, that He may find again the memory of You, and of Your Son as You created Him.

## LESSON 233 (GROWTH LINE)
*I give my life to God to guide today.*

1. Father, I give You all my thoughts today. I would have none of mine. In place of them, give me Your own. I give You all my acts as well, that I may do Your will instead of seeking goals which cannot be obtained, and wasting time in vain imaginings. Today I come to You. I will step back and merely follow You. Be You the Guide, and I the follower who questions not the wisdom of the Infinite, nor Love whose tenderness I cannot comprehend, but which is yet Your perfect gift to me.

2. Today we have one Guide to lead us on, and as we walk together, we will give this day to Him with no reserve at all. This is His day, and so it is a day of countless gifts and mercies unto us.

## LESSON 310  ( DEMATERIALIZATION LINE)
*In fearlessness and love I spend today.*

1. This day, my Father, would I spend with You, as You have chosen all my days should be, and what I will experience is not of time at all. The joy that comes to me is not of days nor hours, for it comes from Heaven to Your Son. This day will be Your sweet reminder to remember You. Your gracious calling to Your Holy Son, the sign Your grace has come to me, and that it is Your will that I be set free today.

2. We spend this day together, you and I, and all the world joins with us in our song of thankfulness and joy to Him who gave salvation to us, and who set us free. We are restored to peace and holiness. There is no room in us for fear today, for we have welcomed love into our hearts.

## CHAPTER 9
# THE PEACEMAKER

"The holy instant does not come from your little willingness alone. It is always the result of your small willingness combined with the unlimited power of God's will."

(T.355/381 ACIM)

# A HEALTHY PEACEMAKER "9"
# ACCORDING TO
# A COURSE IN MIRACLES

I will be still an instant and go home (T.p.339).

*Healthy Peacemakers deep down are nice people who are autonomous and content. They radiate fulfillment in their emotional stability. They are optimistic in their equanimity and they are supportive of others. They radiate a sense of "divine angelhood."*

The deep contentment of self-possession within Healthy Peacemakers is "safe harbor" for anyone who trusts their presence of unpretentiousness and engaging receptivity. They embrace all of life with equal weight of meaning. This leads to their sense of equalizing all people and ideas in their own sense of personal balance where nothing is any more important than anything else. This also leads to their sense of indulgence as they have this sense that everything is "all right" because their sense of peace with the world is endogenous.

## LESSON 182

*I will be still an instant and go home.*

1. This world you seem to live in is not home to you, and somewhere in your mind you know that this is true. A memory of home keeps haunting you, as if there were a place that called you to return, although you do not recognize the voice, nor what it is the voice reminds you of. Yet still you feel an alien here, from somewhere all unknown. Nothing so definite that you could say with certainty you are an exile here. Just a persistent feeling, sometimes not more than

a tiny throb, at other times hardly remembered, actively dismissed, but surely to return to mind again.

2. No one but knows whereof we speak. Yet some try to put by their suffering in games they play to occupy their time, and keep their sadness from them. Others will deny that they are sad, and do not recognize their tears at all. Still others will maintain that what we speak of is illusion, not to be considered more than but a dream. Yet who, in simple honesty, without defensiveness and self-deception, would deny he understands the words we speak?

3. We speak today for everyone who walks this world, for he is not at home. He goes uncertainly about in endless search, seeking in darkness what he cannot find; not recognizing what it is he seeks. A thousand homes he makes, yet none contents his restless mind. He does not understand he builds in vain. The home he seeks cannot be made by him. There is no substitute for Heaven. All he ever made was hell (T.p.339).

4. Perhaps you think it is your childhood home that you would find again. The childhood of your body, and its place of shelter, are a memory now so distorted that you merely hold a picture of a past that never happened. Yet there is a child in you who seeks his Father's house, and knows that He is alien here. This childhood is eternal, with an innocence that will endure forever. Where this child shall go is holy ground. It is His Holiness that lights up Heaven, and that brings to Earth the pure reflection of the light above, wherein are Earth and Heaven joined as one.

5. It is this child in you your Father knows as His own Son. It is this child who knows His Father. He desires to go home so deeply, so unceasingly, His voice cries unto you to let Him rest a while. He does not ask for more than just a few instants of respite, just an interval in which He can return to breathe again the holy air that fills His Father's house. You are His home as well. He will return, but give Him just a little time to be Himself, within the peace that is His home, resting in silence and in peace and love.

6. This child needs your protection. He is far from home. He is so little that He seems so easily shut out, His tiny voice so readily obscured, His call for help almost unheard amid the grating sounds and harsh and rasping noises of the world. Yet does He know that in you still abides His sure protection. You will fail Him not. He will go home, and you along with Him.

7. This child is your defenselessness, your strength. He trusts in you. He came because He knew you would not fail. He whispers of His home unceasingly to you. For He would bring you back with Him, that He Himself might stay, and not return again where He does not belong, and where He lives an outcast in a world of alien thoughts. His patience has no limits. He will wait until you hear His gentle voice within you, calling you to let Him go in peace, along with you, to where He is at home and you with Him.

8. When you are still an instant, when the world recedes from you, when valueless ideas cease to have value in your restless mind, then will you hear His voice. So poignantly He calls to you that you will not resist Him longer. In that instant He will take you to His home, and you will stay with Him in stillness, silent and at peace beyond all words, untouched by fear and doubt, sublimely certain that you are at home (T.p.339–340).

9. Rest with Him frequently today, for He was willing to become a little child that you might learn of Him how strong is he who comes without defenses, offering only love's messages to those who think he is their enemy. He holds the might of Heaven in His hand and calls them friend, and gives His strength to them, that they may see He would be Friend to them. He asks that they protect Him, for His home is far away and He will not return to it alone.

10. Christ is reborn as but a little Child each time a wanderer would leave his home; for he must learn that what he would protect is but this child, who comes defenseless and who is protected by defenselessness. Go home with him from time to time today. You are as much an alien here as He is.

11. Take time today to lay aside your shield which profits nothing, and lay down the spear and sword you raised against an enemy without existence. Christ has called you friend and brother. He has even come to ask your help in letting Him go home today, completed and completely. He has come as does a little child, who must beseech his father for protection and for love. He rules the universe, and yet He asks unceasingly that you return with Him, and take illusions as your gods no more.

12. You have not lost your innocence. It is for this you yearn. This is your heart's desire. This is the voice you hear, and this the call which cannot be denied. The holy Child remains with you. His home is yours. Today He gives you His defenselessness, and you accept it in exchange for all the toys of battle you have made; and now the way is open, and the journey has an end in sight at last. Be still an instant and go home with Him, and be at peace a while (T.p.340–341).

## IV. THE OBSTACLES TO PEACE

1. As peace extends from deep inside yourself to embrace all the Sonship and give it rest, it will encounter many obstacles. Some of them you will try to impose. Others will seem to arise from elsewhere: from your brothers, and from various aspects of the world outside. Yet peace will gently cover them, extending past completely unencumbered. The extension of the Holy Spirit's purpose from your relationship to others, to bring them gently in, is the way in which He will bring means and goal in line. The peace He laid, deep within you and your brother will quietly extend to every aspect of your life, surrounding you and your brother with glowing happiness and the calm awareness of complete protection; and you will carry its message of love and safety and freedom to everyone who draws nigh unto your temple where healing waits for him. You will not wait to give Him this, for you will call to Him and He will

answer you, recognizing your call for the call of God; and you will draw Him in and give Him rest, as it was given you.

2. All this will you do; yet the peace that already lies deeply within must first expand, and flow across the obstacles you placed before it. This will you do, for nothing undertaken with the Holy Spirit remains unfinished. You can indeed be sure of nothing you see outside you, but of this you can be sure. The Holy Spirit asks that you offer Him a resting place where you will rest in Him. He answered you, and entered your relationship. Would you not now return His graciousness, and enter into a relationship with Him? for it is He who offered your relationship the gift of holiness, without which it would have been forever impossible to appreciate your brother (T.p.406–407).

3. The gratitude you owe to Him, He asks but that you receive for Him; and when you look with gentle graciousness upon your brother, you are beholding Him; for you are looking where He is, and not apart from Him. You cannot see the Holy Spirit, but you can see your brothers truly; and the light in them will show you all that you need to see. When the peace in you has been extended to encompass everyone, the Holy Spirit's function here will be accomplished. What need is there for seeing, then? When God has taken the last step Himself, the Holy Spirit will gather all the thanks and gratitude that you have offered Him, and lay them gently before His Creator in the name of His most Holy Son; and the Father will accept them in His name. What need is there of seeing, in the presence of His gratitude?

## A. THE FIRST OBSTACLE: THE DESIRE TO GET RID OF IT

1. The first obstacle that peace must flow across is your desire to get rid of it; for it cannot extend unless you keep it. You are the center from which it radiated outward, to call the others in. You are

its home, its tranquil dwelling place from which it gently reaches out, but never leaving you.I f you would make it homeless how can it abide in the Son Of God? If it would spread across the whole creation, it must begin with you, and from you to reach everyone who calls, and bring him rest by joining you.

2. Why would you want peace homeless? What do you think that it must dispossess to dwell with you? What seems to be the cost you are so unwilling to pay? The little barrier of sand still stands between you and your brother. Would you reinforce it now? You are not asked to let it go for yourself alone. Christ asks it of you for Himself. He would bring peace to everyone, and how can He do this except through you? Would you let a little bank of sand, a wall of dust, a tiny seeming barrier, stand between your brothers and salvation? Yet this little remnant of attack you cherish still against your brother is the first obstacle the peace in you encounters in its going forth. This little wall of hatred would still oppose the Will of God, and keep it limited.

3. The Holy Spirit's purpose rests in peace within you. Yet you are still unwilling to let it join you wholly. You still oppose the Will of God, just by a little; and that little is a limit you would place upon the whole. God's Will is one, not many, but it has no opposition, for there is none beside it. What you would still contain behind your little barrier and keep separate from your brothers seems mightier than the universe, for it would hold back the universe and its Creator. This little wall would hide the purpose of Heaven, and keep it from Heaven (T.p.407–408).

4. Would you thrust salvation away from the giver of salvation? For such have you become. Peace could no more depart from you than from God. Fear not this little obstacle. It cannot contain the Will of God. Peace will flow across it, and join you without hindrance. Salvation cannot be withheld from you. It is your purpose. You cannot choose apart from this. You have no purpose apart from your brother, nor apart from the one you asked the Holy Spirit to

share with you. The little wall will fall away so quietly beneath the wings of peace; for peace will send its messengers from you to all the world, and barriers will fall away before their coming as easily as those that you interpose will be surmounted.

5. To overcome the world is no more difficult than to surmount your little wall; for in the miracle of your holy relationship, without this barrier, is every miracle contained. There is no order of difficulty in miracles, for they are all the same. Each is a gentle winning over from the appeal of guilt to the appeal of love. How can this fail to be accomplished, wherever it is undertaken? Guilt can raise no real barriers against it, and all that seems to stand between you and your brother must fall away because of the appeal you answered. From you who answered, He who answered you would call. His home is in your holy relationship. Do not attempt to stand between Him and His holy purpose, for it is yours; but let Him quietly extend the miracle of your relationship to everyone contained in it as it was given.

6. There is a hush in Heaven, a happy expectancy, a little pause of gladness in acknowledgment of the journey's end; for Heaven knows you well, as you know Heaven. No illusions stand between you and your brother now. Look not upon the little wall of shadows. The sun has risen over it. How can a shadow keep you from the sun? No more can you be kept by shadows from the light in which illusions end. Such was the journey; such it's ending. And in the goal of truth which you accepted, must all illusions end.

7. The little insane wish to get rid of Him whom you invited in and push Him out must produce conflict. As you look upon the world, this little wish, uprooted and floating aimlessly, can land and settle briefly upon anything, for it has no purpose now. Before the Holy Spirit entered to abide with you it seemed to have a mighty purpose: the fixed and unchangeable dedication to sin and its results. Now it is aimless, wandering pointlessly, causing no more than tiny interruptions in love's appeal (T.pp.408–409).

8. This feather of a wish, this tiny illusion, this microscopic remnant of the belief in sin, is all that remains of what once seemed to be the world. It is no longer an unrelenting barrier to peace. Its pointless wandering makes its results appear to be more erratic and unpredictable than before. Yet what could be more unstable than a tightly organized delusional system? Its seeming stability is its pervasive weakness, which extends to everything. The variability the little remnant induces merely indicates its limited results.

9. How mighty can a little feather be before the great wings of truth? Can it oppose an eagle's flight, or hinder the advance of summer? Can it interfere with the effects of summer's sun upon a garden covered by the snow? See but how easily this little wisp is lifted up and carried away, never to return, and part with it in gladness, not regret. For it is nothing in itself, and stood for nothing when you had greater faith in its protection. Would you not rather greet the summer sun than fix your gaze upon a disappearing snowflake, and shiver in remembrance of the winter's cold? (T.p.409).

## I TRUST MY BROTHERS, WHO ARE ONE WITH ME.

1. Trusting your brothers is essential to establishing and holding up your faith in your ability to transcend doubt and lack of sure conviction in yourself. When you attack a brother, you proclaim that he is limited by what you have perceived in him. You do not look beyond his errors. Rather, they are magnified, becoming blocks to your awareness of the self that lies beyond your own mistakes, and past his seeming sins as well as yours.

2. Perception has a focus. It is this that gives consistency to what you see. Change but this focus, and what you behold will change accordingly. Your vision now will shift, to give support to the intent which has replaced the one you held before. Remove your

focus on your brother's sins, and you experience the peace that comes from faith in sinlessness. This faith receives its only sure support from what you see in others past their sins; for their mistakes, if focused on, are witnesses to sins in you; and you will not transcend their sight and see the sinlessness that lies beyond.

3. Therefore, in practicing today, we first let all such little focuses give way to our great need to let our sinlessness become apparent. We instruct our minds that it is this we seek, and only this, for just a little while. We do not care about our future goals, and what we saw an instant previous has no concern for us within this interval of time, wherein we practice changing our intent. We seek for innocence and nothing else. We seek for it with no concern but now (W.337).

4. A major hazard to success has been involvement with your past and future goals. You have been quite preoccupied with how extremely different the goals this course is advocating are from those you held before; and you have also been dismayed by the depressing and restricting thought that even if you should succeed, you will inevitably lose your way again.

5. How could this matter? The past is gone; the future but imagined. These concerns are but defenses against present change of focus in perception, nothing more. We lay these pointless limitations by a little while. We do not look to past beliefs, and what we will believe will not intrude upon us now. We enter in the time of practicing with one intent: to look upon the sinlessness within.

6. We recognize that we have lost this goal if anger blocks our way in any form; and if a brother's sins occur to us, our narrowed focus will restrict pure sight, and turn our eyes upon our own mistakes, which we will magnify and call our "sins." So for a little while, without regard to past or future, should such blocks arise we will transcend them with instructions to our minds to change their focus, as we say:

"I trust my brothers, who are one with me."

7. And we will also use this thought to keep us safe throughout the day. We do not seek for long-range goals. As each obstruction seems to block the vision of our sinlessness, we seek but for surcease an instant from the misery the focus upon sin will bring and uncorrected will remain.

8. Nor do we ask for fantasies; for what we seek to look upon is really there, and as our focus goes beyond mistakes, we will behold a wholly sinless world. When seeing this is all we want to see, when this is all we seek for in the name of true perception, are the eyes of Christ inevitably ours. The love He feels for us becomes our own as well. This will become the only thing we see reflected in the world and in ourselves.

9. The world which once proclaimed our sins becomes the proof that we are sinless; and our love for everyone we look upon attests to our remembrance of the holy self which knows no sin; and never could conceive of anything without its sinlessness. We seek for this remembrance as we turn our minds to practicing today. We look neither ahead nor backward. We look straight into the present, and we give our trust to the experience we ask for now. Our sinlessness is but the Will of God. This instant is our willing one with His (T.pp.337–338).

## V. HERALDS OF ETERNITY

1. In this world, God's Son comes closest to himself in a holy relationship. There he begins to find the certainty his Father has in him, and there he finds his function of restoring his Father's laws to what was held outside them, and finding what was lost. Only in time can anything be lost, but never lost forever. So do the parts of God's Son gradually join in time, and with each joining is the end of time brought nearer. Each miracle of joining is a mighty herald of eternity. No one who has a single purpose, unified and

THE PEACEMAKER

sure, can be afraid; no one who shares his purpose with him cannot be one with him.

2. Each herald of eternity sings of the end of sin and fear. Each speaks in time of what is far beyond it. Two voices raised together call to the hearts of everyone, to let them beat as one; and in that single heartbeat is the unity of love proclaimed and given welcome. Peace to your holy relationship, which has the power to hold the unity of the Son of God together. You give to your brother for everyone, and in your gift is everyone made glad. Forget not who has given you the gifts you give, and through your not forgetting this, will you remember who gave the gifts to Him to give to you.

3. It is impossible to overestimate your brother's value. Only the ego does this, but all it means is that it wants the other for itself, and therefore values him too little. What is inestimable clearly cannot be evaluated. Do you recognize the fear that rises from the meaningless attempt to judge what lies so far beyond your judgment you cannot even see it? Judge not what is invisible to you or you will never see it, but wait in patience for its coming. It will be given you to see your brother's worth, when all you want from him is peace; and what you want for him you will receive (T.p.434).

4. How can you estimate the worth of him who offers peace to you? What would you want except his offering? His worth has been established by his Father, and you will recognize it as you receive his Father's gift through him. What is in him will shine brightly in your grateful vision, that you will merely love him and be glad. You will not think to judge him, for who would see the face of Christ and yet insist that judgment still has meaning; for this insistence is of those who do not see. Vision or judgment is your choice, but never both of these.

5. Your brother's body is as little use to you as it is to him. When it is used only as the Holy Spirit teaches, it has no function; for minds need not the body to communicate. The sight that sees the body has no use which serves the purpose of a holy relationship;

and while you look upon your brother thus, the means and end have not been brought in line. Why should it take so many holy instants to let this be accomplished, when one would do? There is but one. The little breath of eternity that runs through time like golden light is all the same; nothing before it, nothing afterward.

6. You look upon each holy instant as a different point in time. It never changes; all that it ever held or will ever hold is here right now. The past takes nothing from it, and the future will add no more. Here, then, is everything: here is the loveliness of your relationship, with means and end in perfect harmony already; here is the perfect faith that you will one day offer to your brother already offered you; and here the limitless forgiveness you will give him already given, the face of Christ you yet will look upon already seen.

7. Can you evaluate the giver of a gift like this? Would you exchange this gift for any other? This gift returns the laws of God to your remembrance; and merely by remembering them, the laws that held you prisoner to pain and death must be forgotten. This is no gift your brother's body offers you. The veil that hides the gift hides him as well. He is the gift, and yet he knows it not. No more do you, and yet have faith that He who sees the gift in you and your brother will offer and receive it for you both. Through His vision will you see it, and through His understanding recognize it and love it as your own (T.p.435).

8. Be comforted, and feel the Holy Spirit watching over you in love and perfect confidence in what He sees. He knows the Son of God, and shares His Father's certainty the universe rests in his gentle hands in safety and peace. Let us consider now what he must learn to share His Father's confidence in Him. What is he that the Creator of the universe should offer it to him and know it rests in safety? He looks upon himself not as His Father knows Him; and yet it is impossible the confidence of God should be misplaced (T.p.436).

2. Only minds communicate. Since the ego cannot obliterate the impulse to communicate because it is also the impulse to create, it can only teach you that the body can both communicate and create, and therefore does not need the mind. The ego thus tries to teach you that the body can act like the mind, and is therefore self-sufficient. Yet we have learned that behavior is not the level for either teaching or learning, since you can act in accordance with what you do not believe. To do this, however, will weaken you as a teacher and a learner because, as has been repeatedly emphasized, you teach what you do believe. An inconsistent lesson will be poorly taught and poorly learned. If you teach both sickness and healing, you are both a poor teacher and a poor learner.

3. Healing is the one ability everyone can develop, and must develop, if he is to be healed. Healing is the Holy Spirit's form of communication in this world, and the only one He accepts. He recognizes no other, because He does not accept the ego's confusion of mind and body. Minds can communicate, but they cannot hurt. The body in the service of the ego can hurt other bodies, but this cannot occur unless the body has already been confused with the mind. This situation, too, can be used either for healing or for magic, but you must remember that magic always involves the belief that healing is harmful. This belief is its totally insane premise, and so it proceeds accordingly.

4. Healing only strengthens. Magic always tries to weaken. Healing perceives nothing in the healer that everyone else does not share with him. Magic always sees something "special" in the healer, which he believes he can offer as a gift to someone who does not have it. He may believe that the gift comes from God to him, but it is quite evident that he does not understand God if he thinks he has something that others lack.

5. The Holy Spirit does not work by chance, and healing that is of Him always works. Unless the healer always heals by Him the

results will vary. Yet healing itself is consistent since only consistency is conflict-free, and only the conflict-free are whole. By accepting exceptions and acknowledging that he can sometimes heal and sometimes not, the healer is obviously accepting inconsistency. He is therefore in conflict, and is teaching conflict. Can anything of God not be for all and for always? Love is incapable of any exceptions. Only if there is fear does the idea of exceptions seem to be meaningful. T.p.120)

5. Whenever you are not wholly joyous, it is because you have reacted with a lack of love to one of God's creations. Perceiving this as "sin" you become defensive because you expect attack. The decision to react in this way is yours, and can therefore be undone. It cannot be undone by repentance in the usual sense, because this implies guilt. If you allow yourself to feel guilty, you will reinforce the error rather than allow it to be undone for you.

6. Decisions cannot be difficult. This is obvious, if you realize that you must already have decided not to be wholly joyous if that is how you feel. Therefore, the first step in the undoing is to recognize that you actively decided otherwise. Be very firm with yourself in this, and keep yourself fully aware that the undoing process, which does not come from you, is nevertheless within you because God placed it there. Your part is merely to return your thinking to the point at which the error was made, and give it over to the Atonement in peace. Say this to yourself as sincerely as you can, remembering that the Holy Spirit will respond fully to your slightest invitation:

7. *I must have decided wrongly, because I am not at peace. I made the decision myself, but I can also decide otherwise. I want to decide otherwise, because I want to be at peace. I do not feel guilty, because the Holy Spirit will undo all the consequences of my wrong decision if I will let him. I choose to let Him by allowing Him to decide for God for me* (T.pp.89–90).

## B. TO HAVE PEACE, TEACH PEACE TO LEARN IT

1. All who believe in separation have a basic fear of retaliation and abandonment. They believe in attack and rejection, so that is what they perceive and teach and learn. These insane ideas are clearly the result of dissociation and projection. What you teach you are, but it is quite apparent that you can teach wrongly, and can therefore teach yourself wrong. Many thought I was attacking them, even though it was apparent I was not. An insane learner learns strange lessons. What you must recognize is that when you do not share a thought system, you are weakening it. Those who believe in it therefore perceive this as an attack on them. This is because everyone identifies himself with his thought system, and every thought system centers on what you believe you are. If the center of the thought system is true, only truth extends from it; but if a lie is at its center, only deception proceeds from it.

2. All good teachers realize that only fundamental change will last, but they do not begin at that level. Strengthening motivation for change is their first and foremost goal. It is also their last and final one. Increasing motivation for change in the learner is all that a teacher need do to guarantee change. Change in motivation is a change of mind, and this will inevitably produce fundamental change because the mind is fundamental (T.p.106).

3. The first step in the reversal or undoing process is the undoing of the getting concept. Accordingly, the Holy Spirit's first lesson was

*"To have, give all to all."*

I said that this is apt to increase conflict temporarily, and we can clarify this still further now. At this point, the equality of having and being is not yet perceived. Until it is, having appears to be the opposite of giving. Therefore, the first lesson seems to contain a contradiction, since it is being learned by a conflicted mind. This means conflicting motivation, and so the lesson cannot be learned consistently as yet. Further, the mind of the learner projects its own conflict, and thus does not perceive consistency in the minds of others, making him suspicions of their motivations. This is the real reason why, in many respects, the first lesson is the hardest to learn. Still strongly aware of the ego in others, you are being taught to react to both as if what you do believe is not true.

4. Upside down as always, the ego perceives the first lesson as insane. In fact, this is its only alternative since the other possibility, which would be much less acceptable to it, would obviously be that it is insane. The ego's judgment, here as always, is predetermined by what it is. The fundamental change will still occur with the change of mind in the thinker. Meanwhile, the increasing clarity of the Holy Spirit's voice makes it impossible for the learner not to listen. For a time, then, he is receiving conflicting messages and accepting both.

5. The way out of conflict between two oppressing thought systems is clearly to choose one and relinquish the other. If you identify with your thought systems, and you cannot escape this, and if you accept two thought systems which are in complete disagreement, peace of mind is impossible. If you teach both, which you will surely do as long as you accept both, you are teaching conflict and learning it. Yet you do want peace, or you would not have called upon the voice for peace to help you. Its lesson is not insane; the conflict is.

6. There can be no conflict between sanity and insanity. Only one is true, and therefore only one is real. The ego tries to persuade you that it is up to you to decide which voice is true, but the Holy Spirit teaches you that truth was created by God, and your decision cannot change it. As you begin to realize the quiet power of the Holy Spirit's voice, and its perfect consistency, it must dawn on your mind that you are trying to undo a decision that was irrevocably made for you. That is why I suggested before that you remind yourself to allow the Holy Spirit to decide for God for you (T.p.107).

7. You are not asked to make insane decisions, although you can think you are. It must, however, be insane to believe that it is up

to you to decide what God's creations are. The Holy Spirit perceives the conflict exactly as it is. Therefore, His second lesson is:

*"To have peace, teach peace to learn it."*

8. This is still a preliminary step, since having and being are still not equated. It is, however, more advanced than the first step, which is really only the beginning of the thought reversal. The second step is a positive affirmation of what you want. This, then, is a step in the direction out of conflict, since it means that alternatives have been considered, and one has been chosen as more desirable. Nevertheless, the term "more desirable" still implies that the desirable has degrees. Therefore, although this step is essential for the ultimate decision, it is clearly not the final one. Lack of order of difficulty in miracles has not yet been accepted, because nothing is difficult that is wholly desired. To desire wholly is to create, and creating cannot be difficult if God Himself created you as a creator.

9. The second step, then, is still perceptual, although it is a giant step toward the unified perception that reflects God's knowing. As you take this step and hold this direction, you will be pushing toward the center of your thought system, where the fundamental change will occur. At the second step progress is intermittent, but the second step is easier than the first because it follows. Realizing that it must follow is a demonstration of a growing awareness that the Holy Spirit will lead you on (Gloss., p. 108).

## THE AVERAGE "9" ACCORDING TO A COURSE IN MIRACLES

I will be still an instant and go home (T.p.339).

*Average Peacemakers become fatalistic and tend to give up rather than make the effort to change circumstances. In their sense of equanimity of giving equal weight to circumstances that scotch the "smart outcome,"* they escape by living other people's lives to their own self-effacement. Thus they put themselves on "autopilot," approaching reckless abandon.

## I. IRRECONCILABLE BELIEFS

2. Do you not realize a war against yourself would be a war on God? Is victory conceivable? If it were, is this a victory that you would want? This is no war, only the mad belief the will of God can be attacked and overthrown. You may identify with this belief, but never will it be more than madness. Fear will reign in madness, and will seem to have replaced love there. This is the conflict's purpose, and to those who think that it is possible, the means seem real (T.p.486 2:8–11).

*Average Peacemakers in their suppressing anger will stagnate themselves and everyone and everything around them as they vortex down in self-imposed indecision, confusion, and regret for being helplessly immobile. They minimize problems to appease others in their resignation and fatalism. Everyone around them realizes the price of peace is too high when they realize the lost opportunities as a result of indecision, compromise, or living with the atmosphere of stubborn negativism that fosters the indecision. Average Peacemakers will live out what other people expect of them, even when they realize those same people "really" don't care about the Peacemakers' outcome. They coast into obliviousness and unresponsiveness.*

2. While you believe that bodies can unite, you will find guilt attractive and believe that sin is precious. For the belief that bodies limit minds leads to a perception of the world in which the proof of separation seems to be everywhere; and God and his creation seem to be split apart and overthrown (T.p.405 7:2).

*Average Peacemakers are apathetic, disengaged, and removed in their willful, stubborn complacency. They "will" not decide, and as a result live in a self-imposed state of indecision and confusion, making others mad at them for compromising too many opportunities for growth and development. This is their "class act" self-effacement. How can you teach someone the value of something he has deliberately thrown away? (T.p.68).*

## III. THE UNREALITY OF SIN

1. The attraction of guilt is found in sin, not error. Sin will be repeated because of this attraction. Fear can become so acute that the sin is denied the acting out; but while the guilt remains attractive the mind will suffer, and not let go of the idea of sin. Guilt still calls to it and the mind hears it, and yearns for it, making itself a willing captive to its sick appeal. Sin is an idea of evil that cannot be corrected, and yet will be forever desirable. As an essential part of what the ego thinks you are, you will always want it; and only an avenger, with a mind unlike your own, could stamp it out through fear.

2. The ego does not think it possible that love, not fear, is really called upon by sin, and always answers; for the ego brings sin to fear, demanding punishment. Yet punishment is but another form of guilt's protection, for what is deserving punishment must have been really done. Punishment is always the great preserver of sin, treating it with respect and honoring its enormity. What must be punished must be true, and what is true must be eternal, and will be repeated endlessly. For what you think is real you want, and will not let it go.

3. An error, on the other hand, is not attractive. What you see clearly as a mistake you want corrected. Sometimes a sin can be repeated over and over, with obviously distressing results, but

without the loss of its appeal; and suddenly, you change its status from a sin to a mistake. Now you will not repeat it; you will merely stop and let it go, unless the guilt remains. For then you will but change the form of sin, granting that it was an error, but keeping it uncorrectable. This is not really a change in your perception, for it is sin that calls for punishment, not error.

4. The Holy Spirit cannot punish sin. Mistakes He recognizes and would correct them all as God entrusted Him to do; but sin but He knows not, nor can He recognize mistakes that cannot be corrected. For a mistake that cannot be corrected is meaningless to Him. Mistakes are for correction, and they call for nothing else. What calls for punishment must call for nothing. Every mistake must be a call for love. What, then, is sin? What could it be but a mistake you would keep hidden; a call for help that you would keep unheard and thus unanswered?

5. In time, the Holy Spirit clearly sees the Son of God can make mistakes. On this you share His vision. Yet you do not share His recognition of the difference between time and eternity; and when correction is completed, time is eternity. The Holy Spirit can teach you how to look on time differently and see beyond it, but not while you believe in sin. In error, yes, for this can be corrected by the mind, but sin is the belief that your perception is unchangeable, and that the mind must accept as true what it is told through it. If it does not obey, the mind is judged insane. The only power that could change perception is thus kept impotent, held to the body by the fear of changed perception, which its Teacher, who is one with it, would bring (T.p.404).

6. When you are tempted to believe that sin is real, remember this: if sin is real, both God and you are not. If creation is extension, the Creator must have extended Himself. And it is impossible that what is part of Him is totally unlike the rest. If sin is real, God must be at war with Himself. He must be split, and torn between good and evil, partly sane and partially insane. He must

## THE PEACEMAKER

have created what wills to destroy Him, and has the power to do so. Is it not easier to believe that you have been mistaken than to believe in this?

7. While you believe that your reality or your brother's is bounded by a body, you will believe in sin. While you believe that bodies can unite, you will find guilt attractive and believe that sin is precious. For the belief that bodies limit the mind leads to a perception of the world in which the proof of separation seems to be everywhere; and God and His creation seem to be split apart and overthrown. For sin would prove what God created holy could not prevail against it, nor remain itself before the power of sin. Sin is perceived as mightier than God, before which God Himself must bow, and offer His creation to its conqueror. Is this humility or madness?

8. If sin is real, it must forever be beyond the hope of healing. For there would be a power beyond God's capable of making another will that could attack His will and overcome it, and give His Son a will apart from His, and stronger. Each part of God's fragmented creation would have a different will, opposed to His, and in eternal opposition to Him and to each other. Your holy relationship has, as its purpose now, the goal of proving this is impossible. Heaven has smiled upon it, and the belief in sin has been uprooted in its smile of love. You see it still because you do not realize that its foundation has gone. Its source has been removed and so it can be cherished but a little while before it vanishes. Only the habit of looking for it still remains (T.p.405).

9. And yet you look with Heaven's blessing on your sight. You will not see sin long. For in the new perception the mind corrects it when it seems to be seen, and it becomes invisible. Errors are quickly recognized and quickly given to correction, to be healed, not hidden. You will be healed of sin and all its ravages the instant that you give it no power over your brother; and you will help him overcome mistakes by joyously releasing him from the belief in sin.

10. In the holy instant you will see the smile of Heaven shining on both you and your brother; and you will shine upon him, in glad acknowledgment of the grace that has been given you. For sin will not prevail against a union Heaven has smiled upon. Your perception was healed in the holy instant Heaven gave you. Forget what you have seen, and raise your eyes in faith to what you now can see. The barriers to Heaven will disappear before your holy sight, for you who were sightless have been given vision, and you can see. Look not for what has been removed, but for the glory that has been restored for you to see.

11. Look upon your Redeemer, and behold what He would show you in your brother, and let not sin arise again to blind your eyes. For sin would keep you separate from him, but your Redeemer would have you look upon your brother as yourself. Your relationship is now a temple of healing, a place where all the weary ones can come and rest. Here is the rest that waits for all after the journey, and it is brought nearer to all by your relationship (T.p.406).

No one who learns from experience that one choice brings peace and joy while another brings chaos and disaster needs additional convincing. Learning through rewards is more effective than learning through pain, because pain is an ego illusion, and can never induce more than a temporary effect. The rewards of God, however, are immediately recognized as eternal. Since this recognition is made by you and not the ego, the recognition itself establishes that you and your ego cannot be identical. You may believe that you have already accepted this difference, but you are by no means convinced as yet. The fact that you believe you must escape from the ego shows this, but you cannot escape from the ego by humbling it or controlling it or punishing it. (p.68)

4. The ego and the spirit do not know each other. The separated mind cannot maintain the separation except by dissociating. Having done this, it denies all truly natural impulses, not because

the ego is a separate thing, but because you want to believe that you are. The ego is a device for maintaining this belief, but it is still only your decision to use the device that enables it to endure.

5. How can you teach someone the value of something he has deliberately thrown away? He must have thrown it away because he did not value it. You can only show him how miserable he is without it, and slowly bring it nearer so he can learn how his misery lessens as he approaches it. This teaches him to associate his misery with its absence, and the opposite of misery with its presence. It gradually becomes desirable as he changes his mind about its worth. I am teaching you to associate misery with the ego and joy with the spirit. You have taught yourself the opposite. You are still free to choose, but can you really want the rewards of the ego in the presence of the rewards of God?

6. My trust in you is greater than yours in me at the moment, but it will not always be that way. Your mission is very simple. You are asked to live so as to demonstrate that you are not an ego, and I do not choose God's channels wrongly. The Holy One shares my trust, and accepts my Atonement decisions because my will is never out of accord with His. I have said before that I am in charge of the Atonement. This is only because I completed my part in it as a man, and can now complete it through others. My chosen channels cannot fail, because I will lend them my strength as long as theirs is wanting. If the ego is the symbol of the separation, it is also the symbol of guilt. Guilt is more than merely not of God. It is the symbol of attack on God. This is a totally meaningless concept except to the ego, but do not underestimate the power of the ego's belief in it. This is the belief from which all guilt really stems. (T.p.68).


3. The ego is the part of the mind that believes in division. How could part of God detach itself without believing it is attacking Him? We spoke before of the authority problem as based on the

concept of usurping God's power. The ego believes that this is what you did because it believes that it is you. If you identify with the ego, you must perceive yourself as guilty. Whenever you respond to your ego, you will experience guilt, and you will fear punishment. The ego is quite literally a fearful thought. However ridiculous the idea of attacking God may be to the sane mind, never forget that the ego is not sane. It represents a delusional system, and speaks for it. Listening to the ego's voice means that you believe it is possible to attack God, and that a part of Him has been torn away by you. Fear of retaliation from without follows, because the severity of the guilt is so acute that it must be projected (T.p.84).

4. Whatever you accept into your mind has reality for you. It is your acceptance of it that makes it real. If you enthrone the ego in your mind, your allowing it to enter makes it your reality. This is because the mind is capable of creating reality or making illusions. I said before that you must learn to think with God. To think with Him is to think like Him. This engenders joy, not guilt, because it is natural. Guilt is a sure sign that your thinking is unnatural. Unnatural thinking will always be attended with guilt, because it is the belief in sin. The ego does not perceive sin as a lack of love, but as a positive act of assault. This is necessary to the ego's survival because, as soon as you regard sin as a lack, you will automatically attempt to remedy the situation, and you will succeed. The ego regards this as doom, but you must learn to regard it as freedom.

5. The guiltless mind cannot suffer. Being sane, the mind heals the body because it has been healed. The sane mind cannot conceive of illness because it cannot conceive of attacking anyone or anything. I said before that illness is a form of magic. It might be better to say that it is a form of magical solution. The ego believes that by punishing itself, it will mitigate the punishmentof God. (T.p.84).

# THE PEACEMAKER

## I. THE IRRECONCILABLE BELIEFS

1. The memory of God comes to the quiet mind. It cannot come where there is conflict, for a mind at war against itself remembers not eternal gentleness. The means of war are not the means of peace, and what the warlike would remember is not love. War is impossible unless belief in victory is cherished. Conflict within you must imply that you believe the ego has the power to be victorious. Why else would you identify with it? Surely you realize the ego is at war with God. Certain it is it has no enemy. Yet just as certain is its fixed belief it has an enemy that it must overcome and will succeed.

2. Do you not realize a war against yourself would be a war on God? Is victory conceivable? If it were, is this a victory that you would want? The death of God, if it were possible, would be your death. Is this a victory? The ego always marches to defeat, because it thinks that triumph over you is possible; and God thinks otherwise. This is no war, only the mad belief the Will of God can be attacked and overthrown. You may identify with this belief, but never will it be more than madness. Fear will reign in madness, and will seem to have replaced love there. This is the conflict's purpose; and to those who think that it is possible, the means seem real (T.p.486).

3. Be certain that it is impossible God and the ego, or yourself and it, will ever meet. You seem to meet and make your strange alliances on grounds that have no meaning. For your beliefs converge.

## CHAPTER 10
# "GOD IS INCOMPLETE WITHOUT ME."

The serpentine wisdom of this body of knowledge of the tree of Enneagramatic life reveals the wholeness of God in every life. The omniscience and all-seeingness of God is manifest in his creation. We are living out God's being, and without us God has no means of expressing Himself.

It is man's responsibility to "know thyself" and thus realize God in their life.

There is a proverb that says:
*"The one who does not know he does not know, avoid him.*
*The one who knows he does not know is like a child, teach him.*
*The one who knows he knows, follow him."*

# ABOUT THE AUTHOR

Reverend Tim Morgan is a professional speaker, National Guild of Hypnotists instructor, Certified Handwriting Expert, Legal Forensic Document Examiner Expert, Air Wizard Company owner, ordained minister, and author.

He accomplished his undergraduate work at Rutgers University in New Brunswick, New Jersey. He received his PhD and ThD from Almeda University in Boise, Idaho. He graduated from the New Jersey State Troopers Police Academy and has a Master's of Science in Criminal Justice Administration. He is a graduate of The Soul-Esteem Center Ministerial School in St. Louis, Missouri. He has trained physician clinics in hyperbaric medicine, gives lectures on autism, and is editor-in-chief of the newsletter for the Mild Hyperbaric Research Group of North America. He has served as a guest lecturer at Southeast Missouri State University in the Psychology Department, as well as the Sociology and E nglish departments. He has trained hypnotherapists on the use of the Enneagram as a psychological assessment tool for the past twenty years.

As an ordained minister, Morgan is the spiritual director and founder of the *Light of the Soul Center* in Kelso, Missouri. He is actively teaching, lecturing, counseling, and presenting a weekly Sunday service called *"Light of the Soul"* where A Course in Miracles is taught.

Reverend Tim Morgan lives in Kelso, Missouri, and is available for speaking and workshop engagements. You may contact him at:

Light of the Soul Center
100 S. HWY 61
PO BOX 311
Kelso, MO 63758
(573)264-4260
www.lightofthesoulcenter.com

Printed in Great Britain
by Amazon